SHAPING TRANSFORMATION

SORDO MADALENO ARQUITECTOS

SHAPING TRANSFORMATION

SORDO MADALENO ARQUITECTOS

BARRY BERGDOLL
EDITOR

FUNDACIÓN
SORDO MADALENO

CONTENTS

To my father, who started this story, to my sons, who will continue it, and to the talented team that has collaborated with Sordo Madaleno Arquitectos in these 85 years, with a creative vision of urban transformation.

To those of us who experience the city and contribute daily to transforming it positively.

Javier Sordo Madaleno Bringas

PREFACE

ACTORS IN URBAN TRANSFORMATION

BARRY BERGDOLL

A Aerial view of the UNAM Geology Institute, currently National School of Languages, Linguistics and Translation, Mexico City, 1960.

Shaping Transformation has been chosen as the subtitle for this volume to underscore the ways in which three generations of Sordo Madaleno architects have not simply responded to particular architectural commissions over the decades but have equally been major actors in the dynamic transformation of Mexico itself. The firm, in turn, has been shaped by those very transformations. The reciprocal, iterative relations between architectural designers and the urban, national, and often global contexts in which they work is the subject of this book. Sordo Madaleno Arquitectos (SMA) and the built environment of Mexico in the twentieth and early twenty-first centuries, in short, have shaped one another.

For the better part of a century now, SMA, the architectural firm founded in 1937 by twenty-one-year-old architecture student Juan Sordo Madaleno, has both responded to and shaped the evolving cityscapes and landscapes of Post-Revolutionary Mexico, a nation administered from the oldest capital city in the Americas. SMA has grown over the course of eight decades in tandem with Mexico City's dizzying demographic and territorial expansion, helping give form to the metropolis's modernization. From their home base in Mexico City—a
64 sprawling landscape of diverse close-knit neighborhoods that is also the linchpin of the country and increasingly a nodal point in global networks—SMA has steadfastly honed an ar-
356 chitecture that is both urban and urbane.

From Juan Sordo Madaleno's earliest commissions, the firm has been a pioneer not simply in elegantly detailed modernist buildings, but in architectural designs that are inherently urban, and function as building blocks of cities—cities defined at once by complex networks of exchange and by places of neighborhood focus, cities of overlapping scales. No less has the firm been engaged since Juan Sordo Madaleno's iconic
220 Presidente Acapulco Hotel in 1958 with the transformation of the larger territory, both its spatial planning and the place it plays in Mexico's cultural imagination. This has placed SMA in the field of overlapping forces that shape the built environment of the twenty-first century, between state-directed development and increasingly in recent decades the market forces at the heart of modern development. Public sector proj-
90 ects formed an important part of Juan Sordo Madaleno's practice, notably in his participation in the great national project of building a new campus for the National Autonomous University of Mexico (UNAM) with the design of the Geology In-
52 stitute with José Luis Certucha and Luis Martínez Negrete
48 in 1953 (A). Both the office building of the Dirección de Policía

A

y Tránsito of Mexico City (1956) and the Palacio de Justicia (1964) followed.

After launching his practice with his selection to design the Centro Internacional Prensa for the 1986 Mexico City World Cup, Javier Sordo Madaleno Bringas would focus on private architectural practice rather than governmental commissions; although in the neo-liberal economic environment, since the 1980s, the private sector increasingly has built some of the most significant public spaces in cities worldwide. Some of the most exemplary achievements in this regard have come in SMA's urban work in crafting veritable city centers that serve not only as destinations for city dwellers but also as emblematic spaces for contemporary Mexico.

The range of building types on which the firm has worked comprises most of the components of modernity and modernization, beginning with some of the earliest office buildings that changed the face of Mexico City immediately after the Second World War—notably including the building at Reforma and Morelos where Juan Sordo Madaleno opened his office on the top floor in 1946. Expertise was rapidly developed in other technically demanding programs ranging from modern factories—a type that began to ring the Federal District, such as Merck, Sharp & Dohme of 1960 or Cartuchos deportivos of 1962 (B)—to the specialized hospitals such as the

B | Cartuchos Deportivos, Cuernavaca, Morelos, 1962. Southern facade of production building. Roof structural design by Félix Candela.

B

Ángeles de Puebla Hospital by Javier Sordo Madaleno Bringas of 2006, and the large urban hotels which have been important areas of design by all three generations of the firm. Furthermore, SMA has pioneered new types of mixed-used apartment houses that defined the streetscape of such neighborhoods as Roma, Juárez, and Cuauhtémoc, created some of the country's first retail shopping centers tied to an expanding automobile culture and burgeoning consumer society, and dramatically redefined the possibilities of church design.

The daily lives of Mexicans and the experiences of an ever-growing tourist sector in the country's economy have played out in settings crafted by three generations of SMA. Mexican modernity, we might even say, has evolved in buildings and places given compelling artistic and spatial form by Juan Sordo Madaleno (1916–1985), his son, Javier Sordo Madaleno Bringas (b. 1956), and his grandsons, Javier (b. 1985) and Fernando (b. 1991)—both as architectural directors—as well as José Juan Sordo Madaleno de Haro (b. 1986)—director of real estate. Recent discoveries of long-forgotten archives have illuminated the development of the practice from a family concern in which even Juan Sordo Madaleno's dynamic wife, Malena, played a key role as a connector and animator of the professional and artistic circles in which her husband operated. Today, the studio has evolved into a highly complex organization of over 350 people with departments of architecture and interior design, associated with the real estate development firm SOMA (formerly Grupo Sordo Madaleno).

While at one time or another nearly every function of modern life has been studied in the design practice of SMA, what is dramatically clear in the large array of projects selected to illustrate the theme of "shaping transformation" is the ever-greater hybridity of uses that mark SMA's projects over the last twenty years. Projects of the 1930s, '40s, and '50s are relatively easy to categorize as the distinct functional components of a modernizing city; even if an office building might contain shops on the ground floor or house a cinema; even if an urban hotel, such as Juan Sordo Madaleno's masterful Presidente Chapultepec Hotel of 1977, by its very nature 78 is multifunctional and serves both guests and the larger urban community in its restaurants and lofty atrium, which serves as a public plaza. The retail projects of the early 1970s such as Plaza Satélite—designed by Juan Sordo Madaleno with José 190 Adolfo Wiechers and José I. de Abiega—provided the new forms for life at the urban fringe with planned metropolitan expansions, notably the development of Ciudad Satélite to the north of Mexico City from the late 1950s. Shopping and residential life were planned in distinct zones, and architectural practices followed the city in its tentacular spread, where nearly the entire mountain- and volcano-ringed Valley of Mexico was urbanized by the end of the last century.

By then, as in other countries, the tide had turned as the suburban shopping mall typology, radically reconsidered, came to serve as a catalyst for inner-city regeneration, often in previously industrial and manufacturing zones. In place of the destination reached by car or bus, new retail developments emphasized pedestrian access, urban connectivity, and a mixture of functions and services that created new hybrids between retail and public space. The urban mixes that had been discouraged by modernist functional zoning were replaced by new cities-within-cities, and any clear boundaries between an architectural project and a project of urban design are productively blurred. Antara in Mexico City, Andares 116, 130 in Jalisco (C) on the edge of Guadalajara as well as the new Landmark and Midtown projects there, are vibrant and highly 300, 210 successful examples of city regeneration through the deliberate intermingling of functions. These projects are designed for round-the-clock activity and include apartments and office buildings, shopping and restaurant plazas, and cultural facilities such as the nearby museums at Antara and the incorporation of cinemas and an artistic program at Artz Pedregal. 173 Since the turn of the twenty-first century, SMA has developed—sometimes as real estate developer as well as architectural designers—some of the most complex mixed-use urban districts of our post-industrial culture. From buildings inserted into the urban fabric, the firm's work has begun to build the urban fabric itself.

c Aerial view of Andares Masterplan in Zapopan, Jalisco, 2009–2017. From left to right, The Landmark, Andares Corporate, Andares Shopping Mall, residential building and the Andares Hyatt Regency Hotel.

c

To bring together in this volume only a select group of the firm's nearly four hundred projects to date has required conceiving an unconventional architectural monograph. Rather than a complete catalogue of projects built and unbuilt, this volume places many of the office's most ambitious projects in the context of transformation, taking up the theme that architectural projects both shape and are shaped by their context and by the very flux of transformation that is modernity's primary characteristic. In a world in which global flows have rendered existence ever freer of spatial address, SMA has been actively involved in crafting the physical environment in which contemporary life gains richness and in which cities are reinventing themselves from within to establish new paradigms of urban living. Publishing on the firm's eighty-fifth anniversary and with contributions of some of the leading thinkers on architecture and urban form writing today, the aim
84 of *Shaping Transformation* is also to underscore the consistent development of an architectural approach and set of commitments sustained across multiple generations of a single family of architects.

In the most recent work, the exploration of Juan Sordo Madaleno's early use of curtain walls has continued in the complex geometries of the recently completed curtain walls of a wholly new sort in the Artz Pedregal complex. In such projects
242 as the Solaz Los Cabos resort and condominium complex, as well as in projects under study as this volume goes to print, SMA has moved increasingly into new thinking about the sustainable occupation of fragile ecologies. If the work of Sordo Madaleno was well known to me as an architectural historian and curator engaged for some years with the history of Mexican design, the project of conceiving a hybrid book to complement the ever-greater hybridity of the firm's projects has offered a chance to reflect on how a practice can respond progressively to new challenges while maintaining a strong architectural tradition. Some of the most compelling designs presented in this volume are projects where SMA has either had ongoing involvement—such as in the development of Antara Masterplan—or where it has returned to rethink earlier projects in light of today's demands; for example, the transformation of Plaza Satélite from an inward-turning shopping mall set amongst acres of parking—an ideal that epitomized progressive modernity a half-century ago—into an innovative integration of landscape park, shopping, and accommodation of automobiles.

On an even grander scale is the work—ongoing as this volume goes to print—on one of the most symbolic places in the urban life of Mexico City, the Glorieta de Colón rond-point on the Paseo de la Reforma. This key urban crossroads was already transformed early in the career of Juan Sordo Madaleno, and it is to his father's work that Javier Sordo Madaleno Bringas now comes to restore, revivify, and extend that project for a Mexican capital always in dynamic change. Paseo de la Reforma commemorates reform, revision, and critical engagement as a national project. In this sense, the SMA firm is emblematic of the necessity of a modern architectural practice to be planning not static solutions but dynamic contributions to the very process of transformation. This book is, therefore, not conceived as a conventional monograph of an architectural practice; although a large selection of the most consequential and accomplished projects realized by three generations

D

D | Exterior view of Londres and Niza, 1953.

is documented here—often in original architectural drawings recently rediscovered and period photographs that provide a sense of the palimpsest of a city still in transformation since the founding of México-Tenochtitlan seven centuries ago in 1325.

While well known, the masterful photographs by two of the twentieth century's greatest architectural photographers—the Mexicans Guillermo Zamora (1915–2002) and Armando Salas Portugal (1916–1995)—in addition to newly commissioned models, illustrate the interplay between the modern city and architectural projects at the heart of the practice. If these iconic photographs seem even more familiar to some than the buildings they portray, it is because they played a key role in the international fame of Mexican modern architecture, including the early work of Juan Sordo Madaleno, found in international publications and in exhibitions such as the Museum of Modern Art's 1955 influential *Latin American Architecture Since 1945*. There, Zamora's photograph of the office building at the corner of Londres and Niza (1953) (D) formed part of a composite street of Latin American International Style office buildings. Historian Henry-Russell Hitchcock crafted these collaged pages of glazed facades to argue that the elegant background morphological components of the modern city had been forged in Mexico, Brazil, Colombia, Peru, and Argentina, as Latin America provided models for the whole world of what a modern metropolis could be. It was with Zamora's dramatic photographs of the astounding shifted floor plates of the 555 Palmas tower, Juan Sordo Madaleno's declaration of a sculptural turn in his late architectural practice, that I was able—in the absence of the original drawings which I could not find—to represent that stunningly original office building in the exhibition *Latin America in Construction: Architecture 1945–1980*, which I organized at the Museum of Modern Art in New York in 2015, in collaboration with Jorge Francisco Liernur, Carlos Eduardo Comas, and Patricio del Real.

A major impetus for *Shaping Transformation* was the dramatic discovery in 2018 of a large cache of original drawings and documents from Juan Sordo Madaleno, stashed in a rarely accessed residual space in his house at 2076 Reforma. This archival find has made it possible to analyze more fully his design process, inspiring ideas for an exhibition that could bring together original materials that bear witness to the hand of the architect and his office. The rapid organization of these materials—remarkably well preserved because they had been isolated from damaging light and humidity for so many years—was a major resource for the group of authors we invited to think about aspects of the firm's work and it is hoped for future researchers on the history of Mexican modern architecture and urban development.

From the first we decided to take an unconventional approach to the treatment of a veritable dynasty of architects, not seeking to divide the work by chronology per se, which would have obscured the continuities across generations as well as the ways in which each generation has learned form, and at times even renovated or reworked, earlier work by the firm. The sixteen authors who have contributed interviews and essays have not, for the most part, written previously about the firm's work in the architectural press or even in the two excellent reference monographs published by Arquine on Javier Sordo Madaleno (2011) and Juan Sordo Madaleno (2013). Rather, we have brought together here a group of authors whose expertise contextualizes and sheds light on the two-way transformation that is the ethos and hypothesis of the volume. In addition to architects—one of whom, Jose Castillo, has his own architectural practice on several floors of 555 Palmas (1975), the last major work of Juan Sordo Madaleno before his untimely death—facets of the production of the firm are taken up by an economist, a historian of urban morphology, and architectural historians and critics from Mexico, the United States, Germany, and Spain. To supplement interviews conducted with Javier Sordo Madaleno Bringas and his sons, Javier and Fernando, by Martha Thorne from Madrid, we invited Louise Noelle, a pioneering leader in the study of Mexican modernist architecture, to provide a type of retrospective

348

interview—an account of Juan Sordo Madaleno informed by her own work with him toward the end of his career in the 1970s and early 1980s, notably in the pages of Mario Pani's *Arquitectura México*.

The contextualizing essays are organized into two major sections: a first group situates the strategies of design and major projects, both built and unbuilt—beginning as early as Juan Sordo Madaleno's thesis project of 1939 for mixed-use "Edificios de Comercios y Departamentos"—within the dynamic force field of urbanization, isolating what is unique to twentieth-century Mexican urban development and those forces that are continental, even global. A second group takes up many of the building types and programs to which the firm has brought innovations, defining many of the elements of modern life in the country. In this way, the two sections themselves evoke the perpetual dynamic between the larger forces that shape any architectural practice—politics, economic developments and shifts, social life—and the active role that creative architectural design and problem-solving plays in the changing face of a country and its daily life.

Economist and urban planner Manuel Perló Cohen traces the evolution of SMA in the decades from the 1940s to the 1980s in relationship to the nexus between politics and economy, between the state as builder—not the least at UNAM, where building and nation building went hand-in-hand under President Miguel Alemán—and private market forces of investment and development. The dynamic between state and market forces is indeed one of the many overlapping fields in which both the city and architectural practices were to move. Architectural historian Eduardo Alarcón and Juan José Kochen, director of Fundación ICA, invite us to take a closer look at specific key locations on the map of Mexico City to witness those transformations at play, and nowhere west of the Zócalo itself more importantly in this regard than the Glorieta Reforma Colón, a place named for two of the largest forces in the development of Mexico. This roundabout, the veritable focal point of the city's westward expansion since the nineteenth century, when the colonial center began to lose its predominance, is arguably the epicenter of Mexican life. Economists speak of cycles, and thus in multiple senses from the biographical to the patterns of a city continually building and rebuilding itself, Reforma Colón is both a place of origin and place of return for SMA. Here, of course, Juan
94
Sordo Madaleno moved his office at a moment when it was expanding with the federal city in the late 1940s, and here, almost 70 years later, the SMA firm has returned in designing and shepherding an enormous urban revitalization of this area in the heart of the sprawling twenty-first-century metropolis. The project, the only one yet to be completed that is featured in this volume, is detailed here by Rosalba Rojas, Media and Marketing Director of SMA, to explain the daunting complexity of the undertaking, the largest project in the history of the firm—even as it is but one of some 80 projects underway at various stages in the office as this volume goes to press.

The late twentieth century witnessed the explosive emergence of megacities that are centers not only of national commerce but of global and globalizing forces. Mexico City's extensive metropolitan area now rivals the two other megacities of the Americas, São Paulo and New York, sharing with them many of the characteristics and challenges faced by megacities worldwide. Along with a demographic revolution, the center of Mexico City has witnessed the removal of the heavy industry which motored urban growth in the twentieth century, thus joining the roster of cities characterized by urban analysts as "post-industrial," despite Mexico remaining an important manufacturing economy. SMA is at the epicenter of this phenomenon with what developers have nicknamed Nuevo Polanco, having both designed and now working from Antara Masterplan, the multi-use commercial and office center built on the lands of the former General Motors de Mexico plant and warehouses. This phenomenon is discussed in the first part of the volume by Felipe Correa, Ecuadorian-born historian of the morphology of contemporary urbanization.

To these essays which position the work of SMA in relationship to forces of urban change and transformation, Kenneth Frampton offers an appreciation of the perpetually redefined idea of the "city in miniature" in the firm's urban strategy focused on the complex of Artz Pedregal. Frampton takes an even longer historical view by placing this complex of shopping, entertainment, offices, art, and restaurants into a larger trajectory of complex urban types. He traces which might be called the agora of the modern city since the heyday of Paris's Palais Royal as an urban hub in the late eighteenth and early nineteenth century to some of the recent large-scale, multi-functional urban projects developed since the turn of the century by SMA. These places create dynamic settings for the spectacle of urban life, concentrating the excitement and spontaneity of the city and mixing commercial functions with centers for artistic expression. It is interesting to note that the large-scale cinema—notably Cine Ermita (1951) and Cine París (1954), which was a novel element of public assembly designed by Juan Sordo Madaleno for several generations of

E | Presidente Acapulco Hotel, Guerrero, 1958. North and west facades. The motor lobby on the Costera Miguel Alemán Highway. *Los amantes* (The Lovers) by Mathias Goeritz greets the guests.

E

Mexicans—return in the Artz Pedregal complex, now accompanied by an art gallery space and a robust program of outdoor sculpture through the non-profit organization Arte Abierto. Here, as in the UNAM, but a short distance away, a synthesis of the arts is brought together.

In the second group of essays, each takes an individual building type as a focus, moving thus from the complex interlocked infrastructures of the modern metropolis, with mixed-use projects which are very present across the three generations of SMA, to building types that are either novel or that have been fundamentally transformed by modern life since the 1940s. With the exception of churches—of which outstanding works by Juan Sordo Madaleno in Polanco (San Ignacio de Loyola Church, 1961) and by Javier Sordo Madaleno Bringas (San Josémaría Escrivá de Balaguer Parish, 2009)—most of the building types are inherently mixed-use in nature, emphasizing the urban complexity of architecture for SMA. Ivan San Martín considers churchs in relation to changing functions of ecclesiastical space as a result of Vatican Council II of 1965 and ever since. Here the emergence of sculptural form in architecture in the later work of Juan Sordo Madaleno and in the work of his son and grandsons underscores the extent to which the modern city needs monuments and focal points. The ability of the firm to seek a balance between the integration of their work in the fabric of the city, and the need for rapid, sometimes uncontrolled, urban development like Santa Fe, is one of the defining contributions the architects have made to Mexican urban society. The deeply felt religious belief of the family itself is underscored by one of Zamora's iconic photographs of Juan Sordo Madaleno, in his office with Mathias Goeritz's crucifix (1954)—a favorite work that emerged from one of his many friendships with key avant-garde artists in the mid-century Mexican scene.

As modern urban life was increasingly characterized by the separation of spheres of work and spheres of living, by the end of the twentieth century, along with it the office building came to be a new architectural, social, and economic type. Juan Sordo Madaleno was one of those who pioneered the office building as a complex urban actor, offering public services and spaces alongside the specialized and sequestered places of business on upper floors. The evolution of the office building as a major task for SMA is studied here by Jose Castillo, a Mexican architect. As he underscores, commercial space was an integral part of many of these buildings which animated the street level through public functions rather than controlling access, a balance that Javier Sordo Madaleno negotiates brilliantly, for instance, in the ways which the Antara
complex in Colonia Granada allows crisscrossing circulation 322
through a dense development even as the upper reaches offer
prime office space. The history of this modern transformation 332
of shopping—in which models came overwhelmingly from the United States—is studied here by German architectural historian Vera Simone Bader, offering insights into the influences from abroad on Sordo Madaleno's work in creating the retail landscape over more than half a century and underscoring aspects which are unique to Mexico and to the firm's work.

Both the individual house and vanguard designs of new types of apartment buildings have occupied SMA almost continuously and offer two scales of living. Sordo Madaleno's innovations with mixed-use urban building block are analyzed by Sara Topelson and Jimena Orvañanos. Designing individual family houses, which prompted new forms of integrating suburban nature and garden, particularly in Mexico City where most of the residential work is concentrated, is studied by one of the great specialists in the history of the Mexican modern house, Lourdes Cruz.

Sophisticated mixed-used projects of ever-increasing complexity have been the hallmark of the Sordo Madaleno firm. A synthesis of this comes in the history of the firm's work in hotel design, from the acclaimed Presidente Acapulco Hotel (1958) (E) to the remarkable work of integrated architectural and landscape design in a recent masterpiece, Solaz Los Cabos (2018) (F). Architectural historian Cate Ettinger reveals the role these brilliant and iconic designs play in the national and commercial strategies of developing the coast for tourism, integral parts of national highway planning and in recent decades striking a balance between preserving natural environments and developing tourist sites. Solaz Los Cabos,

F Solaz Los Cabos, Baja California Sur, 2018.

F

for instance, is a veritable microcosm of the urbanization of leisure, a coastal pendant to Artz or Andares in Zapopan, Jalisco, as cities in miniature.

In a completely different architectonic register is the large body of work undertaken pro bono since 1999 for the Teletón
364 Children's Rehabilitation Centers (CRIT) to literally create a universe for children suffering from handicaps. Here is an architecture that provides a joyous and hopeful environment even for the most challenged youth. Sara Topelson analyzes the entirely different register in which color is used, not to represent some "mexicanidad" in the tradition of Chucho Reyes and Luis Barragán, but rather a playful environment that underscores a commitment that architecture can improve lives, creating settings in which the most challenging but also the most hopeful aspects of modern medicine can be practiced. Each design is unique, representing the fact that in all the building forms in which the firm has excelled, a type is continually refined but never as a template to repeat, always to be adapted to the specifics of setting, region, and brief. From Baja California to San Antonio, Texas, the CRITS of SMA represent a commitment to architecture as one of the building blocks not only of the city, but of society as a whole.

Although today the scale of projects on which SMA is working has achieved almost the complexity of many small cities, the principles of an innovative use of the means of modern construction, of elegant detailing at every scale from hardware to the integration of exterior and interior space, and of sensitivity to the urban qualities of the city as it exists and can be forged. These are hallmarks of the design work that remains consistent with the ethos that launched Juan Sordo Madaleno into practice 85 years ago.

REFLECTING ON CONVERSATIONS WITH JUAN SORDO MADALENO

LOUISE NOELLE GRAS

A Portrait of Juan Sordo Madaleno with *Auschwitz Savior* by Mathias Goeritz, Mexico City, late 1940's.

A

> There is no doubt that an architect changes and evolves as a human being...
>
> Juan Sordo Madaleno[1]

When I had the honor of meeting and conversing with Juan Sordo Madaleno[2] in the late 1970s, he was already an architect with several major projects behind him both in Mexico and abroad. By then, he had been selected as one of the fourteen architects "with the greatest implications for our medium"[3] included in the 100th anniversary issue of the magazine *Arquitectura México* in 1968. Nevertheless, he had the ease of one who has no need to prove himself, and this made him generous and amiable in his dealings as a professional. This meant it was always pleasant to visit him at his studio on Darwin in Mexico City to discuss the publication of his design work in the magazine. In thinking back now about him and his architecture, the course of those interesting conversations is in a way resumed; words and memories that are still relevant are brought into the present.

This analysis must begin several decades earlier, as it was then that two events took place with decisive consequences for his future. The first was his marriage on June 20, 1941, to Magdalena Bringas, with whom he had three children: José Juan, Magdalena, and Javier. This happy occurrence proved fundamental in giving him a budding family for which he built some very successful residences, such as the house at 725
252 Sierra Fría in Lomas de Chapultepec (1946)[4] or the one on Paseo de la Reforma, 2388 Reforma (1952),[5] which has regrettably disappeared. Of the latter, its architect recalled, "The growth of the family gradually sets the course for the architectural solution. The decisions taken are not the architect's whims but a result of the conditions that arise."[6]

But let us go back to December 4, 1939, the day he graduated as an architect from the National School of Architecture of the UNAM. While his works evolved over time, as he said himself, they also reflected a constant desire to belong to the vanguard of modernity. It should be added that even in his thesis, "Edificios de Comercios y Departamentos" (Mixed-use spaces: commercial and apartment buildings), he already proposed "seeking the way to ensure evolution of the routine type of constructions destined for habitation."[7] This sheds light on a statement he made in 1968: "I started building with glass, with glass windows so big that they were really glass walls."[8]

---

1. Louise Noelle, "Diálogo con el Arquitecto Juan Sordo Madaleno," *Arquitectura México*, July–August, no. 117 (1978): 11.
2. Juan Sordo Madaleno was born in Mexico City on October 28, 1916 and died in the same city on March 13, 1985.
3. Mario Pani, "Del Director," *Arquitectura México*, April-July, no. 100 (1968): 3.
4. This residence was published in the book *18 residencias de arquitectos mexicanos* (Mexico City: Ediciones Mexicanas, 1951); "Casa habitación. Juan Sordo Madaleno, Arq." *Arquitectura México*, September, no. 35 (1951); and *Guía de arquitectura mexicana contemporánea* (Mexico City: Editorial Espacios, 1952).
5. "Residencia de un arquitecto," *Arquitectura México*, June, no. 42 (1952); and "Casa de un arquitecto," *Espacios*, May, no. 15 (1953).
6. *Espacios*, no. 15.
7. Juan Sordo Madaleno, "Edificios de Comercios y Departamentos," thesis to obtain the degree of architect, Mexico City, Escuela Nacional de Arquitectura, UNAM (1939). Such proposals were made by some other modern architects, particularly Mario Pani, who carried out projects like the Presidente Alemán Residential Complex a decade later.
8. "Juan Sordo Madaleno," *Arquitectura México*, April–July, no. 100 (1968): 79.

B | Interior of the office of Juan Sordo Madaleno on Reforma and Morelos, Mexico City, 1946.

B

C Juan Sordo Madaleno visiting the construction of the Anáhuac Tower, Mexico City, circa 1957.
D Juan Sordo Madaleno in his composition class, UNAM National Architecture School, Mexico City, circa 1952.
E Juan Sordo Madaleno presents Plaza Universidad to the mayor of Mexico City, Alfonso Corona del Rosal, Mexico City, circa 1968.

C

D

E

These first works were built in partnership with fellow architecture student, Augusto H. Álvarez (1914–1995),[9] who graduated a few months before him. Coincidentally, it was also around that time that the first woman architect, María Luisa Dehesa, presented her thesis, an indication of the changes then taking place in the profession. The series of projects built by these two young architects was framed within the burgeoning of the so-called International Style in the new districts or *colonias* of Mexico City and its principal avenues, and they had no qualms in affirming that "we did what had to be done: apartments, houses, offices."[10]

286 The ten-year partnership of Álvarez and Sordo Madaleno produced many buildings, some still standing while others have sadly been swept away by the avarice of the property market. In the first ones, seventy years after they were built, it is still possible to appreciate not only the quality of the project but also the care taken with their structural calculations and the choice of finishes. One of these outstanding buildings forms part of the unique grouping on Plaza Melchor Ocampo, where it stands harmoniously alongside apartment blocks produced by the talent of Enrique del Moral and Luis Barragán in association with Max Cetto or José Creixell. These four buildings opt for individual creativity within a total respect for heights and alignments; the one by Álvarez and Sordo Madaleno stands out for its careful use of materials and the rationality of its design with modernity and comfort sought for its users.

Among those demolished, another excellent example was their 1947 building of shops and apartments at the iconic corner of Paseo de la Reforma, Mariano Escobedo, and Melchor Ocampo, a nine-story edifice whose ground floor housed for many years a shop selling sweets called Larín that fed the dreams of thousands of children. To showcase the historic plaza from which Simón Bolívar once rode off to other latitudes, the building, which has two apartments per floor, has as its most memorable feature a concave facade punctured by large

9. Lourdes Cruz González Franco, *Augusto H. Álvarez, arquitecto de la modernidad* 8 (Mexico City: Facultad de Arquitectura, UNAM, 2008).
10. "Madaleno," *Arquitectura México*, 79.

windows providing ample views over the Bosque de Chapultepec (Chapultepec Forest). Two features underscore the rationality of the designers: the centralization of the vertical circulation, and the structure based on columns whose shafts tapered as they approached the top floors. These columns allowed the personalized distribution of partitioning walls.

At the end of this period, Sordo Madaleno was honored with an invitation to be part of the group of architects who took part in the design of the campus of the UNAM (National Autonomous University of Mexico), between 1950 and 1952, under the overall direction of Enrique del Moral and Mario Pani, the designers of the masterplan. In his case, he took charge of the Geology Institute[11] in collaboration with Luis Martínez Negrete and José Luis Certucha, and with the geological engineers Eduardo Schmitter and Teodoro Flores acting as consultants. The new university campus was the result of a significant and visionary action on the part of the authorities of the UNAM at that time, and was listed by UNESCO as a World Heritage Site in 2007. The institute designed under the auspices of Sordo Madaleno was composed of two separate blocks, "a taller one of five stories on a north-south axis, joined by a bridge to a lower one aligned east-west,"[12] with a modern character rooted in Le Corbusier, and amalgamating university departments used today by the National School of Languages, Linguistics and Translation.

By the 1950s, Juan Sordo Madaleno had come to realize "that for my part, I had never lived, or wanted to live, in a glass cage exposed to everyone's view. And it's even less pleasant to have to hide behind curtains."[13] In the face of this, he decided to build "in accordance with my own wish, which is to seek isolation... [since] the home must be a refuge where one can enjoy a sense of freedom."[14] Consequently, he designed a series of memorable houses such as the one on Paseo de la Reforma, unfortunately now demolished,[15] and also the ones at 100 Conscripto and 940 Corregidores. Moreover, he took the committed and visionary view that "the task of architecture, whether the architect likes it or not, currently consists of providing lodging for the popular masses in a more civilized way. Luis Barragán and I," he added, "have been trying to combine city planning with views in such a way that people can live pleasurably."[16] This assertion underlines his close friendship with both Barragán and Mathias Goeritz, sharing interests with the former that surprises us with novelty and facilitated the participation of the latter in his projects. Especially memorable is Goeritz's sculpture *Auschwitz Savior* (A), which seemed to watch over the work done in Sordo Madaleno's office, and in a way encouraged him to state that "in short, we are trying to construct a focus on being more civil and therefore more civilized to the extent that our derailed civilization will allow."[17]

At the same time as he moved personally towards a style of residential design that prefigured what is today called regionalism, his broad talents also led him to work in other modernist genres. Apart from various office buildings, he also designed two cinemas, Cine Ermita (F) and Cine París (G), that 94
were paradigmatic in the mid-twentieth century.[18] It was probably this type of highly specialized project that led him to assert that "we Mexican architects know the importance of technique in our profession, and each day we apply this knowledge more."[19] This command of technique also allowed him to make successful incursions into other genres like hotels, factories, and shopping centers, although this is not the place for a minute review of these diverse contributions, which will be detailed later on.

The architect himself reflected on this, concluding that "it is an imminent need for specialties to be developed in our country at the same rate as in the countries with the most advanced techniques," since he believed:

> The future of construction in Mexico demands it, owing to the country's demographic explosion and industrial boom, and if we want our architecture to preserve the humanism that characterizes it, and we do not want pure technique to drag us down into subordination rather than subordinating it to architectural ideas, then we must stay abreast of technical advances so as to apply them to our current and future architecture.[20]

These were concepts fundamental to the architectural creed that he not only expressed cogently but also took pains to put

256
260

11. "Instituto de Geología," *Arquitectura México*, September, no. 39 (1952): 281–283.
12. "Instituto de Geología," *Arquitectura México*, 281.
13. "Madaleno," *Arquitectura México*, 79.
14. "Madaleno," 79.
15. "Residencia en la ciudad de México," *Arquitectura México*, June, no. 42 (1953).
16. "Madaleno," *Arquitectura México*, 79.
17. "Madaleno," 79.
18. "Cine Ermita," *Arquitectura México*, June, no. 34 (1951); "Cine París," *Espacios*, August, no. 20 (1954).
19. "Madaleno," *Arquitectura México*, 82.
20. "Madaleno," *Arquitectura México*, 82.

F Interior view of the lobby of Cine Ermita, Juan Sordo Madaleno, 1951.

F

into practice, producing work that won recognition both at
home and abroad. He was therefore able to undertake large
projects that marked the capital's skyline, such as the Direc-
48 ción de Policía y Tránsito building in Tlaxcoaque and Mexico
64 City's central court of law, the Palacio de Justicia (H),[21] not for-
getting his novel and in many ways pioneering shopping malls.
Special mention should be made of his contributions to indus-
78 trial architecture, a genre that few architects take on.[22] It is
quite a challenge to combine administrative facilities with safe
and functional buildings for workers, giving everyone the dig-
nity that they deserve in the workplace. The Merck, Sharp &
52 Dohme Laboratories (I),[23] located in southern Mexico City, are
designed over three blocks, with a bold circular structure for
the production area "combined and duly proportioned with two
rectangular volumes, [which] provided a solution to the re-
quirement of including publicity in the overall effect."[24] Car-
tuchos Deportivos, a factory in the outskirts of Cuernavaca,
posed the particular challenge of planning a zone for working
with explosives that would "comply with the necessary safety conditions in accordance with the risk represented by the operation" within an attractive and coherent complex.[25]

The 1970s, when my friendship with Juan Sordo Madaleno began, was a propitious time for him to reap the harvests of much of what he had designed and been able to realize in the preceding years. An example was the Presidente Chapultepec Hotel,[26] which he designed and built in association with José

21. "Palacio de Justicia de la Ciudad de México," *Arquitectura México*, March, no. 89 (1965).
22. On this subject, see *Arquitectura México*, April, no. 104 (1971).
23. These laboratories were designed in collaboration with Imanol Ordorika and José Adolfo Wiechers. See "Merck, Sharp & Dohme de México," *Arquitectura México*, April, no. 104 (1971), and "Merck, Sharp & Dohme de México," *Calli*, April, no. 7, (1963).
24. "Merck, Sharp & Dohme de México," *Calli*, 22.
25. "Cartuchos Deportivos," *Arquitectura México*, Mexico City, Editorial Arquitectura April, no. 104 (1971): 17.

Adolfo Wiechers between 1976 and 1977, as it forms part of his work for the same hotel chain, for whom he had already worked in Acapulco in the 1950s and continued in Cozumel and Cancún. Nor can we overlook his participation in the design of the famous María Isabel Hotel,[27] in collaboration with his former teacher, José Villagrán García, or the hotels built in Madrid, the Villamagna and Meliá Castilla. Sordo Madaleno said himself to us of that hotel: "I have made a lot of buildings, but this one is very special because of its size, its volume, its design, and because it belongs to the current phase of my professional development. There is no doubt that an architect changes and evolves as a human being, and the Presidente Chapultepec Hotel satisfies me fully because it responds to my current thinking about architecture."[28] It is also interesting to note that in these buildings for intense use by tourism, he secured the inclusion of works by colleagues like Félix Candela, with his La Jacaranda nightclub, or renowned artists like Mathias Goeritz with *The Lovers* in Acapulco (J), Ángela Gurría with *The Kapok Tree*, and Ernesto Paulsen with *The Triangles* in Mexico City. This could be said to have been an approach to artistic integration, an important aspect of Mexican modernism.[29]

That period was also the moment when he came full circle with his architectural work by resuming a fruitful relationship with Augusto H. Álvarez, who not long before had said: "For thirty years we architects have enjoyed almost complete liberty. I do not think we have abused it. We have turned this conscience of liberty into collective work by forming a collective creative spirit."[30] They combined their talents once more to win the competition for the Centro Operativo Bancomer,[31] a building that displays a particular geometrical rationality without neglecting the comfort of the numerous workers who occupied its offices. The proposal called for a horizontal construction organized like a chessboard, using a grid pattern to insert several courtyards that provided all the office workers with natural light. The tragic renovation of this building for a supposed modernization of the center is difficult to accept.

"Architecture has always been and will continue to be art. Architecture is creation. At present, though... the goal is rather functionality."[32] These words may act as a corollary to the reminiscences presented here, illuminated by the wise presence of Juan Sordo Madaleno in his words and accomplishments. His legacy is becoming more clearly defined with time, having won wide renown that has persisted into the new century with the warm approval of the many people who have the chance every day to enjoy the architectural ambiences he created.

G Juan Sordo Madaleno and Jaime Ortiz Monasterio, Cine París, Mexico City, 1954. Interior view of the mezzanine and main stairway.

H Juan Sordo Madaleno, José Adolfo Wiechers and Imanol Ordorika, Palacio de Justicia, Mexico City, 1964. Interior view.

G 58

H 352

26. "Hotel El Presidente Chapultepec," *Arquitectura México*, July-August, no. 117 (1978).
27. "Hotel María Isabel," *Arquitectura México*, June, no. 78 (1962).
28. Noelle, "Diálogo," 12.
29. Louise Noelle Gras, "La integración plástica: confluencia, superposición o nostalgia," in *(In)Disciplinas: Estética e historia del arte en el cruce de los discursos* (Mexico City: Instituto de Investigaciones Estéticas, UNAM, 1999).
30. "Augusto H. Álvarez," *Arquitectura México*, April-July, no. 100 (1968): 5.
31. Another architect who contributed to this work was José Adolfo Wiechers (1932–2007), with whom Sordo Madaleno was associated for two decades.
32. "Madaleno," *Arquitectura México*, 81.

I Juan Sordo Madaleno, José Adolfo Wiechers and Imanol Ordorika, Merck, Sharp & Dohme, Mexico City, 1960. Exterior view.
J *Los amantes* (The Lovers) sculpture by Mathias Goeritz in the entrance to the Presidente Acapulco Hotel, 1958.

I

J

CONTINUITY AND CHANGE IN THREE GENERATIONS OF ARCHITECTS

MARTHA THORNE

A Javier Sordo Madaleno Bringas with *Auschwitz Savior* by Mathias Goeritz, Mexico City, 2018.

A

Mexican architecture since the mid-twentieth century is as complex and varied as the country itself. While it is not possible to generalize, in the case of Juan Sordo Madaleno it would be fair to say that his practice was at once strongly influenced by the international language of modern architecture and inflected in relation to local culture and to the unique topography of each place. At the same time, each project is marked by a freshness of approach. His bold forms along with his understanding of the natural features of materials chosen resulted in some of the most outstanding buildings of Mexico from the 1940s through the 1970s.

As I interviewed the next two generations of architects in the Sordo Madaleno family, I was struck both by their respect for the firm's legacy and at the same time by their excitement about new possibilities. Javier Sordo Madaleno Bringas has been challenged not only by the weight of the past but also by the need to take over the family business and make it prosper. He has not only understood and appreciated architecture from an early age and has consistently followed a rigorous process of design, but he has also grown the firm very substantially and developed a structure combining design and real estate, all the while without sacrificing either architectural quality or the ability to try new things. No less, Javier Sordo Madaleno Bringas's deep understanding of the city means that he can envision not only new projects by his firm but also grasp and consider the impact of those projects on the larger city and gauge the ability of those projects to serve as catalysts for future change. This approach has significantly transformed entire urban areas and will continue to do so in the future.

The three sons, two architects and a financial director, are now fully incorporated in Sordo Madaleno Arquitectos and SOMA (formerly Grupo Sordo Madaleno), the real estate arm. They continue with the same entrepreneurial spirit, seeking new opportunities and new frontiers. The success of the firm derives from its well-organized structure and the well-defined roles within the two companies. Yet today's large firm has remained loyal to the established values and criteria of the practice forged in the 1930s and '40s by Juan Sordo Madaleno.

For these interviews, the three architects were generously open in discussion and allowed me to see not only how they work together, but what motivates them individually, and even what are some of the emotions that direct their approach. It is safe to say that all three believe that architecture is a life-long learning experience. They work to create places for people, not simply functional solutions.

While they have been very successful economically, this was never expressed as a priority, even when I pushed them on the business side of the equation. They are sophisticated, organized, committed, and optimistic—qualities that are fundamental for the practice of architecture today. As the founder brought his son fully into the firm, and as Javier has invited his sons into key positions, we can appreciate the changes already underway and those to come. While buildings last for decades, they cannot reflect a past alone; important buildings must also open to a dynamic future and an expression of optimism about what lies ahead. This is evident in the work of SMA.

Interview with Javier Sordo Madaleno Bringas

Did you always want to be an architect? How did you start?
Yes, when I was very small, I was given things to draw and boats to put together. At my home, everything was related to art and architecture. I came to know Luis Barragán and Chucho Reyes very well, and all their contemporaries were part of

my family circle. When I finished my preparatory studies, at the age of nearly sixteen, I started to have doubts, and to find out if I really wanted to devote myself to architecture I worked over the summer at the studio of Ricardo Legorreta, helping with the scale models. Then I worked with Augusto H. Álvarez for a long time, and afterwards with Pedro Ramírez Vázquez; only after that, did I begin to work with my father.

I made up my mind to go into architecture as a career, and gradually, as part of a process of discovery, I moved further into it. I've always been restless, and I found it hard to concentrate on my studies, although I made up on the design part for other subjects. Well, let's just say I wasn't the best student. I realized that architecture was what I really liked, and when I graduated, I was very happy.

What was your father's studio like?

It was a very interesting studio in many ways. He founded it in 1937, when he was very young. It was very innovative for its time, and it evolved. In the mid-1970s, a project came up for Manolo Arango, together with the competition for the Centro Operativo Bancomer. My father then set up two studios, one in conjunction with José Adolfo Wiechers and Augusto H. Álvarez to do the competition, and the other separate, which is where I was. My father was deeply affected by the death of my brother José Juan in 1974, and he lost focus at that point. I didn't start to take the reins of the studio until 1978 or 1979, but it wasn't until 1982 that I became the director of the whole office, as my father contracted cancer in 1981 and died in 1985. I was very young, and at that time we didn't have much work.

How did you secure projects for the studio at such a young age?

Although I had the name of Sordo Madaleno, people didn't know me, and they weren't going to hire me only because of the name. And I therefore became a developer to be able to do the projects. At that time, the studio kept functioning with some commissions I received and some other projects I promoted. I took part in some bids, but the key work was really the building for the Centro Internacional de Prensa for the 1986 World Cup, a project I obtained with Emilio Azcárraga. For some strange reason, I had to give Emilio information so that he would pass it on to the person who was going to carry out the work, but the man didn't show up. I then offered to do a project concept in one night, and the next day we sent him some sketches. He saw them, and he liked them. My father would never have thought they were going to give me that project, and I received the commission a month after his death.

B

C

352

The Centro Internacional Prensa represents a change in my attitude, and from then on, I started to get commissions. 356

Your father's work was closely linked to the Modern movement, and he spoke a great deal about "clarity" of language and "balance" in composition to give a work strength...

Yes, one of his great qualities was his ability to visualize space. He had the idea of space, and he designed in section more than plan. I think my father was a person who was most stimulated by interesting spaces, proportion, double stories, changing volumes. That was really his strength.

Your father did a lot of traveling. Were his travels a source of inspiration for his own works?

Yes, my father traveled a lot, especially to Spain. He did several buildings there, both in Torremolinos and in Madrid, the Meliá Castilla and Villamagna hotels. My father was a Mexican

B Javier Sordo Madaleno Bringas in the presentation of the Project for the Centro Internacional de Prensa, Mexico City, 1985.

C Juan Sordo Madaleno, Reforma and Morelos, Mexico City, 1946. Interior of workshop.

D Southern facade of the Torremolinos Hotel Comp ex in Málaga, Spain, 1963.

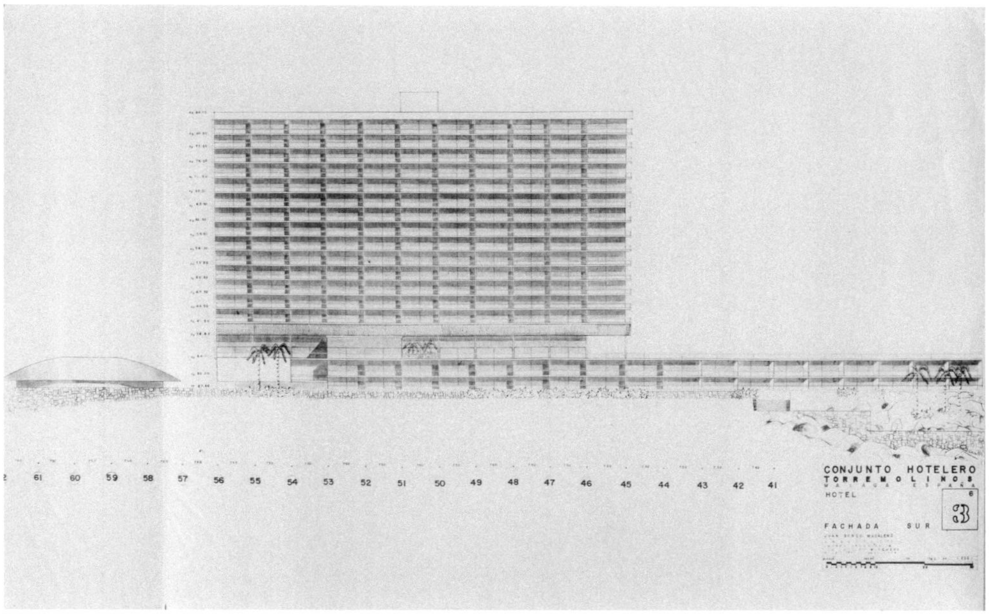

D

architect and couldn't sign the projects in Spain, so only the local architect appears in the credits.

What is there in your own work that is inspired by your father's?

For me, the handling of space is fundamental, and it was from him that I learned the timeless quality of works. I too have tried to make our works timeless, ensuring they keep looking good for a long time. This has to do with proportion, with simplicity, and with the fact that the fewer elements, variables, and complications it has, the easier it will always be to achieve a good result.

Talking of your father's studio and your own, what do you see in your studio that might be termed continuity with the past, and where are the greatest breaks with that past?

The continuity is the vision I share with my father that architecture is composed not only of design but of many other elements as well, and that to secure certain projects, it was necessary to be a developer. The gap I see between my father's studio and mine is in the dependence on the architects. Back
116 then, projects depended more on the individuals who developed them than on a process or structure, as they do now.

My dream was to successfully run an architecture firm with a solid structure of control and quality. I always felt responsibility towards the client. If a person commissions you for an office block, for example, you want the project to be the best, and the client needs to make money with it, so the budget must be controlled. There's traditionally been a tendency towards confrontation between contractors and architects owing to the large amount of money that's at stake.

78 When we were building the Presidente Chapultepec Hotel in 1974, the figure of the "Project Manager" emerged. This was a work coordinator, something that didn't exist when there was direct contact with the builder. Because the builders abused the situation, this figure appeared to point the finger everywhere without having responsibility for anything. Anyway, I always intended this studio to do things properly, to produce the plans with all the necessary data, to ensure that everything had a great quality of design and transcendence. We needed a team where nobody was indispensable, myself included.

In my father's time, there were figures in the office who were sometimes important, but who on other occasions didn't quite accomplish their role. I've always thought that the team of people working in an office is what gives it its character. It wasn't easy to get where we are now, but we've gradually been approaching our goal, and today we have a great architecture firm, one of the biggest in Mexico and in Latin America.

With about 400 people?

Yes, but the most important thing is to know about everything. Of course, you need to have a good internal team for architecture, interior design, engineering, representation, and expression, but you also need people in other promotional roles who know how to operate, how to rent, legalities, and so on. Based on projects like Antara, a mixed-use project in 2006, I developed my philosophy that every element forms part of the experience of a place, from a sign to a poorly let property or a badly organized group of businesses. On the other hand, if the place you're walking through doesn't impress you as pleasant, you're not going to go walking there again. That was really the great leap taken by this studio, doubly important because I had worked before then with department stores, but Antara was the first shopping center I did without them.

At some moment you've remarked that every project is a new starting point for you, and you don't have preconceived formal ideas. However, both in your work and in your father's, the formal aspects are very potent.

E

F

We don't always use the same forms or the same materials. Every region is different, and it's not the same, for instance, to build a hotel in Puerto Vallarta as it is in Cancún or Tulum. You must adapt to the forms of the place and not have preconceived ideas. You have to make sure a project blends with the culture of the specific place, and at the same time makes you feel you're in a particular region. This is fundamental when it comes to hotels. Nowadays, hotels have become so generic that when you arrive, you don't know where you are.

I think it's very important for architecture to be able to interpret each context. Unlike many architects who have become known for using only one material or certain forms, I prefer the idea of freedom. I've always loved proportion and geometry, but freedom is above all that, and a fundamental part of that freedom is that it now gives us the chance to make decisions, to change and experiment depending on the scale, context, and type of project we're working on. It's hard to work successfully with different scales, from micro to macro; but you can if you have that freedom of focus.

How do you see your work with respect to the modern architecture that flourished earlier in Mexico, especially after the Second World War?

What we are today as architects is the full practice we have created over time. In that period, the historic significance of architecture was much more important and symbolic. As technology, technique, culture, and education have advanced, we've become more internationalized and in a way we've lost a little of our identity. But we still have connections with the past, a guiding thread that reflects all we do through all we have done as architects. This basis of thought spins itself out and creates a proximity to history, tradition, and what you're doing as a studio.

How do you see the role of the next generation in your studio? What changes do you expect as a result of the influence of your sons?

Right now, we don't expect a revolution. My sons have been a very important part of the firm for some time now. It's rather like what happened in my father's day, when I started to take part in the affairs of the studio with him. We started to revolutionize everything. He continued to make decisions, as I did, but the decisions were now focused from another viewpoint. This part is very enriching, and it makes the creative process today so positive and successful. We involve the knowledge of three generations in everything that goes on. And so,

E Juan Sordo Madaleno and Javier Sordo Madaleno Bringas, 2076 Reforma, Mexico City. Interior of the workshop of Sordo Madaleno Arquitectos, circa 1992.

F Juan Sordo Madaleno and Javier Sordo Madaleno Bringas, 2076 Reforma, Mexico City. Interior of the workshop of Sordo Madaleno Arquitectos, 2015.

G From left to right in the SOMA/SMA offices, Antara Corporate II: José Juan Sordo Madaleno de Haro, Javier Sordo Madaleno Bringas, Fernando and Javier Sordo Madaleno de Haro, Mexico City, 2017.

G

I think the studio will go from strength to strength, because we continue to learn every day of our lives. I've improved many things through the insistence of my sons, who won't let us get complacent but come with questions and demands.

Your idea of a multidisciplinary studio doesn't seem very standard, and your focus in the field of real estate is very different from that of traditional real estate firms. It looks like rather a lonely road, doesn't it?

When I started to work, I made plans for others because I couldn't get the projects I wanted. When I went to see an agent with the plans and convinced them to do something, I realized that the things I was proposing to them came out well financially, and they were doing good business. Antara came up when I was developing the department store El Palacio de Hie-
198 rro in Polanco, at Molière Dos22, and the available lands were close by. I then realized the enormous potential of the place. Department stores at that time were tightly structured around what they wanted, and they didn't like to experiment any further. There were very strict "norms" for shopping centers, such as that they had to have a straight central passageway, that both doors had to be visible, that they had to have a width of ten meters, et cetera. I wanted to break away from those conventions because I found them very boring. When I go somewhere, I like to find a place that inspires me and makes me want to go back.

You remarked that the Antara project was special for you. Why?

For me, Antara was a very special exercise because it confirmed that we could also be successful as developers. The previous projects worked well, but Antara was a star project with a completely different concept. I am the biggest critic of my own projects, and I base my practice on my experiences. I think that if I like it and if I sense and feel a place, then most people are going to like it as well. This site was located between two streets. One was Miguel de Cervantes, a very pretty street with trees, pleasant for walking but very difficult to appreciate, while the other side was on Avenida Ejército Nacional, which continues to be a harsh and inhospitable street.

When I presented the project to my partners, the first building I proposed was a top category hotel. However, I didn't manage to get the idea accepted, and so I finally decided to do an office building. Housing was another major issue at that time. My partners told me that if we couldn't get a hotel into the project, we could make apartments, but I opposed this strongly, as my vision of the project I wanted to do was not suited to the level of dwelling that was then possible in that area.

Another great battle with my partners was getting the shopping center opened onto Calle Miguel de Cervantes. They were against this solution because it meant losing a lot of meters because of the doors, but I was convinced that the building had to be permeable on an urban level, and that it had to be open and allow people to pass through. And that contributed to its success. I always imagined Antara Masterplan as a new center that everyone would pass through, and that's what we achieved, because today we have around sixteen million visitors a year. Projects must generate positive changes and help cities to alter, customs to evolve, and barriers to be torn down.

Many of your city projects incorporate various building types or functions. What do you see for the future?

Indeed, we've designed several mixed-use projects within the urban fabric of different cities. That approach comes from my father, although it was less common at that time. It is important to realize that the city is mixed, and that variety gives it wealth and makes it interesting. I think that's why mixed-use complexes like Antara and Artz Pedregal in Mexico City and Andares in Guadalajara have worked so well, growing in phases and maturing over time. Those projects created new city centers that are alive all day and all through the week, by comparison with single-use developments that can stay alive during the week but die on the weekends or vice versa. The flow generated by one use helps the other, and community is gradually built.

The future will probably bring even more projects and new concepts that we will progressively incorporate. It will be a combination of things, some more traditional and others more contemporary, because everything must be steadily interrelated and has to be congruent. Someone who's giving to live in the place has to feel part of it. It must arouse a sense of belonging.

In many projects, you incorporate a substantial amount of art. It looks like another example of an advance in mixed-use developments, or at least an unusual path for a developer. Why do you do it?

The idea for Artz Pedregal (2018) came from the availability of some real estate that was regarded as the best in the south of the city, and I was adamant from the start that the place had to be a very special destination, with the finest offering of restaurants, shops, entertainment, and large areas of greenspace. I wanted it to be an evolution of Antara. Art is further away from everyone all the time. Museums are fixed and permanent collections don't change that much, so it's very important to bring art to people so that it will recover all the importance it should have in our lives.

When we started to do artistic interventions at Antara Masterplan, we realized those interventions were much better than any publicity. The people who visited them took photos and shared them, and those photos were suddenly in a lot of places online, something no advertising would ever have achieved. For instance, I wanted to inaugurate Antara with an exhibition by the sculptor Javier Marín, but he wanted to exhibit in a museum, not a shopping center. That was how the idea for Artz Pedregal was born, with Javier Marín as the most interested beneficiary. I think Artz Pedregal is the first project that changes the concept and the distance between art and retail by having art in the open air and interior spaces dedicated exclusively to art.

Changing the subject, let's talk about cities. You've done large-scale projects that have therefore been high-risk. What are the ideas that guide those projects? 173

I think I have the sensibility to realize how the city functions, 130
how it evolves and how it can change. In major interventions it's important to bring about a change—though it's important too in small interventions—by inspiring people or the government to help you put that change into effect. I've learned a lot over the years, as you gain from experience. I've realized that the most valuable thing is not the capital gain of your building, but the capital gain your building brings to its surroundings. That is what's given back to you and the area, and that's where the investment is recouped. There are many examples of renovations of urban areas that have had a great impact. However, certain areas would have been much better off if they had had urban planning from the start. In our country, unfortunately, the governments have six-year terms, so there's a new vision every six years. There's no way to generate a long-term view, and for the future of a city it's essential to be able to plan fifteen or twenty years ahead.

If we think of the city as an ecosystem, what would it need to have?

You must have diversity in the population to make a place attractive, and your product has to invite it. One current concept is that young people can share apartments and don't need to

H | Sordo Madaleno Arquitectos, SOMA/SMA offices, Antara Corporate II, Mexico City, 2017.

H

follow traditional ideas on homeowning, which is a starting point that leads to lots of variants. The same is true of hotels. The most advanced ones have rooms of different sizes and prices to achieve diversity. Based on diversity, you generate the architecture that in the end reflects the concept. Afterwards it must be finished off with everything to do with commercialization, the business premises that are needed, the communal areas, the gardens, the open spaces, the art, and everything that's going to help to build an integral community. Projects come to form part of the city's fabric, they encourage the formation of a community around them, and they enable new types of relationships. For me, that's the future. The only way forward is to take risks, and to do that, the design, the context, and the promotion have to be studied in depth.

Are there other factors that affect the way the city progresses?
I'll give you an example. If you ask other architects about my work, they may well say: "He's a developer." If you ask promoters, they'll say: "He's an architect." Although they appear to be very different professions, I've managed to strike the difficult balance between not cutting corners on the design, learning from experience, starting up projects that make positive changes to their environment, and at the same time doing business. I think it's always best to give more, and I know that the more you give, the more you get back.

I learned a lot from a project of my father's, Plaza Satélite, the shopping center in the north-west region of Mexico City that was inaugurated in 1971. When he did the shopping center, there was nothing around it. It was originally a go-kart track, and there was only empty land next to it. When the shopping mall opened, it was those next-door lands that made the most money. Everyone, then, must generate their own added value, but in the long term decisions can't be simply numerical; they have to be based on concept and vision.

You're an architect with a great appreciation and knowledge of cities. What is unique about Mexico City, and what does it share with any great metropolis anywhere in the world?
Mexico City is where I was born and where I've spent all my life. I know it well, and the truth is that I've learned to find its magical parts, its wonderful corners, and its culture. I've also lived through the policies that have influenced the city. I've seen how the city has gradually lost its intimacy as it's grown bigger. Mexico City is special because it has a very sophisticated culture and a very important history. I've seen many cities around the world, and cities always have cycles. They can go through a period when things seem to be getting worse, and then suddenly enter a phase when they get better. They start to improve because people rediscover those values that were being lost. The lifestyle of Mexico City is probably more European than American. It's a blend of history and culture, with tremendous social problems owing to the contrasts among its population, but it's a city that has many wonderful flavors for those living in it, as sophisticated as anywhere else in the world. You come to realize that in certain respects, Mexico City is very close to what's going on elsewhere and has parallel experiences.

I'd say the most interesting part is what comes next. In our city, we're all now starting to think about not using the car. The solution is not only public transport but also the relocation and creation of new centers, which means less movement. Mexico City is starting along a new road that I think could be beneficial for the city's future. New directions should always be made to lead to positive actions. Little by little, things get done and people join in.

How does Reforma Colón come to form part of this vision of the city?
The most important project we have in the studio today is the
Reforma Colón project, based on this principle of a new center. 136
The project approaches the city in a completely different way. It's the first project in this country and this city to consider the
relocation of people and mobility for pedestrians and cyclists 190
as priorities, although it also incorporates public transport, spaces for mobility, and some private transport operators.

The fundamental thing is to weave this social fabric. What is very important for Reforma Colón, and what most excites me about it, is that the area around it has every socio-economic level in Mexico City, from Colonia Guerrero, one of the poorest districts, to the wealthier Condesa and Roma. Everyone from the owner of a company to the courier could live in this development. They wouldn't have to live at the edge of the city and travel into the center every day. That's what I see as the important solution and contribution. We've done an analysis and mapping of 400 hectares around this project so that there can be housing, parks, amenities, and connections. The goal is for this whole project also to be a cause for people to return to Mexico City's great Historic Center.

The Reforma Colón project proposed elliptical towers. Why was this shape chosen? Does it have something to do with the need to create powerful buildings in a city of such size and personality?
Partly, perhaps, because the site is like a triangular polygon and it's very difficult to harmonize the two towers with square

or straight forms. You need a gentler encounter between them so that they will strike up a dialogue. Otherwise, the idea is to build an office block on a very large plan—about 3,000 square meters for the largest—because it's more efficient. The result gives you a very good form for the distance between the central core and the facade. We considered many shapes, but finally, because the towers are relatively close together, we preferred the curved form as a means of softening the encounter between the buildings. As in every project, you resolve all the aspects little by little. As the plan is very large, we made the tower slightly wider on the lower floors and shaped it to grow slenderer as it rises.

***Besides architecture and real estate development, do you do work* pro bono?**
Yes, when Fernando Landeros, the president of Teletón-México, came to see me, we understood each other. They make facilities for handicapped children in Mexico, and I thought it was wonderful to work for children in need. I've taken part in the
364
design and construction of more than twenty children's rehabilitation centers over two decades.

Their designs were based on color and geometric shapes, both inspired by children's toys. The children had to feel they were coming to a place that was theirs. At the same time, the interiors also had to have the same spirit while containing everything necessary for a rehabilitation center. A lot of things have to be taken into account. During therapies, for example, the children spend a long time looking at the ceiling or the walls. All elements must be worked on, not only the physical ones but also sensory aspects like the light, so that the children will be entertained at every moment. We sought inspiration in the locations of the centers, since each one is different according to its context. Another important aspect of *pro bono* work is everything you learn from it. The people in my office also feel great satisfaction at being able to help. They want to help, and this is a very palpable way of doing it.

Do you think the projects for Teletón pay tribute to the traditions of Mexican architecture?
No doubt about it. The inspiration in our history and culture comes from different sources in Mexico. I feel the influence of Chucho Reyes, because when it comes down to it, I think he was the discoverer of color in Mexican architecture. Really, what Chucho did was one thing, what Luis Barragán did was another, and what I've done in the Teletón projects is something else again. Not everything that uses color has the same meaning. The important thing is that with Teletón we used the tradition of color of Chucho Reyes, and this, combined with reminiscences of traditional Mexican toys (like the spinning top), is reflected in the geometrical forms of the buildings. Why Mexican toys? Because the Teletón buildings are for children, and the intention is that the children should always relate to the architecture. That's why the interior always has textures, colors, and drawings—things that interest children. I think the Teletón architecture is directly related and pays a clear tribute to our culture and our tradition, always extremely colorful.

Is there some building you would like to do or which remains for you to do in your career?
I'd love to do an airport. I have several ideas for making changes in current airports. You're often forced to pass through spaces that don't interest you like the duty free. There are no pleasant areas; they're all utilitarian. Airports lack heart, and I'd like to implement a few ideas to give them one.

What changes do you see on the horizon for the architectural profession?
A lot more figures are going to appear in architecture, at least in our country. When I started, there weren't many architects who were also developers, but in the future, there are going to be more multidisciplinary offices. Nowadays, to be just an architect, pure and simple, you really have to be a genius, and that's for very few. It's going to get harder all the time to be a genius, with so much information and so many things around! You must have the support of a team. For example, to find out about new materials and collaborate with those who are developing them, or to study the social aspects of a project and its community effect as well as its implications for its surroundings.

Interview with Javier Sordo Madaleno de Haro

You started to work in the architecture studio when you were a student, combining the academic and professional worlds. What did you gain from each of those experiences?
I was very lucky to be able to combine university with the studio. The academic part was good, but I think academic curricula in Mexico still have to grow. I feel that the academic degree course is not practical enough. In the studio, I learned a lot about the technical part and the reality of the profession. Fortunately, I was able to transfer that experience to the university.

What do you find most fulfilling about your professional work?
What I like are projects that change the paradigm, the "game changers," to explore different programs rather than repeating the traditional way of doing things. I'm also very partial to projects with a cultural component.

It seems that a lack of complacency is an intrinsic part of architecture, that aspect of the profession rooted in imagining an unknown future...
Architecture allows you to imagine the future. It opens your mind in many ways and lets you understand things from another perspective. Without architecture, I wouldn't have the creativity to be able to work on all these projects at once. I don't like to remain bound by pure design. I like challenges in the program and in social affairs. If a project is really successful, it's because it brings together many components apart from a good design.

Let´s talk a little about Artz Pedregal. Where did the idea come from to combine art and commerce? I understand you were the driving force.
I've always liked art to decorate private spaces but taking it to the public can attract new audiences, and the experience of retailing is greatly changed. In this case, it was perhaps also a restless urge to give rise to something new. A lot of people talk about generating new experiences, but few actually do it. Achieving it is very interesting, as it involves an integral conceptualization of the project. The project is the architecture, the way it's done commercially: the brands, the restaurants, the art, the greenspace, and a whole series of integrated elements. That's how the design process was focused.

Are you trying to change the concept of the shopping center to allow shoppers to have more activities at their disposal, or are you trying to promote art?
People come for the pleasure of the space but also for the art, which is an important part of the project. I've always liked challenges, and I think this is the biggest I've taken on. When I started with the project for the Fundación Arte Abierto (Open Art Foundation), very few people believed it was possible to mix art and retail, or to have an exhibition venue and a cultural program inside a shopping mall. It wasn't easy to explain to the Board that you were going to invest in spaces for art with no direct return. In time, however, when they saw the final project, the way it could be done and the experiences it would provide, they grew convinced that the concept was sound and that the returns would come in other forms by stimulating culture and creativity.

Talking of technology, it seems to hold great promise in every phase, from design to construction.
I think technology is a very interesting tool for thinking through the possibility of doing something different, as in the case of prefabs or modular construction. For instance, we recently took part in a tender with a proposal for a totally modular hotel in Saudi Arabia, with every room designed as an independent module. In general, though, these are technologies in progress. The traditional systems still dominate the market.

Right now, technology is more important in the design phase than in construction, where it's not yet demanded by developers. They're tools for design and representation. Using technological resources helps clients to understand the project more easily, and they offer many advantages for an architecture studio when used well.

Tell me about time. In architecture, many people seem to try to cut time down on the principle that "time is money". That doesn't seem to be the way at Sordo Madaleno Arquitectos, but it would be logical to reduce times, since technology allows immediacy in communications and many other things.
I don't think very fast things are good. Everything needs its time. For example, the development of the Antara project lasted seven years, the same as Artz Pedregal. There's a design process and a construction process, and with time you can rectify and improve the project. I feel that good things take time. Doing a very good, very well-thought-out project, with all the necessary components put together, is very complicated. I'm a restless spirit; but I like to do things well.

How has the studio evolved since you started in 2006? Where will it go in the future?
In 2006, the office was very different from today's, and my father's office in the nineties was traditional in its way of doing

I Sordo Madaleno Arquitectos, Middle East Masterplan proposal, 2020.

I

things. The great change took place with the progression from a medium-sized studio to a large one, with international collaborators and alliances with other firms. The breaking of the barriers to exercising the profession in Mexico really came when we opened up to other countries, other processes, other ways of doing things, and above all to attracting important talent. I'm a firm believer that it's essential to know who makes up the studios. I believe a studio is not a one-man show but the entirety of the human team you form.

The foundations of the future are already laid. The firm is very solid and will keep growing. We have been nurturing support areas like technology, human resources, communication, and marketing, very good for making the studio stronger and better organized. I think the next natural step will be to participate in more international projects and perhaps establish
242 satellite offices to handle projects in other countries.

Interview with Fernando Sordo Madaleno Haro

How did you first start out in the world of architecture?
I studied at the Universidad Iberoamericana, where I took my degree in architecture between 2010 and 2014. Since 2012, my professional career has been with Sordo Madaleno Arquitectos (SMA). At the beginning I started working through all the stages, as I think it's very important to understand the practice from different viewpoints—from that of the draftsman, the manager, the project director, and now as director of architecture.

When I joined the office, I was still studying, and I obviously had a lot of things to learn. Today, I still have a good deal to learn. My father and I thought the best procedure would be to learn from both school and the studio. He gave me the chance to earn a position in very conspicuous projects. Solaz Los Cabos was the first project I was involved in. I had to work on the design of something very specific, the *cañadas*

J | Fernando Sordo Madaleno de Haro reviewing the project, Mexico City, 2018.
K | Sordo Madaleno Arquitectos, SOMA/SMA offices, Antara Corporate II, Mexico City, 2017.

J

K

or "ravines," and that was my introduction. From then on, my ideas went down well, and I moved on to a slightly higher level of design, not just a draftsman. Speaking sincerely, it was a very valuable process.

There's a traditional separation between architects and developers, but it seems the two are very closely integrated in SMA. Why is that?
I think we'd have to go back to the DNA of the office and the context of its beginnings. It was founded by my grandfather in 1937, at a moment when Mexico was growing. The architects of that time were the ones who planned the cities. Then my grandfather had the vision of building the first shopping centers in Latin America, with Plaza Universidad in 1969 and Plaza Satélite in 1971. Today we see that these centers are regenerating different urban centers in their turn. I think architecture and city planning have always been connected, and I think too that putting these pieces together is also the job of architects. Today we have to collaborate with specialists in urban macro-scales for these projects, something that's been in our DNA and has evolved since the office was founded.

As an architect, what's your vision of Mexico City? How do you understand it?
As an architect, working here and born in Mexico City, I think the context is enormously enriching, because we have many cities in one. For example, Colonia Condesa or Colonia Roma have different scales. Each district has its own identity. That's why it's so important that we understand the context in depth when we carry out a project in a city as big as this one and know how it was generated and how it's evolved. I certainly love this city, and I think its diversity is very rich.

For you, what is the context when you're going to start a project?
For me, the context or the place is without doubt the most important thing in the phase of conceptualization, because it's a source of inspiration. I believe a great deal in the conceptual phase of a project, not only to produce a pretty piece of architecture but also to make sure it belongs and has meaning in that specific place. I think I feed constantly off the conditions of the site and its analysis as a basis for the creative process. I like to look at everything, as I love history and I think it's very enriching. We have to know how we have arrived at the particular site, the things with which people identify and how you want your project to be identified too.

Before starting on a project, we embark on a phase of very deep research. Besides the historical, social, and cultural questions, there are other important factors to be considered, like the climate, the topography, the orientations, and the vernacular architecture. All that feeds our creativity. When you see a Sordo Madaleno building, whether it's a picture, a rendering, or the finished project, you notice a very interesting formal diversity. That's because we begin with a blank sheet of paper but also with very well-established criteria and a process for our investigation and analysis. To arrive at a solution, there is

L

L Sordo Madaleno Arquitectos, Chablé Sea of Cortez, La Paz, Baja California Sur, 2020, rendering.

a guiding thread in all those steps we've taken beforehand. Nevertheless, the materiality, the conceptual sense, and the formal result are very different in each project.

Tell me a little about the materials and the construction processes, as there is much talk now of new materials, industrialization, modular construction, and sustainability. How do you see these new frontiers?
The history of architecture has always been related to the technology of its time. The twentieth century was marked by the use of concrete, and designs were greatly influenced by metal structures. I think it is always necessary to be very up to date with these technologies because they're the thing that molds architecture and puts it in the present. Architecture is a witness to what is happening at a given period, and we have to stay abreast with ours. Sustainability and sustainable materials are certainly a priority, although construction ultimately runs somewhat counter to sustainability. In the Chablé Sea of Cortez (L) project that we're doing in La Paz, Baja California Sur, you come to a site that hasn't been touched by man, and you have to make sure the project gives more to the place than the place gives us. We can't get value out without putting value in. This is the paradigm that's changing now.

By way of an example, can you tell us about a project that satisfied you and which you regard as a success?
It's often said that the best project is always the next one. That's what keeps me always looking for ways to improve in the things we're doing, learning a great deal in the process. I don't know if I could mention any project in particular among the many very interesting ones we're working on.

What do you find the most enriching thing about architecture? Where's your architectural passion?
My passion for architecture is huge, and I can assure you it hasn't changed since I was a boy. I think I'm greatly attracted by the blank sheet. The creative process involved in starting a project and investigating the context is without a doubt what most impassions me. I think a lot of challenges come afterwards. The concept is the purest idea, and then other factors come into it that we architects are sometimes unable to control: the engineering, the budgets, the construction, and other parameters that ought to be opportunities but sometimes aren't. I think the pure idea of the concept is what most impassions me.

Where do you see the studio going in the future? Or to put it another way, what do you want to take with you of the history of SMA?
Having a studio with more than eighty years of history has always been a challenge for me, but also an enormous opportunity given to me by my grandfather and now my father. Having that platform and starting to work on architecture from a very young age presents a great many challenges and difficulties that I eagerly confront. The normal process of the architect is much slower. I'm twenty-nine, and we have some eighty projects under way. It's an accelerated process that carries a lot of responsibility. In the future we want to see SMA as a Mexican architecture studio with an international reputation, a course we have already begun. My vision is that we will be recognized internationally as a Mexican architecture studio.

What makes SMA different from other studios?
What's different at SMA is our real understanding of what we're planning and the acquiescence of all the social and economic players—the context and the environment—that we can bring to the table to analyze. All this is part of our makeup, from reconnaissance to the creative process. I think we're able to come up with very different and interesting solutions.

I.

URBAN TRANSFORMATION

1.

TWO ARCHITECTS IN THE URBAN TRANSFORMATION OF THE METROPOLIS

MANUEL PERLÓ COHEN

A Aerial photograph of the Colonia Roma, Mexico City, 1957.

Jointly spanning eighty-seven years, the architectural and professional careers of Juan Sordo Madaleno and Javier Sordo Madaleno have left a permanent mark on the physiognomy and landscape of Mexico City. Begun in 1937 by the former and carried forward from 1985 until the present day by the latter, their architectural oeuvre is probably the most extensive in Mexico. It can certainly be argued that the two generations are different, with architectural training, styles, working methods, and historical contexts that diverge to give each personality a distinctive stamp. But it may be asserted nevertheless that the accumulation of knowledge, traditions, and values found are shared and applied by both architects in their work. One element of continuity is the challenge both have faced in working in the city of their birth, the place where they have lived and given shape to their most ambitious projects and proposals. It is a city that has been characterized by vertiginous growth, offering extraordinary opportunities to its millions of residents, professionals and entrepreneurs, and continually presenting enormous challenges in the fields of environmental protection, infrastructure, and planning.

This is perhaps best illustrated by history. At the end of 1939, when the administration of President Lázaro Cárdenas del Río (1934–1940) was in its fifth year, Mexico City had 1.4 million inhabitants, as the census of 1940 later showed. It was a national capital that was not one of the world's largest cities, like London (8.6 million), New York (7.4 million) or Tokyo (7.3 million). It was even less populous than some Latin American cities like Greater Buenos Aires, with its 3.6 million inhabitants, and Rio de Janeiro, which at that time had a population of nearly 1.8 million. During Cárdenas's left-wing nationalist government, the capital did not escape the sweeping social and political transformations implemented by the government on a national scale, including agrarian reform, socialist education, and nationalization. These transformations found expression in the considerable extension of the communal ownership of land at numerous points around the Federal District, the formation of many so-called "proletarian colonies" to the northeast of the capital, and the reduction of the federal government's support for new urban projects in favor of investment in rural areas.

A

At that same time, in December 1939, a young man of twenty-three presented his professional thesis to qualify as an architect at the National School of Architecture of the UNAM (National Autonomous University of Mexico). With experience in professional practice since 1937, Juan Sordo Madaleno entitled his thesis: "Edificios de Comercios y Departamentos" (Mixed-use spaces: commercial and apartment buildings).[1] In the section of his text in which he discussed precedents, he explained his interest in proposing a project aimed at the middle class which now required living space thanks to improved economic prospects. Sordo Madaleno's project was in Colonia Roma, one of the most sought-after residential zones in the city at that time (A). Although its height and modern design departed from the architectural styles of the *colonia*, it did conform with their tradition of mixed use. In the following years, the young practitioner continued to construct buildings on the same scale, and with the same uses, in Colonia Roma as well as the neighboring Juárez and Cuauhtémoc.

Under the next federal administration, headed by General Manuel Ávila Camacho (1940–1946), the country underwent a sharp turn away from the economic policy of his predecessor. Land distribution, nationalizations, and socialist education were curtailed, and industrialization was fostered instead, security was provided for private investment, and workers' demands were reined in. In Mexico City, this change led to greater support from the federal government for the authority

1. Juan Sordo Madaleno, "Edificios de Comercios y Departamentos," thesis to obtain the degree of architect, Mexico City, Escuela Nacional de Arquitectura, UNAM (1939).

B Juan Sordo Madaleno, model of the urban proposal for the intersection of Reforma and Insurgentes, Mexico City, 1954.
C Mario Pani, model of the urban proposal for the intersection of Reforma and Insurgentes, Mexico City, 1944.

B

C

in charge of the Federal District, the DDF (Federal District Department), resulting in public works, the spread of industrial estates, greater incentives for private residential developments, and expropriation of communal lands. The location of the projects and the type of buildings constructed by Juan Sordo Madaleno seem to correspond to the new economic development and the processes of deconcentration and densification that the capital was starting to undergo. In the early 1940s, the first Sears Roebuck store was built on the grounds of the former American School in Colonia Roma, not far from his buildings at Monterrey and Álvaro Obregón and at 15 Tonalá.

Sordo Madaleno's first steps seem to point toward similar projects, typically represented by mixed-purpose buildings with no more than ten floors constructed on relatively small plots. However, recent investigations in the historic archive of Sordo Madaleno Arquitectos reveal that he drew up an audacious project in 1954 for an urban intervention of considerably larger size for the time (B). This was the project for the Reforma-Insurgentes intersection, which envisaged several high-rise buildings, shopping areas, parking lots, and pedestrian zones, and reveals an architect with the ability to conceive large-scale projects as part of the urban fabric. Ten years before, in 1944, Mario Pani also proposed his well-known Reforma-Insurgentes Crossing project, which consisted of a round plaza with three hundred meters in diameter ringed by twelve high-rise towers, the tallest in the city, connected at ground level by areas for shops and pedestrians, with an enormous car park reached by ramps (C).[2]

Neither project was implemented. In the case of Mario Pani's proposal, we know from the writings of Salvador Novo, a prominent journalist and chronicler of Mexico City, that the project had the support of the city authorities, but that strong opposition arose among some property owners in the area, who disagreed with the project and with the costs proposed. "The whole problem," Novo wrote, "will be convincing the blind and recalcitrant conservatives of the city's future development."[3] On the other hand, the political moment was no longer propitious for interventions of such magnitude, since the administrations of President Manuel Ávila Camacho and the head of the DDF, Javier Rojo Gómez, were both entering their final phase.

In 1946, new times arrived for both the nation and the city.
For the first time, Mexico had a civilian president, Miguel 282
Alemán, who had emerged from the ranks of the UNAM. Here was an executive with a strong program of modernization, and architects were invited to give shape and form to his project. In 1947, the recently created Ingenieros Civiles Asociados (ICA), directed by the engineer Bernardo Quintana, began construction of the Multifamiliar (Housing Project) Miguel Alemán, designed by Mario Pani (D). Soon after came the Multifamiliar Benito Juárez, also the result of the triangular relationship between Pani, ICA, and the Federal Government. Major architectural projects of the time include the Secretariat for Hydraulic Resources on the Reforma-Colón plaza, the National Conservatory of Music, and the National Auditorium.

However, perhaps the most important project of the late 1940s and early 1950s was the construction of the UNAM campus to the south of Mexico City, which involved the work

2. Graciela de Garay, "Mario Pani," in *Historia oral de la Ciudad de México. Testimonio de sus arquitectos (1940–1990)* (Mexico City: Conaculta-Instituto Mora, 2000).
3. Salvador Novo, *La vida en México en el periodo presidencial de Manuel Ávila Camacho* (Mexico City: INAH-Conaculta, 1994).

D Mario Pani, Presidente Alemán Housing Project, Mexico City, 1949.
E Aerial photograph of University City, Mexico City, 1960.

D

E

of well-known architects from different generations (E). Near the campus, the most emblematic private residential district in the south of Mexico City, Pedregal de San Ángel, rose on terrain of volcanic origin. Architects Luis Barragán and Max Cetto played a key role in its design and construction.

While Juan Sordo Madaleno did not participate in the wave of public projects, he did make a modest contribution to it in 1953 with the construction of the UNAM Geology Institute at the new Ciudad Universitaria. Instead, he kept more or less to the line of his previous work, responding to the needs of the real estate market and private enterprise. During Miguel Alemán's dynamic six-year term, the architect built the shop and apartment block at 533 Insurgentes (1950), designed in collaboration with Jesús García Collantes, and the residence at 2388 Reforma (1952). He also designed in response to the country's new industrializing demands, as at the Wyeth-Vales pharmaceutical complex (1950).

In the decade from 1940 to 1950, Mexico City experienced unprecedented urban growth, and the population of its metropolitan area grew from 1.4 million to nearly 3 million inhabitants. In some areas of what was then the periphery, like Azcapotzalco, Gustavo A. Madero, Iztapalapa, and Álvaro Obregón, the annual growth rates fluctuated between 11% and 17%. This rapid demographic increase, which was to continue
94 in subsequent decades, was largely due to the natural growth of the population, but a factor was also the torrential arrival in
314 the national capital of migrants attracted by the opportunities and better living conditions it offered.

With the arrival of the new government of Adolfo Ruiz Cortines (1952–1958), many national policies were reformulated, particularly where Mexico City was concerned. Instead of the grand architectural projects of the previous six-year term, the policy now favored was one of constructing such basic services as water supplies, drainage, public markets, and schools. To ensure the fulfilment of his objectives of austerity and social orientation, the president appointed an energetic politician named Ernesto P. Uruchurtu as head of the DDF. His effectiveness and determination kept him in the post for nearly fourteen years, during which time he applied a policy of containment of growth whose effects were seen in a drastic reduction of applications for new residential developments. In December 1953, a new planning law for the Federal District was passed, centralizing approval for new constructions in the city with the head of the DDF, displacing the existing planning committee, and shelving any attempt to draw up an official plan for urban growth.[4]

The check imposed on the horizontal expansion of the city stimulated greater population density in some of the districts formed in the first half of the twentieth century, as well as causing an overflow into the State of Mexico, where the Ciudad Satélite (Satellite City) project began in the 1950s, involving the participation of architects like Mario Pani and Luis Barragán together with major artists like Mathias Goeritz. In this new context for the urban development of the capital, Sordo Madaleno continued to concentrate on the city's vertical expansion with office buildings and cinemas, two of the most outstanding being Cine Ermita (1951) and Cine París (1954). He also undertook architectural projects for religious buildings like the Sanatorio de la Sociedad de la Beneficencia Española

4. Adrián García Cortés (1972), *La reforma urbana de México: Crónicas de la Comisión de Planificación del Distrito Federal*, vol. I (Mexico City: 1972).

Chapel (1955) and was involved during this period in a project for a public edifice, the Dirección de Policía y Tránsito (1956). His crowning achievement in 1958 was without doubt the imposing Anáhuac Tower on the Reforma-Colón plaza, opposite the building designed by Mario Pani in 1950 for the Secretariat for Hydraulic Resources.[5]

With the beginning of the presidency of Adolfo López Mateos (1958–1964), who decided to ratify Uruchurtu as head of the DDF, there was a fresh impetus for the great urban architectural projects that had been lost in the previous administration, though new residential developments were not permitted. The new president wanted the image of Mexico to be clearly projected abroad, not only to attract a growing flow of tourists but also to draw attention to the great social progress that had been achieved and to publicize the country's enormous cultural wealth. To attain these ends, he pursued three major projects. The first was a successful application in 1963 to host the 1968 Olympic Games in Mexico City; the second was the construction of the urban architectural complex of Tlatelolco (F), headed by Mario Pani; and the last was the construction of a complex of museums in Bosque de Chapultepec (Chapultepec Forest), foremost among them the National Museum of Anthropology, under the direction of Pedro Ramírez Vázquez.

Once more, Juan Sordo Madaleno remained almost completely apart from the wave of official projects, but he showed great vision in taking advantage of the new era in the country to boost his own areas of interest. The time had come for the construction of the hotels that would articulate Mexico's new insertion in the international context. The turn came in 1958 for the Presidente Acapulco Hotel, and in 1961 for the inauguration of one of the most iconic hotels in Mexico City to this day, the María Isabel Hotel, designed in collaboration with the architect José Villagrán García. Sordo Madaleno's production intensified and diversified throughout the 1960s. In 1960, he built the striking pharmaceutical complex of Merck, Sharp & Dohme. In 1964, he designed a public building, the Palacio de Justicia (Court of Law) in the central Colonia de los Doctores. In addition, his work now extended to Spain, where he designed a hotel complex in Torremolinos (1963), followed by the Villamagna Hotel (1963) and Meliá Castilla Hotel (1968), both in Madrid. One can only agree with what Juan Manuel Heredia wrote about the intensity and effectiveness of Sordo Madaleno's work: "His studio must have had a surprising level of organization to have successfully completed so much work of quality."[6]

In the mid-1960s came Sordo Madaleno's first metropolitan project, the civic center of Lomas Verdes (1966) (H), designed 48 jointly with Luis Barragán, who had considerable experience in large residential developments like Pedregal de San Ángel 100 and Ciudad Satélite. Without abandoning his projects in the capital, he started to look further afield at other districts in the metropolitan area of Mexico City, as well as in other cities around the country and the world (G, H). The policy of containing growth in the Federal District eventually led to an overflow of population into neighboring municipalities in the State of Mexico, where there was a lack of roads and public transport. In 1960, the population of the Federal District was 4.8 million while the metropolitan municipalities held about 246,000 inhabitants. By 1970, the population of the Federal District had grown to 6.9 million, and the metropolitan municipalities to 1.8 million. The highest rate of population growth was to be found in the State of Mexico.

In the second half of the 1960s, under the administration of President Gustavo Díaz Ordaz (1964–1970), Sordo Madaleno continued to build hotels, one example being the Presidente Cozumel Hotel (1969). It was nearly at the end of the decade that he made his first incursion into the design of what for Mexico was a new urban and commercial concept, the shopping mall. The first was Plaza Universidad (1969), in collaboration with Adolfo Wiechers. Shortly afterwards came Plaza 190 Satélite (1971), the Bosques de las Lomas Complex (1974), 72 and Perisur (1980).

During the 1970s, under the presidency of Luis Echeverría (1970–1976), Sordo Madaleno carried out some of his most iconic projects in Mexico City. They were less numerous than those of the previous decade, but they were very high-profile: 220 the 555 Palmas Tower (1975), the Centro Operativo Bancomer 348, 352 (1976), and the Presidente Chapultepec Hotel in Polanco (1977). 58 78 This phase coincides with the first systematic attempt to initiate urban planning in Mexico City, with the approval of the Planning Law for the Federal District in 1971 and the Urban 52 Development Law for the Federal District in 1976. 64

---

5. For a very thorough review of Juan Sordo Madaleno's work, see Miquel Adriá, *Juan Sordo Madaleno (1916–1985)*, (Mexico City: Arquine, 2013), with texts by Juan Manuel Heredia and photographs by Guillermo Zamora.
6. Juan Manuel Heredia, "Juan Sordo Madaleno y el sentido de la proporción," in *Juan Sordo Madaleno (1916–1985)* (Mexico City: Arquine, 2013).

F Mario Pani, aerial photograph of the Nonoalco Tlatelolco Housing Project, Mexico City, 1965.
G Juan Sordo Madaleno and Luis Barragán, aerial photograph of La Alteña Housing Project, Lomas Verdes, State of Mexico, 1973.
H Juan Sordo Madaleno and Luis Barragán, Lomas Verdes urban planning project, State of Mexico, 1966.

F

G

H

Under the administration of President José López Portillo (1976–1982), large oil reserves were discovered, and the country experienced the illusion of a bonanza that was to end in a terrible economic crisis. The currency was devalued, and the ensuing flight of capital prompted Portillo to nationalize the banks. Right at the peak of the crisis, Juan Sordo Madaleno formalized his partnership with his son Javier to form Sordo Madaleno y Asociados. Born in 1956, Javier Sordo Madaleno studied architecture at the Universidad Iberoamericana, graduating in 1979 at exactly the same age as his father was when he qualified in 1939. From a very early age, he had known famous architects like Luis Barragán, José Villagrán, Augusto H. Álvarez, Ricardo Legorreta, Francisco Serrano, and José A. Wiechers, as well as artists like Chucho Reyes and Mathias Goeritz, who were family friends.

Juan Sordo Madaleno died in 1985, whereupon his son Javier took over the directorship of Sordo Madaleno y Asociados. The country was still deep in a profound economic crisis marked by galloping inflation, falling purchasing power, the bankruptcy of thousands of firms, devaluation, and high unemployment. To make matters worse, two earthquakes on September 19 of that year caused the greatest seismic devastation in Mexico City in centuries.

The location for Javier Sordo Madaleno's first project in his own right, in 1986, was Polanco, a *colonia* that would become for him what Roma and Juárez had been for his father. As Miquel Adrià says:

> With the Centro Internacional de Prensa, which later became the Televisa Cultural Center for Contemporary Art, Javier Sordo saw his opportunity at the age of twenty-seven. He had two weeks to propose a project that he resolved in a single night, imagining first of all the definition of the central gap around which the floors were arranged on the same levels as at the Hotel Presidente, designed by his father, with thoughts of the possibility of joining up the modules in future to form a shopping center. Taking risks, beguiling and persuading formed part of what Henri Cartier-Bresson called the decisive moments. And the decisive moment of Javier Sordo was the presentation of that project. It was convincing.[7]

With the presidency of Carlos Salinas de Gortari (1988–1994), Mexico adopted a policy that privileged a free market and fostered globalization in association with the United States through the North American Free Trade Agreement. New capital flows and investments reached various points of the national territory, above all the tourist centers and the northern border. This new context brought projects like the Westin Regina Hotel, in Los Cabos, Baja California Sur (1994), and the Molière Dos22 (1997), a shopping mall considered by specialists to be one of his most iconic works.

A watershed for the metropolitan area of Mexico City came in 1995. The population of the metropolitan municipalities reached 8.6 million, slightly higher than the Federal District's figure of 8.4 million. This meant a combined population of 17 million people. By 2000, the number of total inhabitants had risen to 18.4 million, making Mexico City the third most populous megalopolis in the world, behind only Tokyo, with its unbeatable 34.4 million, and the Kyoto-Osaka-Kobe corridor, with 18.6 million. This growth stemmed fundamentally from the metropolitan municipalities in the State of Mexico. While this urban conglomerate was forming, the authorities of its component parts—Mexico City, with its sixteen delegations, and fifty-nine municipal conurbations in the State of Mexico[8]—unfortunately failed to generate the laws, institutions, and investments necessary to give it metropolitan governability. Its people were left with a fragmented metropolis.

Before the end of the century, under the presidency of Ernesto Zedillo (1994–2000), changes took place that had an important effect on the internal administration of Mexico City. In 1996, the Political Constitution of Mexico was reformed to modify legislation that permitted the President of the Republic to govern the Federal District through the head of its administration. In 1997, thanks to the change, the administrative head started to be elected by secret and universal ballot, and the same began to occur after 2000 with the election 356
of the sixteen delegates. This transcendent political modification was to change the rules of play in the city, including its plans and projects for urban development. Architects and developers no longer had the president as interlocutor, but now came to depend on local authorities and greater participation by residents.

The fifty-eight-year period covered in this essay, 1939 to 1997, encompasses two generations of architects of the Sordo Madaleno family, who have been joined in recent years by a third generation. During that time, the works they have produced cover a very wide range of construction types: apartment buildings, office blocks, residential houses, industrial facilities, churches, hotels, corporate premises, public buildings, shopping centers, and hospitals. This truly impressive variety is to be found at numerous sites around the metropolitan area of Mexico City, and many others in Mexico and abroad. Only the greatest and most renowned architecture firms can boast such a portfolio.

Juan and Javier Sordo Madaleno have been building with- 230
out interruption in Mexico City since 1937. They have done
so in a city whose demographic, economic, cultural, and po- 198
litical growth has been one of the most spectacular in the world. Even at its most critical moments, this city has never ceased to offer options and opportunities. Each of these men has had his own historical circumstances, particular challenges, and personal responses, but the two have shared a visionary gaze enabling them to understand the time and place of their works, detect and exploit new paths, and drive their proposals forward. Their grasp of urban dynamics, their professional commitment to their projects, their ability to pursue complex undertakings supported by solid teams, and their creativity in stamping their personal architectural hallmark on their works have allowed them to leave a permanent trace in the life of the metropolis.

---

7. Miquel Adrià, "La arquitectura como una estrategia," in *Juan Sordo Madaleno (1916–1985)* (Mexico City: Arquine, 2013).
8. Programa de ordenación de la Zona Metropolitana del Valle de México, Actualización 2012, Síntesis Ejecutiva, Sedesol, Gobierno del Distrito Federal, Gobierno del Estado de México y Gobierno del Estado de Hidalgo.

Population growth in Mexico City (1824–2014)

1956
DIRECCIÓN DE POLICÍA Y TRÁNSITO

Left hand page, above: main facade. Below: eastern facade and Tlaxcoaque Street.

Right hand page, above: access lobby. Below: model, Chapel of the Santísima Concepción (17th century) as the main element of the plaza.

1960
MERCK SHARP & DOHME

MERCK SHARP & DOHME

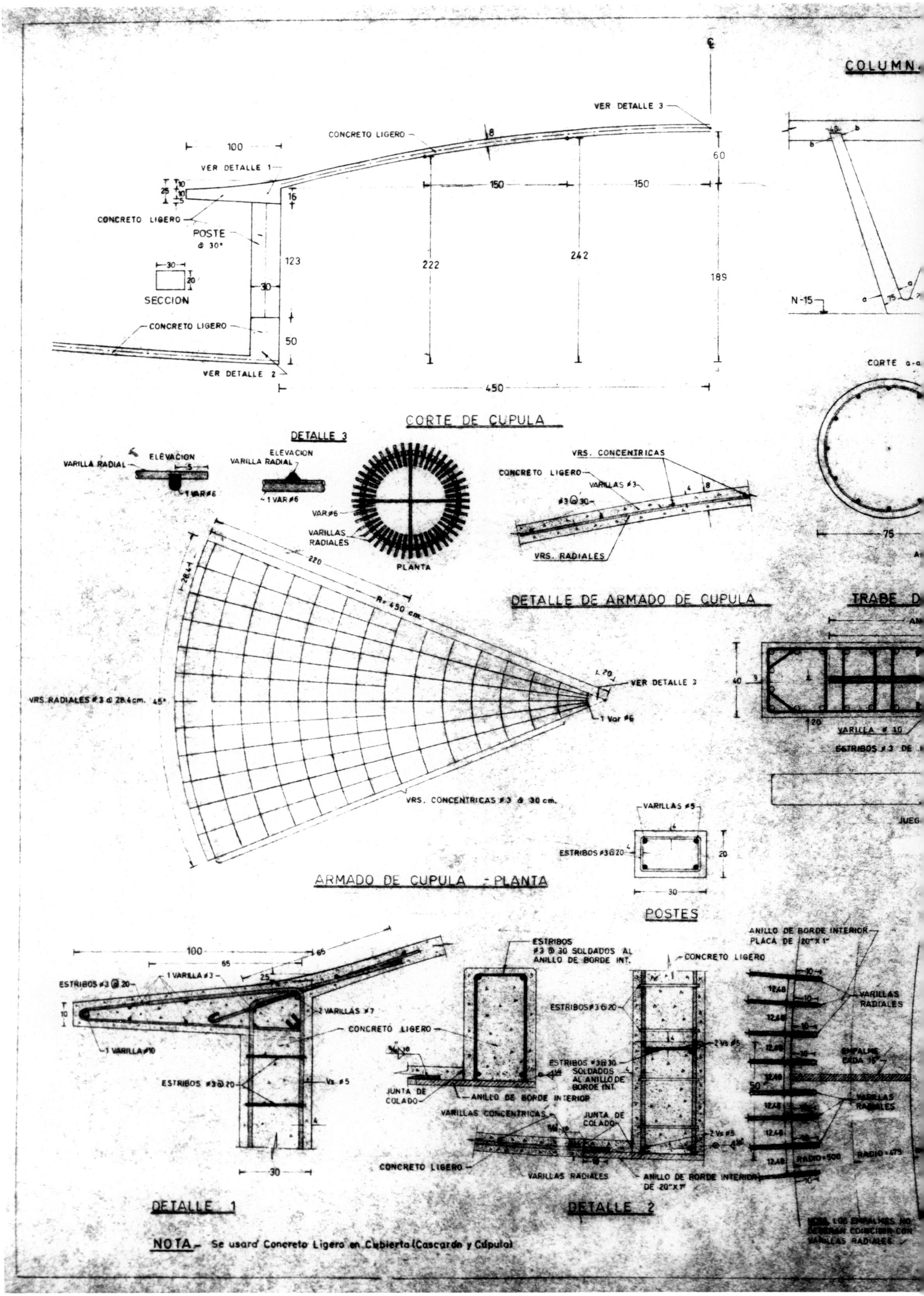

Construction details of the production unit. Leonardo de Zeevaert, consulting engineer.

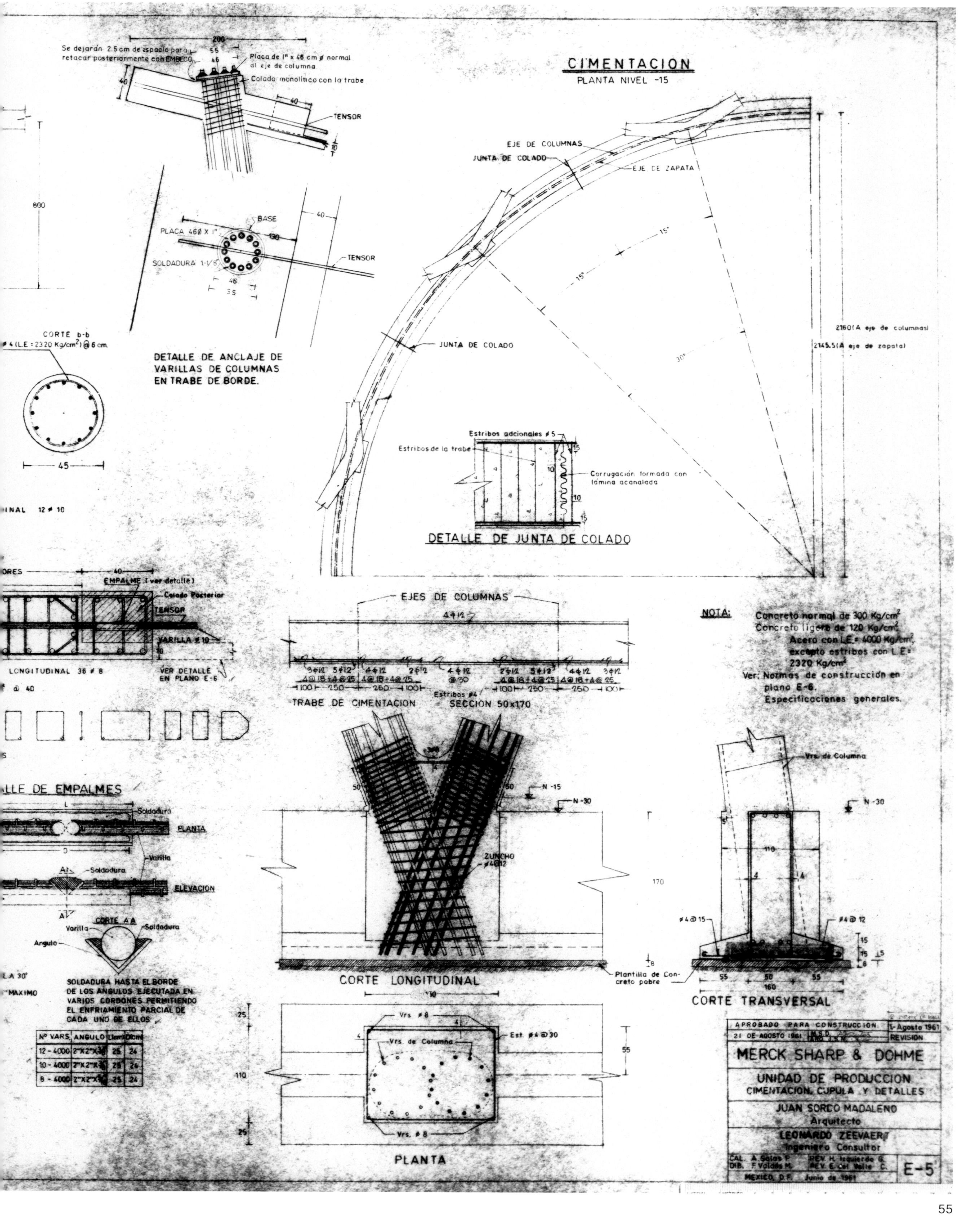

Nº VARS.	ANGULO		
12 - 4000	2"X2"X3/8	25	24
10 - 4000	2"X2"X3/8	25	24
8 - 4000	2"X2"X3/8	25	24

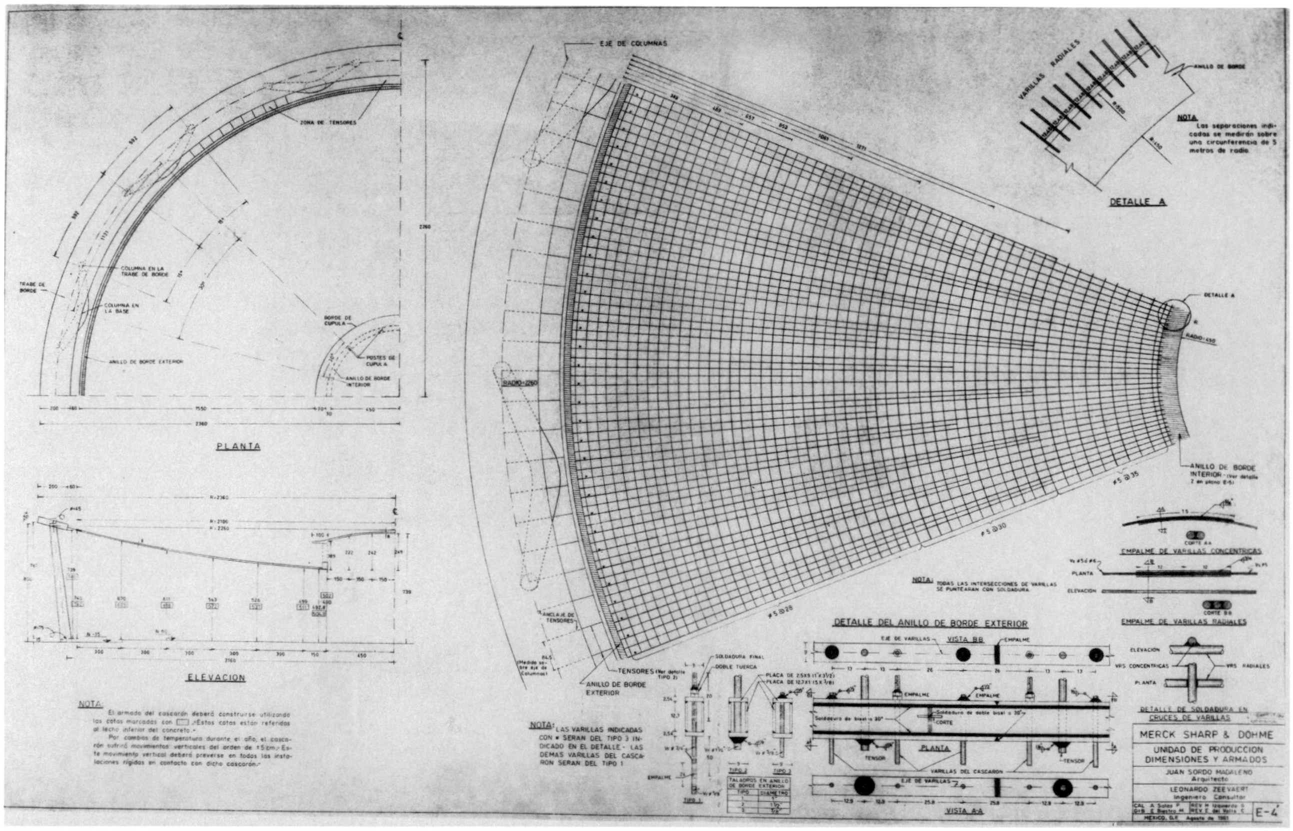

Left hand page: exterior view. Distribution hallway profile for the V-shape columns.

Above: assemblage detail of the dome of the production unit. Leonardo de Zeevaert, consulting engineer.

Below: interior view. Production plant in operation.

1961
MARÍA ISABEL

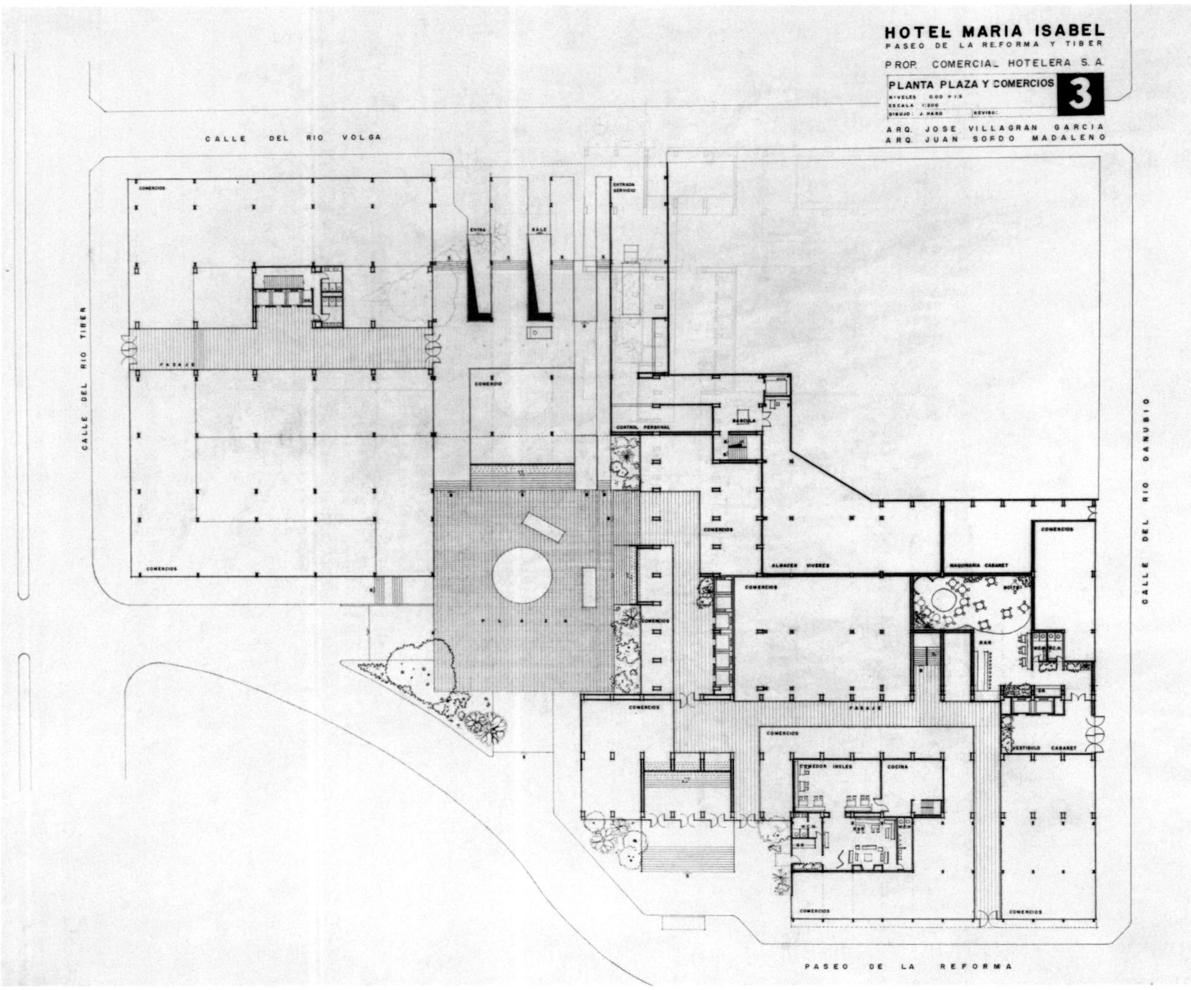

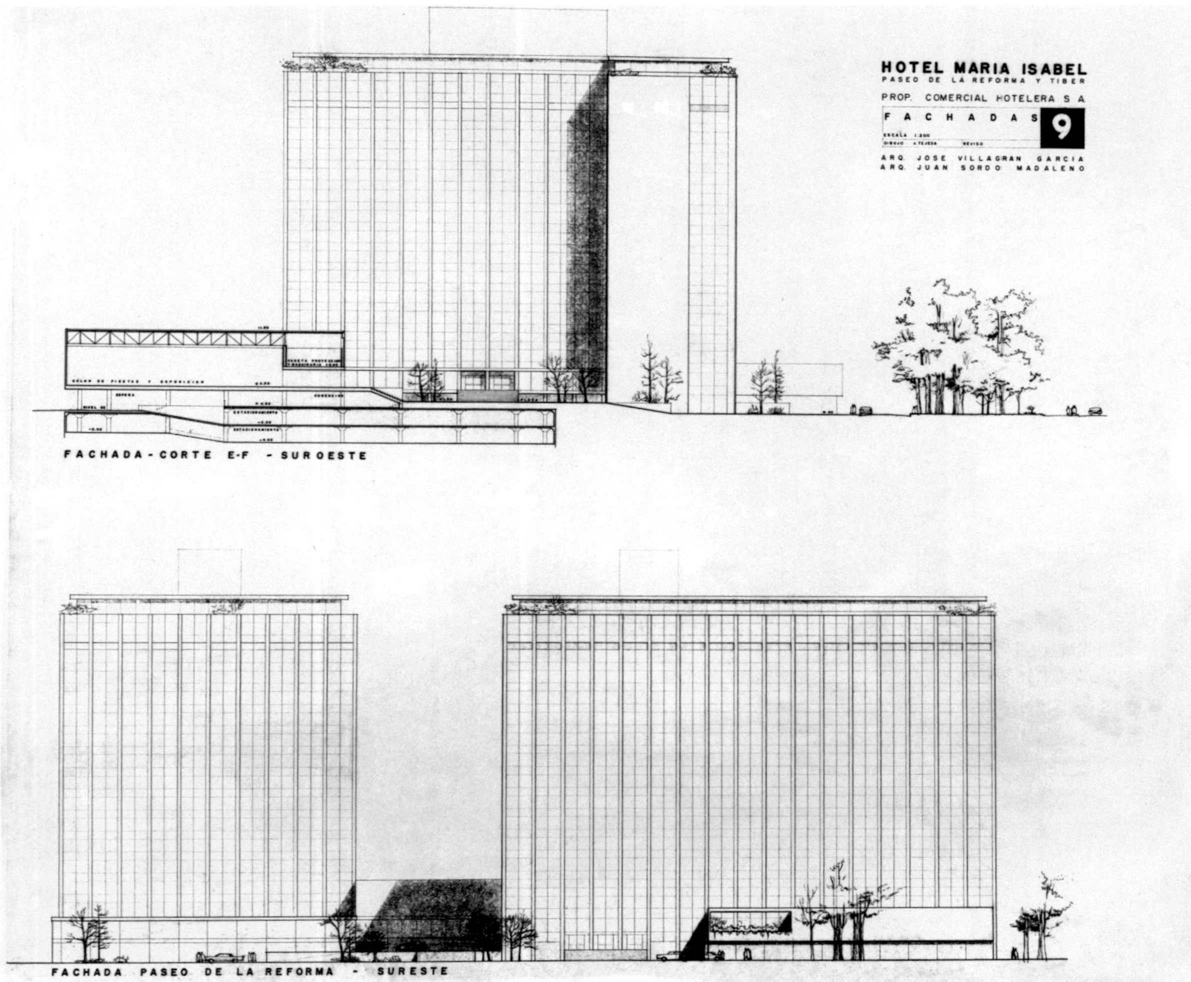

Above: ground floor of plaza and shops. Below: facade of the hotel on Río Tiber and facade on Reforma Complex.

Hotel interior.

Above: entrance plaza to hotel.

Right: perspective of the access plaza.

1964
PALACIO DE JUSTICIA

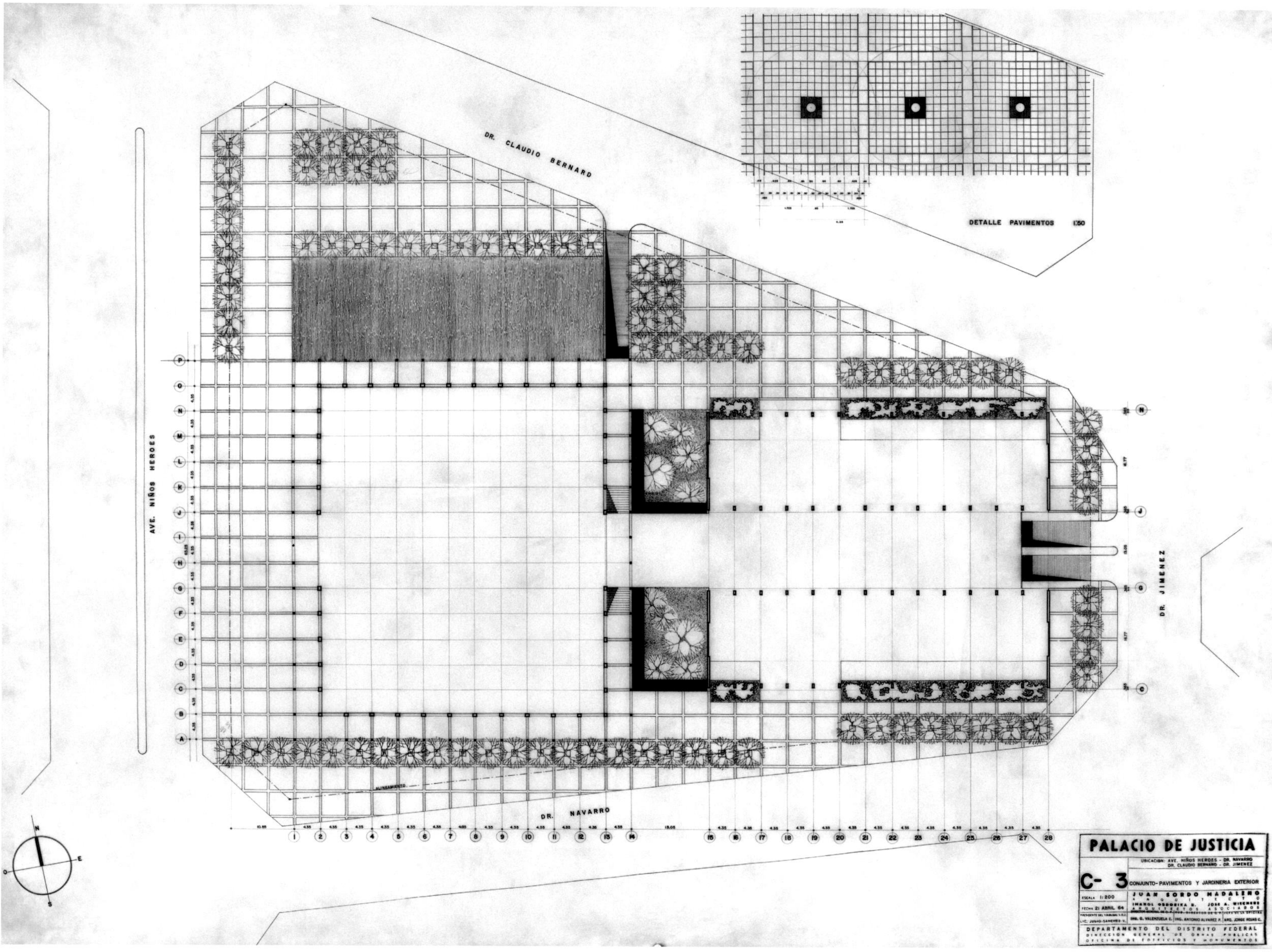

Left hand page, above: principal access to court buildings. Below: exterior portico of courts.

Right hand page: paved roads and inner gardens.

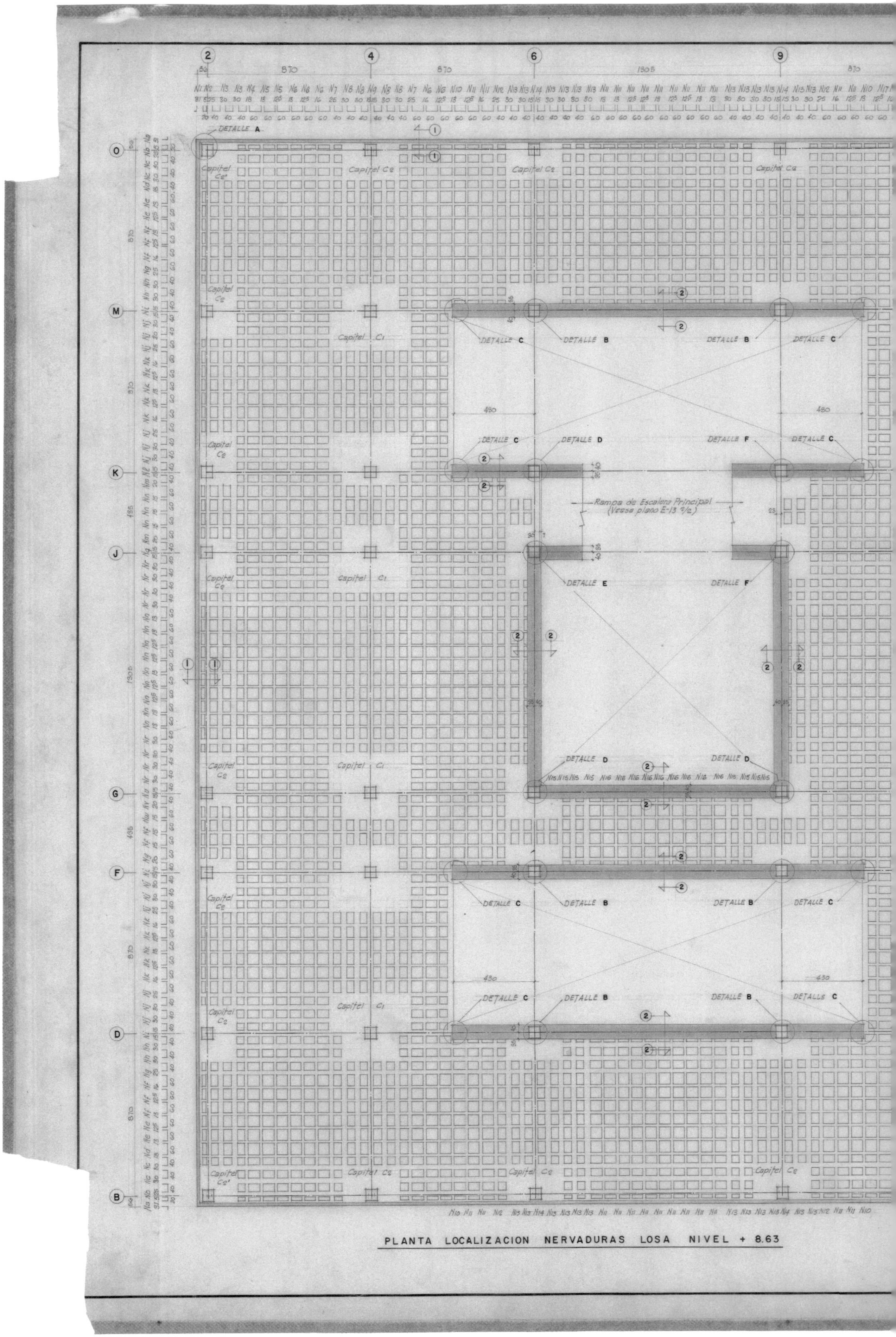

Structural design of the siding on the classrooms building, DIRAC.

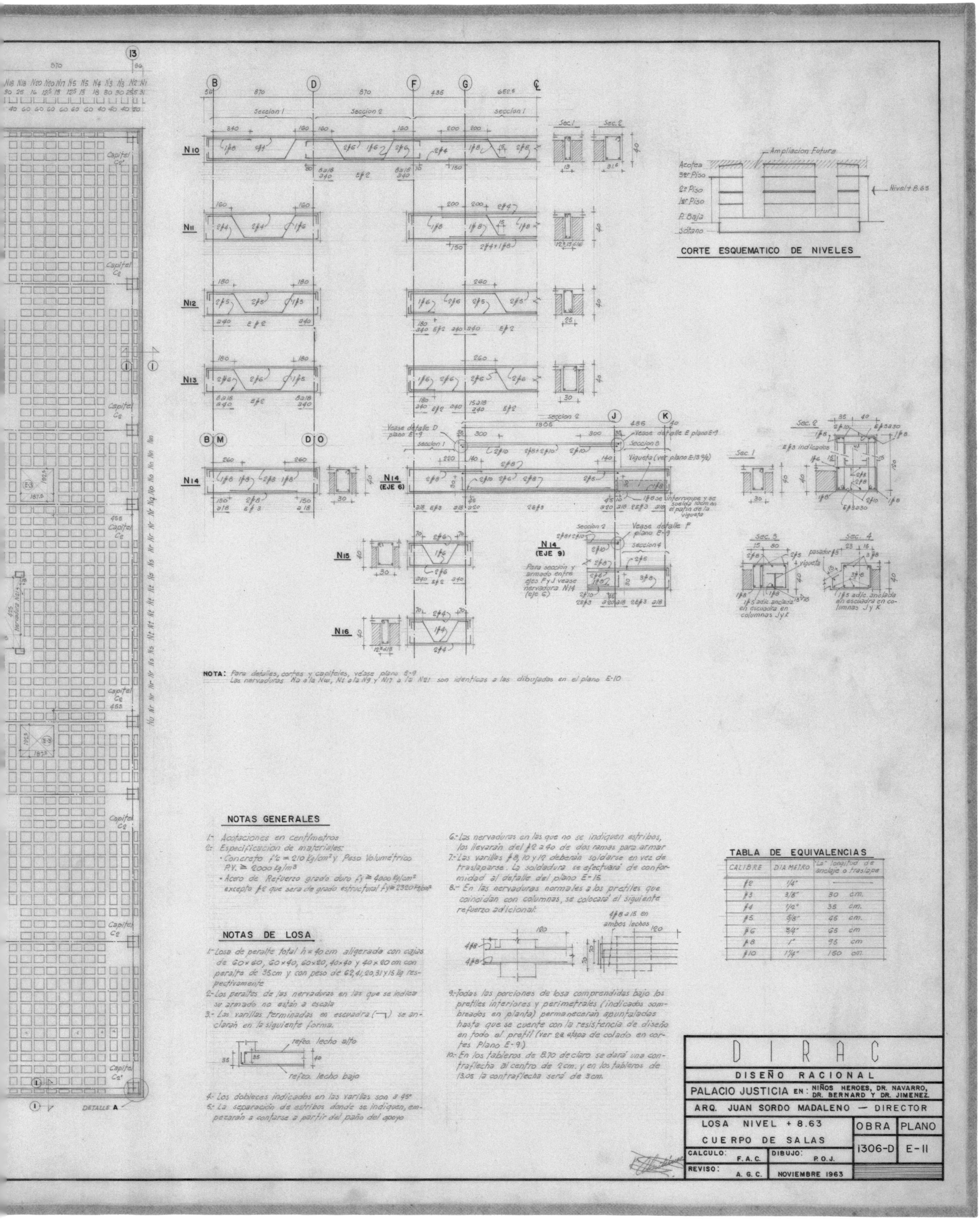

TABLA DE EQUIVALENCIAS

CALIBRE	DIAMETRO	"La" longitud de anclaje o traslape
#2	1/4"	—
#3	3/8"	30 cm.
#4	1/2"	35 cm.
#5	5/8"	45 cm.
#6	3/4"	65 cm
#8	1"	95 cm
#10	1 1/4"	150 cm.

Left hand page: plaza between the tribunal building and the courts tower.

Right hand page, above: view of the plaza from the portico. Below: view of the connection plaza from the bridges that connect to the courts tower.

1974
BOSQUES DE LAS LOMAS COMPLEX

Aerial photograph of Bosques de las Lomas in 1974. Shopping mall and office building in construction within the frame.

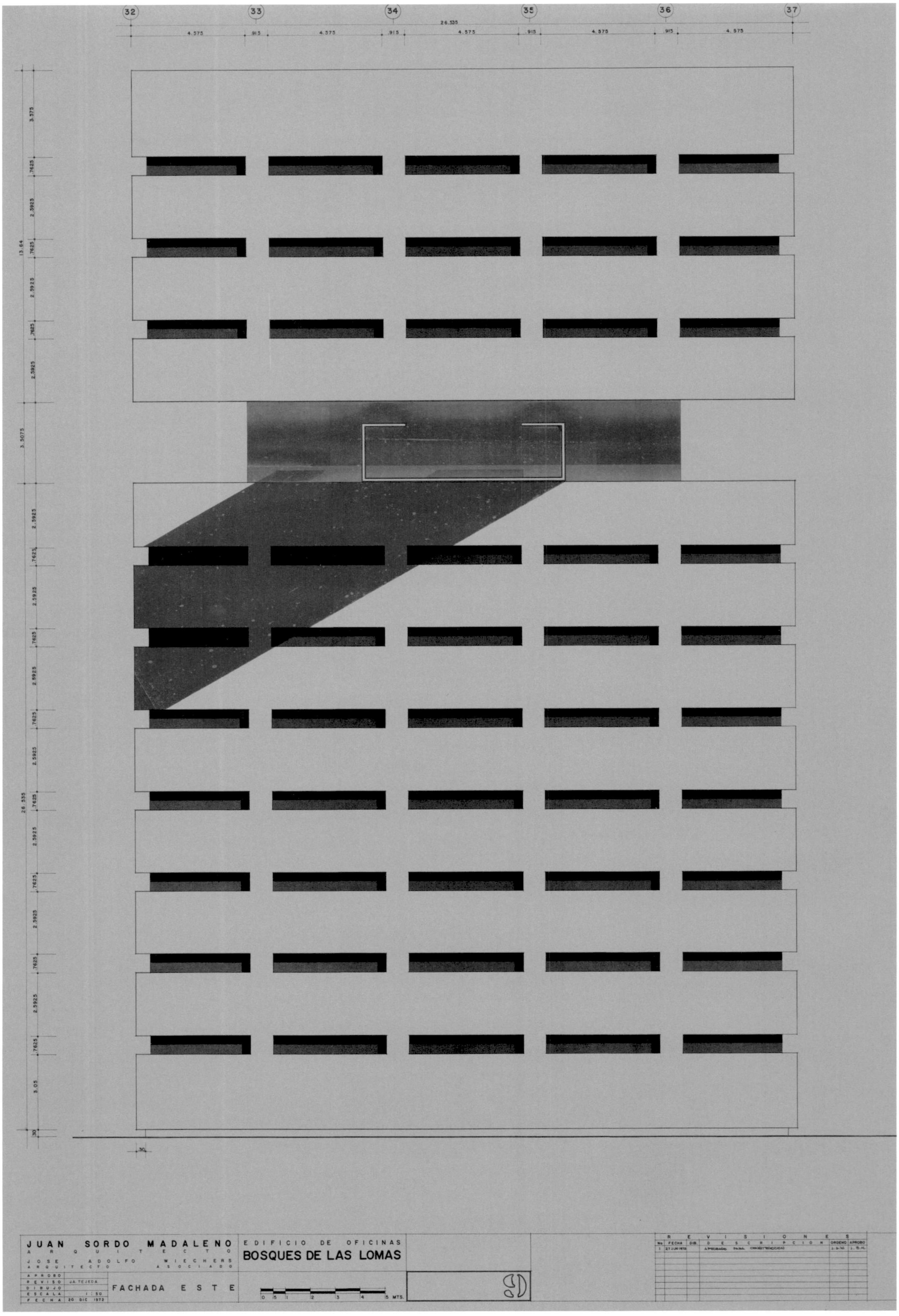

Facade of the office towers.

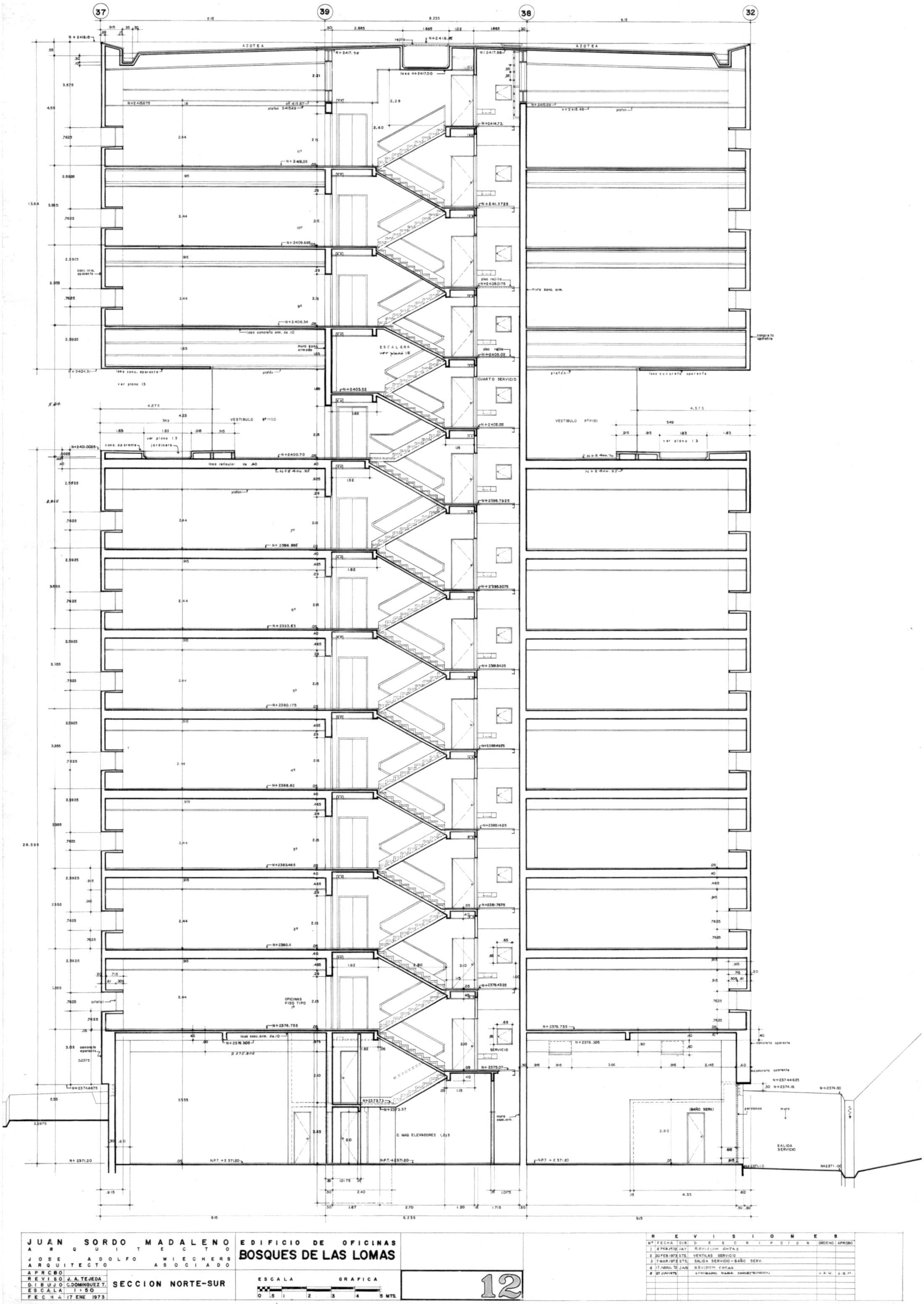

Cross-section.

Left hand page, above: layout of the complex from the original masterplan. Four corporate towers were proposed of which only the first was built, along with the shopping mall. Below: view from the parking lot.

Right hand page, above: access lobby, section of the southern facade. Below: interior view of the commercial area; space in the center of the building with view of the ravine.

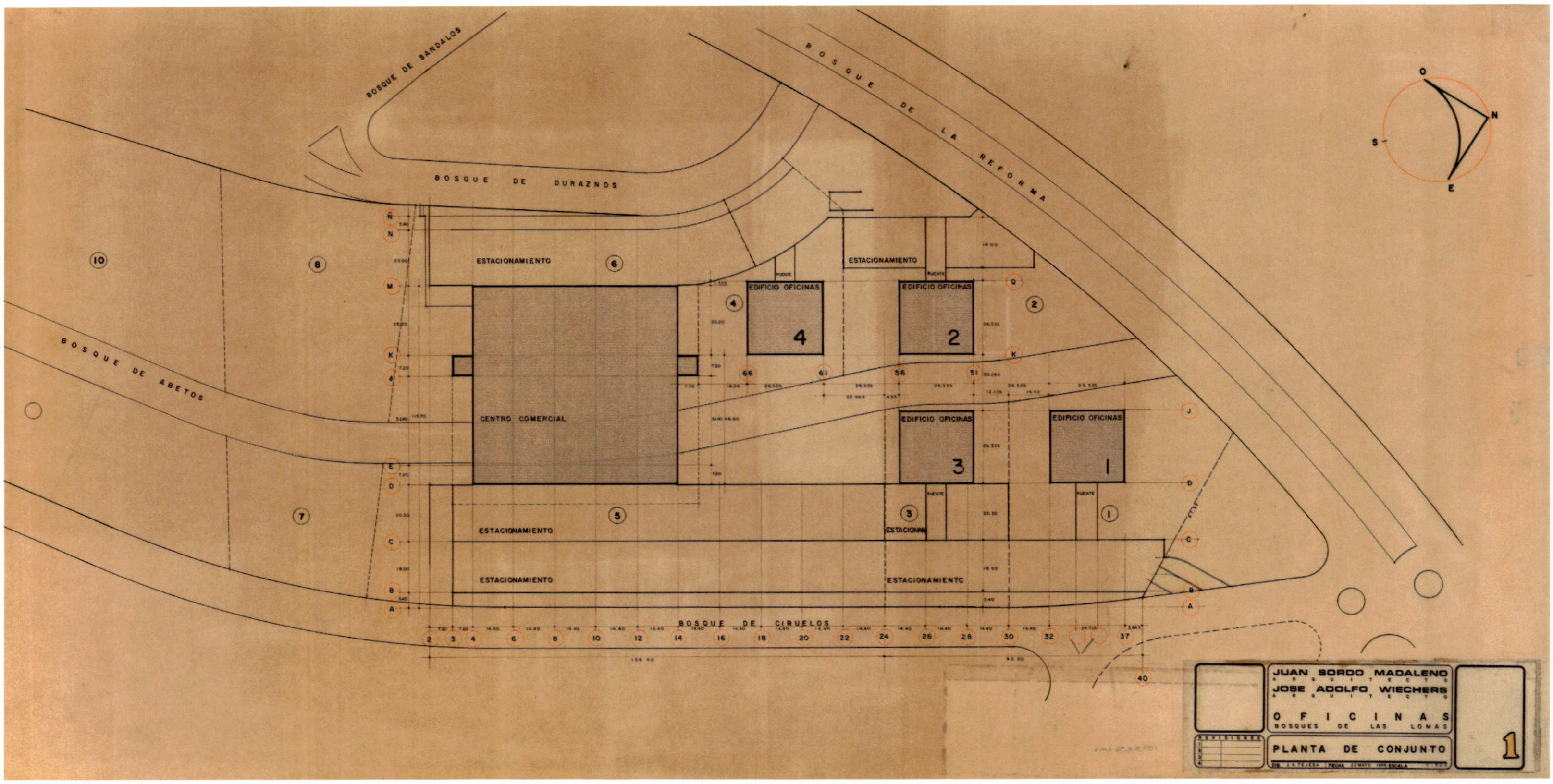

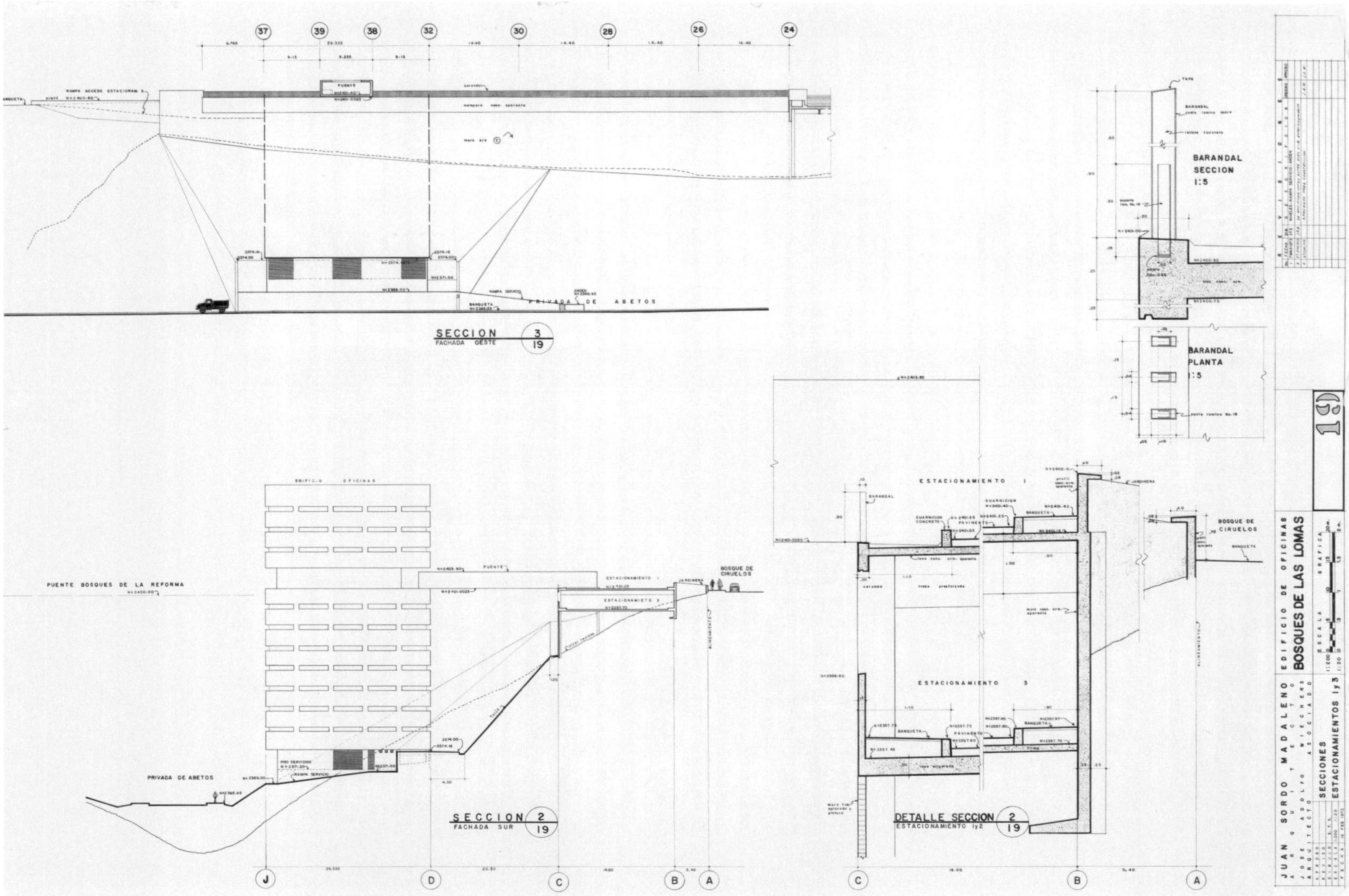

1977
PRESIDENTE CHAPULTEPEC

Facade facing Campos Elíseos, Polanco.

Model of original plan which included a tower for the hotel and another one for residential use which wasn't constructed.

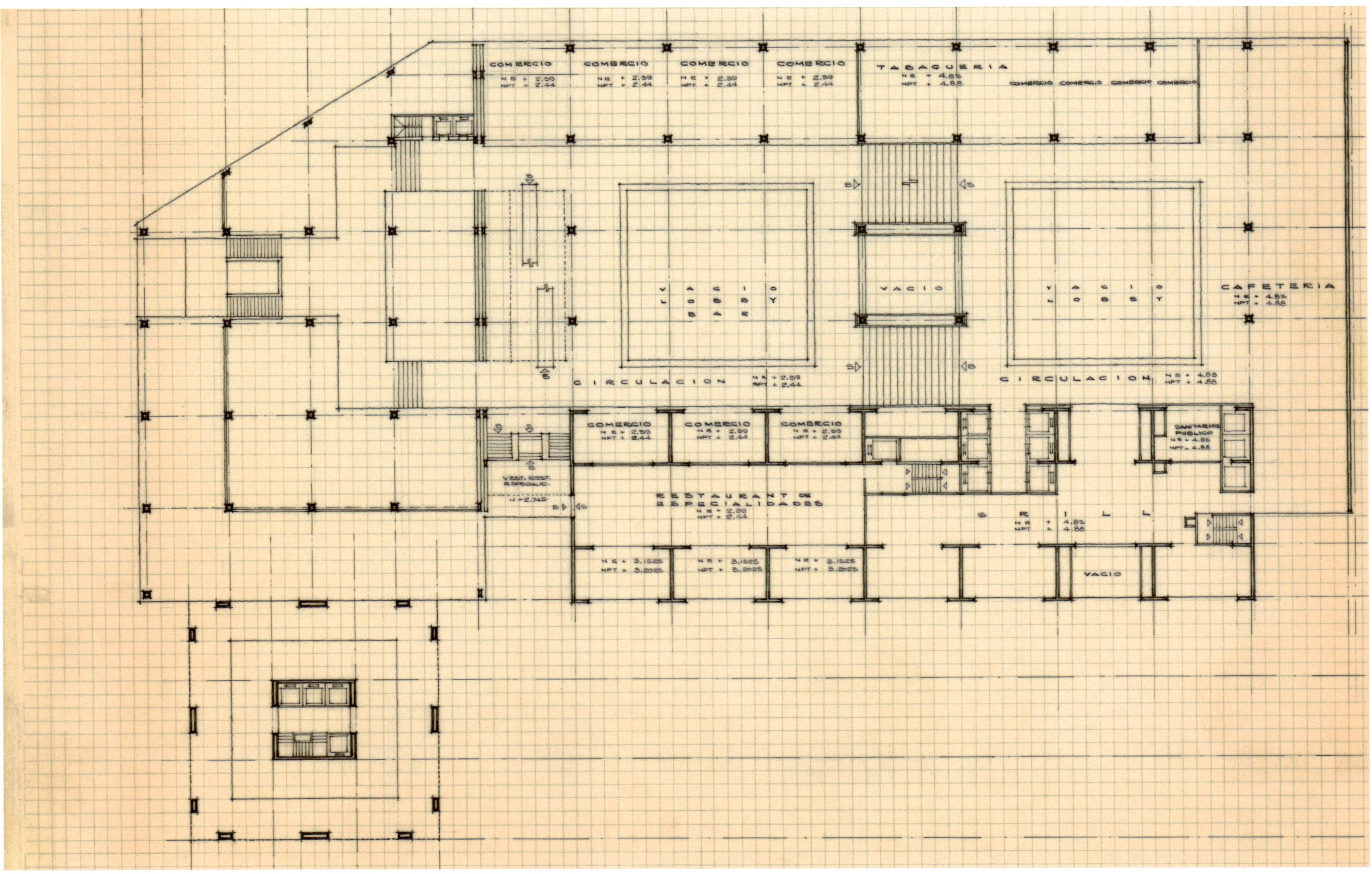

Proposal with floor of shops and café; also shows the second phase of the unbuilt tower.

Above: perspective of the proposal for a motor lobby.

Below: interior view of the reception area.

Perspective of the proposal for the main patio.

2.

REFORMA COLÓN: AN ARCHITECTURAL DIALOGUE (1940–1960)[1]

EDUARDO ALARCÓN AZUELA

A Map of the layout of Reforma in the second half of the 19th century. The Glorieta de Colón can be seen on the right.

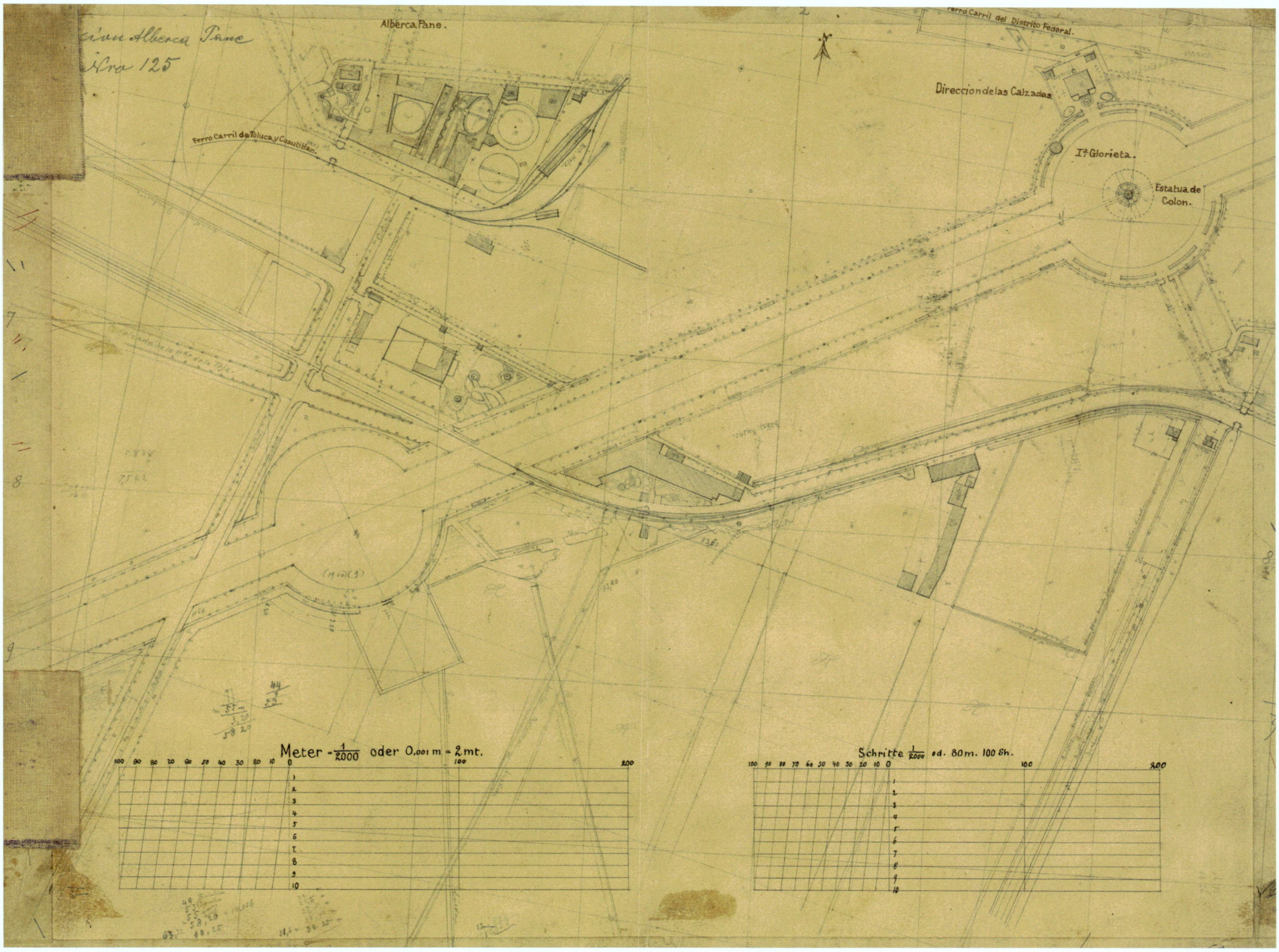

A

Parisian influences

The short-lived empire of Maximilian of Habsburg (1864–1867) left Mexico with a brief but significant legacy that historians have only now started to evaluate fully. Where the urban planning of Mexico City was concerned, one especially important development was the construction of the roadway linking the emperor's residence at Chapultepec Castle with the rest of the city. This thoroughfare was given the name of Paseo de la Emperatriz in honor of the empress, Charlotte of Belgium, and was designed as a great avenue with elegant *glorietas*—traffic circles embellished with a monument and small park at their center—lined on either side with majestic trees, very much in the nineteenth-century city planning style of Baron Haussmann of Paris. After the victory of the Republicans in 1867, the project was not cancelled. Indeed, the growth of the city around the new avenue, renamed Paseo de la Reforma, was now actively promoted.

It was during the *Porfiriato*[2] that the thoroughfare acquired the character of a Parisian boulevard, with major monuments exalting Mexican history located on the main plazas.

1. This article is a result of research on Glorieta de Colón and its immediate surroundings in the mid-twentieth century with the goal of recreating the most representative buildings to have stood around the monument to Columbus, which included five designed by Juan Sordo Madaleno.
2. The period of the administration of Mexican president Porfirio Díaz (1876–1880 and 1884–1911), which includes the presidency of Manuel González (1880–1884).

B

B Reforma and Glorieta de Colón. Photograph taken from the Anáhuac Tower, circa 1965.

C Immediate surroundings of the Glorieta de Colón, from left to right: Secretariat for Hydraulic Resources (1950), Edificio Patricia (1957), Hotel Imperial (1904), Reforma and Morelos (1946), and Reforma and Versalles (1954).

D Charles Cordier, Monument to Christopher Columbus, postcard from 1963.

C

D

Especially prominent was the *glorieta* with the statue of Christopher Columbus, the surroundings of which will be analyzed in the following paragraphs. During Díaz's prolonged mandate, economic growth and social tranquility led to the expansion of the city. Large mansions were built, especially in the area around Paseo de la Reforma, both on the avenue itself and in the nascent adjoining residential districts (*colonias*) of San Rafael, Tabacalera, and Juárez, previously called Colonia Americana. In this way, the properties situated around the great monuments became the most coveted real estate on the avenue, since the buildings constructed on the *glorietas* would enjoy a privileged view and become major city landmarks in their own right. This was the case of the Café Colón, located opposite the statue of Columbus—*Colón* in Spanish—which became very popular among the social and intellectual elites during those years. Facing that building was the most notable building to be erected during the years of Don Porfirio, the Hotel Imperial. Characterized by its wedge shape and its singularly eclectic architecture, it still stands today. According to architect Felipe Leal, this hotel strongly recalls Madrid, since its composition, with its small crowning cupola, is reminiscent of the urban skyline of Madrid's Gran Vía.[3]

From historicist city to modern metropolis

After the Mexican Revolution which began in 1910, the growth of Mexico City remained stable until the end of the 1920s, when new *colonias* for the middle and upper classes, like Polanco and La Condesa, were consolidated. The architectural styles that predominated in these new neighborhoods during the post-revolutionary period were Art Deco and Californian colonial. Emblematic examples include La Nacional, a building by Manuel Ortiz Monasterio that is considered the country's first skyscraper (1930–1932); the Edificio Ermita in Tacubaya by Juan Segura (1930–1931); the shopping arcade in Polanco designed by Francisco Serrano (1938); and the Monument to the Revolution (1933–1938), built very close to Paseo de la Reforma by the architect Carlos Obregón Santacilia, who took advantage of the metal structure of the failed project for Porfirio Díaz's Palacio Legislativo Federal (Federal Legislative Palace).

Architectural expression of this type was also found on Glorieta de Colón. The Edificio Latinoamericano was built in the early 1940s, following the circular line of the roundabout.[4] Its robust Art Deco composition consisted of a ground floor and twelve further storeys with large balconies. It can also be seen in period photographs that there were large open spaces on the roof overlooking the avenue. The building was radically modified in the 1950s, when its solid facades were replaced with huge walls of plate glass in keeping with its new use, as it now housed the Bonos del Ahorro Nacional offices.

3. Felipe Leal (Felipe Leal Difusión), *Programa ciudad de ciudades. Reforma, primera parte*, YouTube, video, 2013, https://www.youtube.com/watch?v=ZUI5AuWy5tE
4. There is very little information on this building, and its architect is unknown.

E Postcard of the Glorieta de Colón on Reforma. In the background, the Revolution Monument, circa 1950.
F Mario Pani, U.S. Embassy building, 1951, circa 1955.

E

F

The first building on Glorieta de Colón to be constructed in a sober architectural vocabulary that followed modernist
90 ideals was located on the corner of Reforma and Morelos, directly opposite the Hotel Imperial. The project was executed in 1946 by the young architects Juan Sordo Madaleno and Augusto H. Álvarez, who had collaborated some years earlier on the design of several apartment buildings. It was built on a rectangular plan with a long, glazed facade facing north and a shorter one finished with natural stone whose discreet windows enjoyed a privileged view of the statue of Columbus. There were plans for shops on the ground floor and offices on the ten remaining floors.

When construction was complete, Juan Sordo Madaleno installed his architecture studio on the top floor, which had a terrace overlooking Paseo de la Reforma, but two more stories were added to the building soon afterwards and the space was enclosed. For many years there was an Eastern Airlines office on the ground floor with a mezzanine level extending its full width. In the meantime, the cartoonist Abel Quezada set up his studio on one of the available floors, confirming that rationalist architecture was embraced by some famous personalities of the time. Another important business that opened a branch office there was Hoteles Unidos S.A., the operator of the Casino de la Selva in Cuernavaca, the Hotel Mocambo in Veracruz, and the Hotel Lincoln in Mexico City. All three tourist centers were financed by Manuel Suárez y Suárez, an entrepreneur of Asturian origin —a region in northern Spain— who was also a patron to several painters and sculptors.

In the late 1940s, the architects and partners Mario Pani and Enrique del Moral designed an office building on the former site of the Café Colón. The new building was acquired shortly afterwards by the federal government to house the Secretaría Recursos Hidráulicos (Secretariat for Hydraulic Resources). It was structurally daring because it rose to more than seventy meters, a very unusual height for the time. The load-bearing system consisted of rigid frames of reinforced concrete. The graceful design was opened out towards the plaza by means of semicircular segments between the floors. The first twelve floors covered the whole of the ground plan while the rest were smaller, with the uppermost level containing a nursery for the workers' children. Convex-concave forms predominated on the rear facades, a particular hallmark of Pani—trained at the École des Beaux-Arts in Paris—who had recently designed the National Conservatory of Music in Polanco. This was a building characterized as an architectural symphony, made up of curved walls that harmonize the overall volumetrics.

The Secretariat for Hydraulic Resources was not to be Pani's only project in the area around the statue of Columbus. In the early 1950s, in partnership with Jesús García Collantes, he constructed the building for the U.S. Embassy (F) at the intersection of Reforma and Calle Lafragua. The height was like that of the previous building, though the construction in this case was wedge-shaped. The first eleven floors covered the whole area of the plot while the rest occupied a smaller volume, with a convex arch facing the point of the wedge. When it opened, the ground floor was used as a shopping area, soon occupied by a branch of Sanborns, a restaurant on Calle Lafragua that was seeking increased capacity.

The presence of these novel architectural languages in Paseo de la Reforma gave an increasingly cosmopolitan character to the immediate surroundings of the statue of Columbus. The buildings around it clearly displayed the image of a modern city undergoing economic development. As Felipe Leal notes, this was the place where the city's first skyscrapers were built to house both government offices and insurance companies.[5] In those years, there was no building to compete in height with the great constructions that rose on Reforma,[6]

G Postcard with aerial photograph of the Glorieta de Colón and surroundings, circa 1965.

and Glorieta de Colón became one of Mexico City's most famous postcard images in the 1950s and 1960s.

In 1954, Juan Sordo Madaleno completed the Reforma and Versalles complex next to the building on Reforma and Morelos. This was also intended to house offices and businesses. The volumes of the project surrounded the *glorieta*, though with the salient feature of a glazed tower with a height of more than sixty meters that was set back into the lot from Calle Versalles. That same year, just a few meters from this compound, the same architect, though this time in collaboration with Jaime Ortiz Monasterio, undertook the construction of a cinema, the Cine París. The new entertainment center announced itself on Paseo de la Reforma with an illuminated sign and typography closely in keeping with the designs of the day, highlighting its name in italic lettering. Spectators entered along a long passage that was flanked by two shops and ended in the main lobby, where elegant staircases led up to an auditorium with 1,500 seats, all facing a large curtain operated by stage machinery to reveal the magnificent screen where the great works of cinema were shown.

Among the architects who helped to form the urban image of Paseo de la Reforma, José Villagrán García should be singled out as the designer of large hospital complexes and the mentor of most of Mexico's modernist architects. Although he is best known today for designing the National School of Architecture on the Ciudad Universitaria UNAM campus,[7] Villagrán was responsible for two important mixed-use complexes in the area around the statue of Columbus. The first is the Lafragua parking garage on the street of the same name, and the other the Cine Paseo on Reforma. The two buildings occupied adjacent properties, and both included a vertical volume 98 to make profitable use of the space.

Another important architect who deserves to be remembered is Juan Martínez de Velasco, a little-known figure despite being the co-designer with Juan O'Gorman and Gustavo Saavedra of the Central Library of the Ciudad Universitaria UNAM campus. In the mid-1950s, Martínez de Velasco erected a notable building opposite the U.S. Embassy. The slender construction, which stood on a site of restricted dimensions, was also intended for offices, although a single apartment was 94 fitted out on the top floor with magnificent views over Paseo de la Reforma. The work was reviewed in the last issue of *Espacios* magazine, edited by Guillermo Rossell de la Lama, where it was called Edificio Patricia.[8]

In the gap between the two buildings designed by Pani and his collaborators, Juan Sordo Madaleno built the Anáhuac 100 Tower in 1958 with a steel structure and a height of about 80 meters, slightly higher than its two predecessors.[9] The new

5. Leal, video, 2014.
6. In the mid-1950s, however, the Torre Latinoamericana was inaugurated. At 180 meters, it was the tallest building in the city for several years.
7. José Villagrán designed the National School of Architecture together with the architects Alfonso Liceaga and Xavier García Lascuraín.
8. *Espacios*, September-December, no. 39–40, 1957.

building stood on the corner of Calle de las Artes[10] and Lafragua, with only a small front on Paseo de la Reforma. Juan Sordo Madaleno's design consisted of a very sober prism, ensuring that the long facade had views over the majestic avenue. The use of glazed walls and metal profiles points undeniably to the influence of the skyscrapers of Ludwig Mies van der Rohe of the early 1950s in New York and Chicago. As Max Cetto has observed, the projects of Pani and Juan Sordo Madaleno overlap in their architectural language—the use of horizontality and the number of stories—besides the fact that they succeeded in turning the location into a singular urban conglomerate.[11]

The last building that helped to form the *glorieta's* architec-
106 tural vocabulary was the headquarters of DM Nacional, a manufacturer of office furniture. Built by Juan Sordo Madaleno in 1963, the building was constructed next to Cine París, and was likewise designed to attract the attention of passersby with great four-story window displays of the firm's new designs. Its dimensions were the same height as the front of the adjacent cinema, but the offices of the furniture store were dispersed on various levels behind the window displays. One of its most striking effects was that of the "DM Nacional" sign lit up at dusk on the facade. Moreover, the large windows overlooking Reforma followed a curved line, as the edge of the site was aligned with the *glorieta*, and it therefore shared the view of the monument to Columbus with its neighbors.

Final considerations

The nineteenth-century layout of Paseo de la Reforma and Glorieta de Colón by no means limited the multiplicity of twentieth-century architectural languages that sprang up around them. On the contrary, all these modern Mexican buildings became major landmarks of both the avenue and the plaza, itself an important urban reference point owing to the privileged views over the boulevard shared by all its buildings. The coexistence of several iconic works of Mexican architecture thus established a friendly dialogue among these modern buildings.

Regrettably, this harmony was to be lost in later decades, since while the capital continued its accelerated growth, new poles of urban development were constructed in other parts of the metropolis. The *colonias* next to the center of the city lost their interest to entrepreneurs, and the middle and upper classes found dwellings farther afield. The buildings that previously represented a period of splendor now began to be displaced by new projects for expansion, especially to the south and west of the city. This process was accompanied by various cultural changes in habits of consumption and entertainment. The cinemas on Paseo de la Reforma, for example, were closed in the 1980s, since large halls for more than a thousand spectators had ceased to be viable. Finally, the earthquakes that shook the heart of the city in September 1985 caused severe damage to many examples of Mexico's modern architecture. This ultimately altered the urban context of Paseo de la Reforma and Glorieta de Colón, which lost its sheen in the last few years of the twentieth century. The revitalization of the historic center and its surroundings would have to wait until the start of the new millennium.

9. This building, known today as Torre Contigo, exists now with severe alterations to its original design.
10. Calle de las Artes has now been renamed Antonio Caso.
11. Max Cetto, *Arquitectura moderna en México* (Mexico City: Museo de Arte Moderno, 2011), 147.

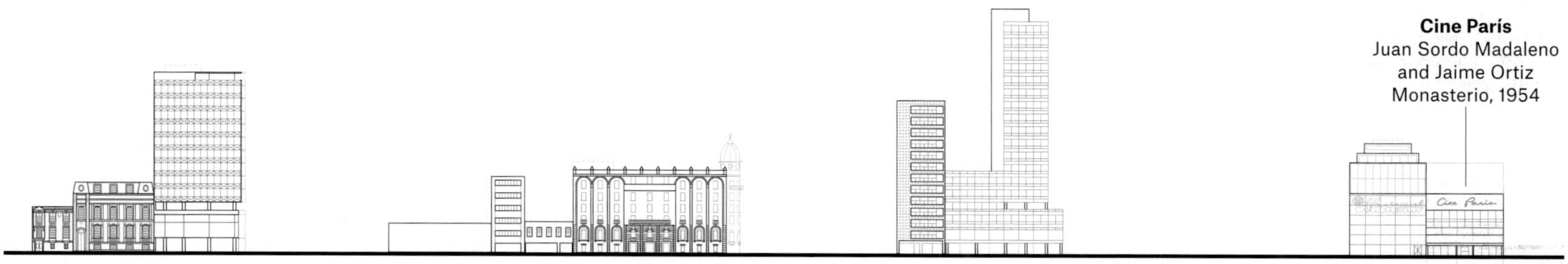

Cine París
Juan Sordo Madaleno and Jaime Ortiz Monasterio, 1954

Edificio Patricia
Juan Martínez de Velasco, 1957

Hotel Imperial
1904

Reforma and Morelos | **Reforma and Versalles**
Juan Sordo Madaleno and Augusto H. Álvarez, 1946 | Juan Sordo Madaleno, 1954

DM Nacional
Juan Sordo Madaleno, Jesús García Collantes and Alfredo Terrazas de la Peña, 1963

1946
REFORMA AND MORELOS

EASTERN AIR LINES
EASTERN AIR LINES
EASTERN
Air Lines

Interior view of the Eastern Airlines ticket office on the building's ground floor and mezzanine.

Above: terrace or the uppermost floor of the building. Two floors were added later.

Below: interior view of the airline's mezzanine.

1954
CINE PARÍS

ANNA

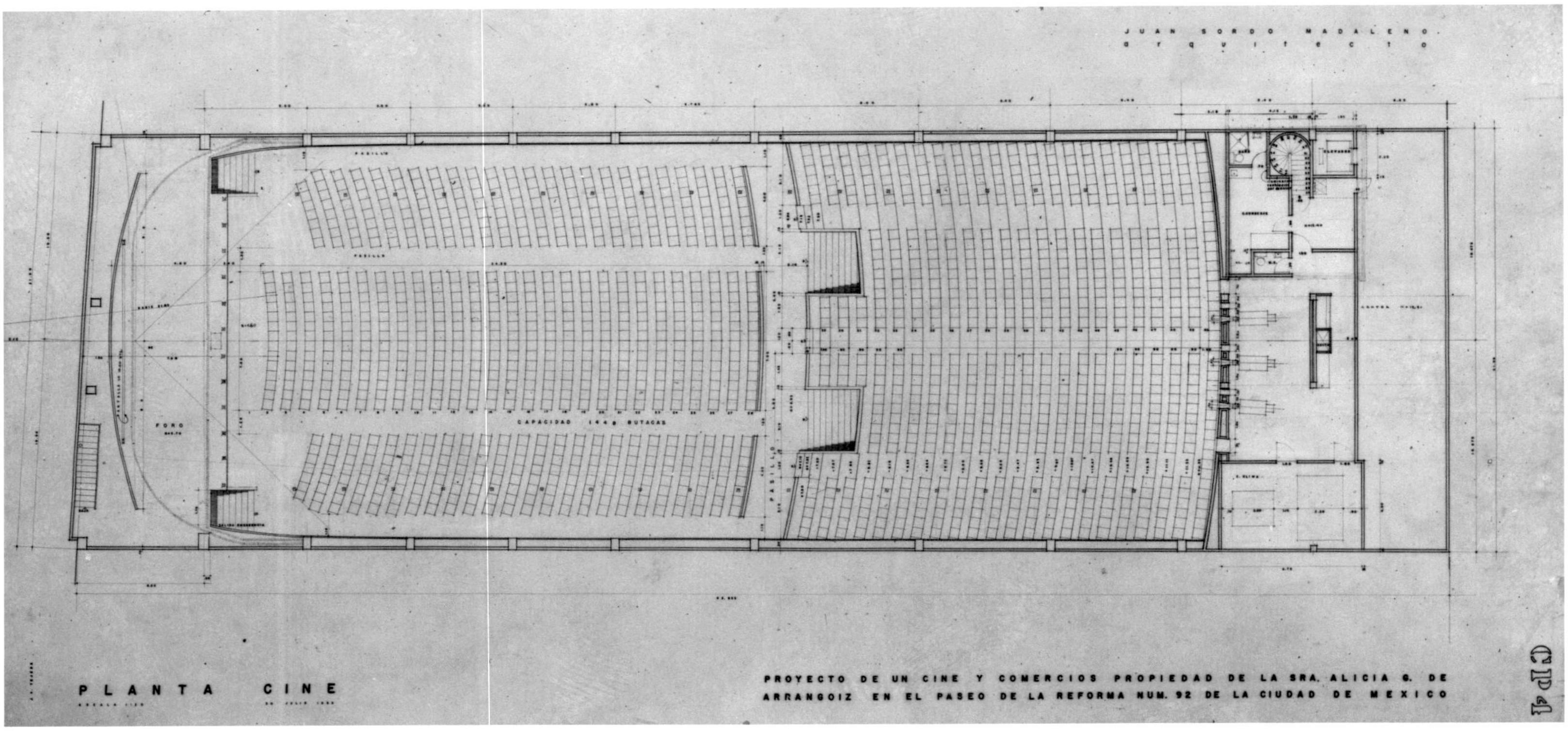

Ground floor of the movie theater.

Longitudinal section in perspective. Detail of the auditorium, the mezzanine and the vertical circulations.

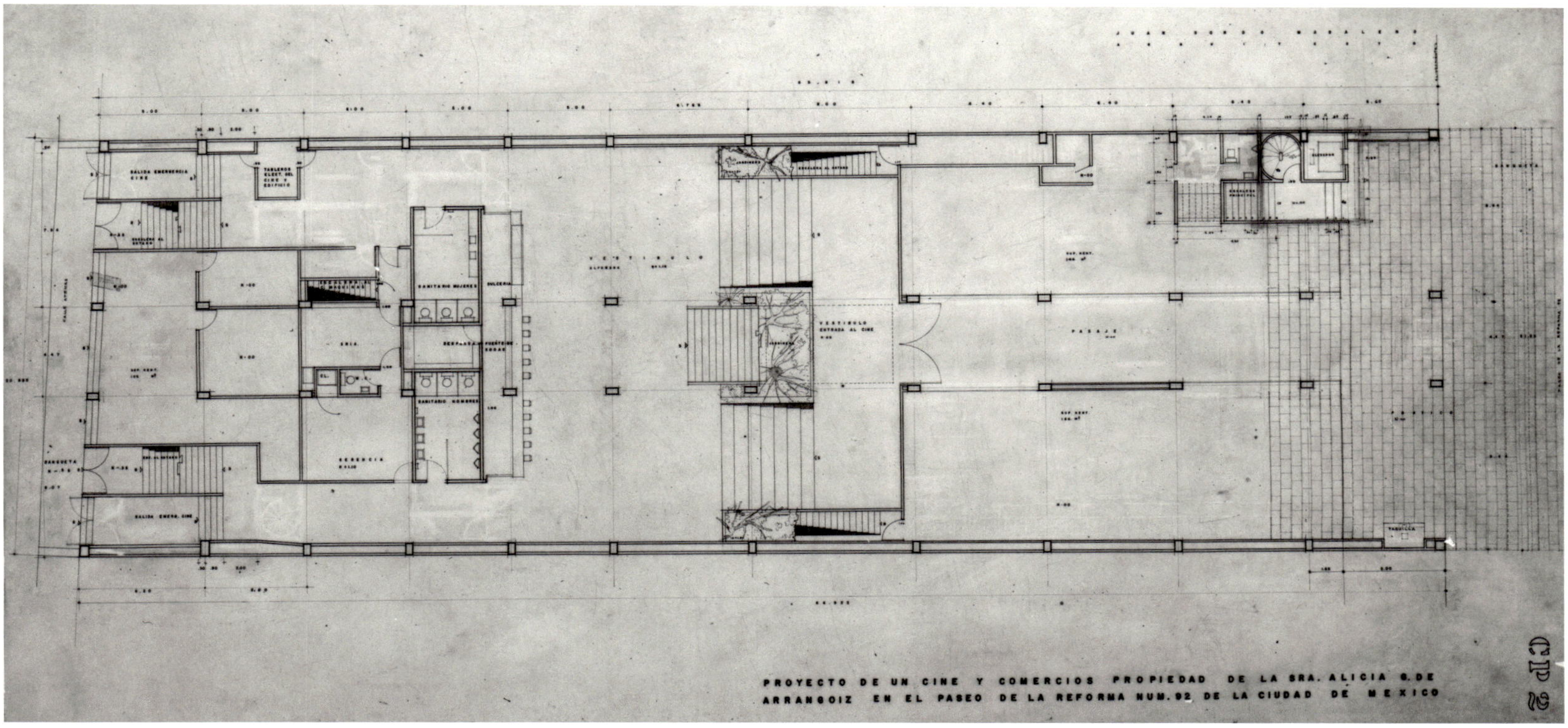

Ground floor lobby and mezzanine.

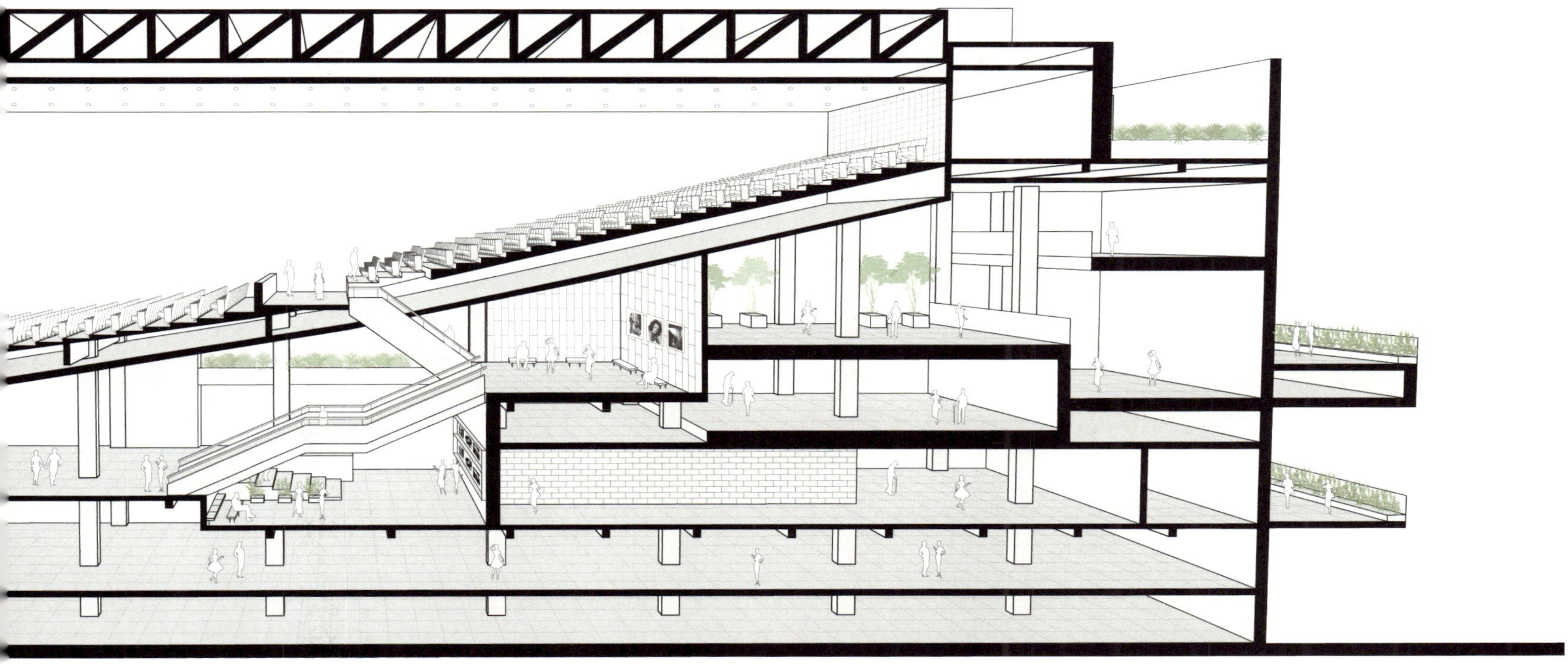

1954
REFORMA AND VERSALLES

Model of preliminary project with surrounding streets and roadways on Reforma.

HOTELES
EASTERN AIR LINES
Copel
BANCO DE COMERCIO

1958
ANÁHUAC TOWER

Photomontage of a model and surrounding area. Preliminary studies of the tower's volume. From left to right: Secretariat for Hydraulic Resources, Anáhuac Tower and U.S. Embassy.

INGENIO POTRERO S A

LA PLANCHA DE ACERO EMPLEADA EN ESTA ESTRUCTURA ES PRODUCTO NACIONAL DE
AHMSA
ALTOS HORNOS DE MEXICO, S.A.
MONCLOVA, COAH.
EN ESTA ESTRUCTURA SE EMPLEAN PERFILES DE LA
CIA. FUNDIDORA DE FIERRO Y ACERO DE MONTERREY, S.A.
TURAL, S.A.
ELEVADORES OTIS
LAC
La Consolidada, S.A.
ASEGURADORA ANAHUAC, S.A.

Left hand page: Construction of the steel frame of the building.

North facade.

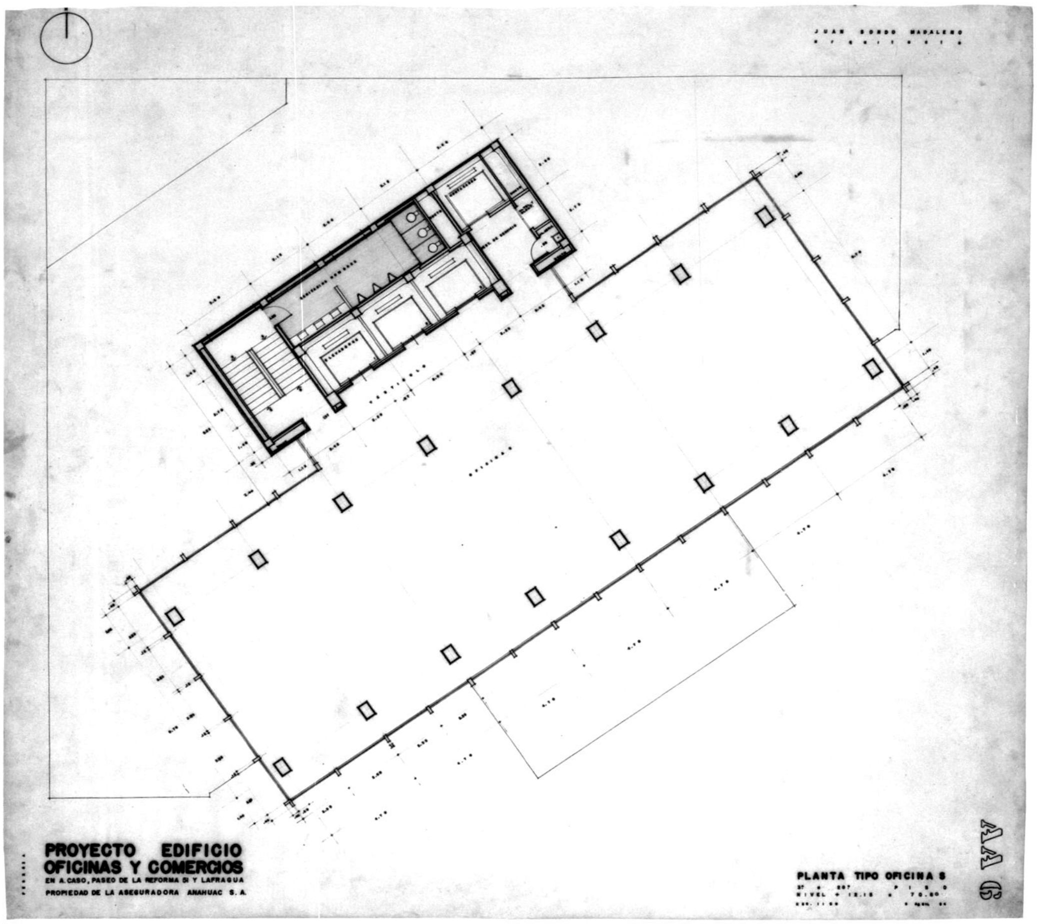

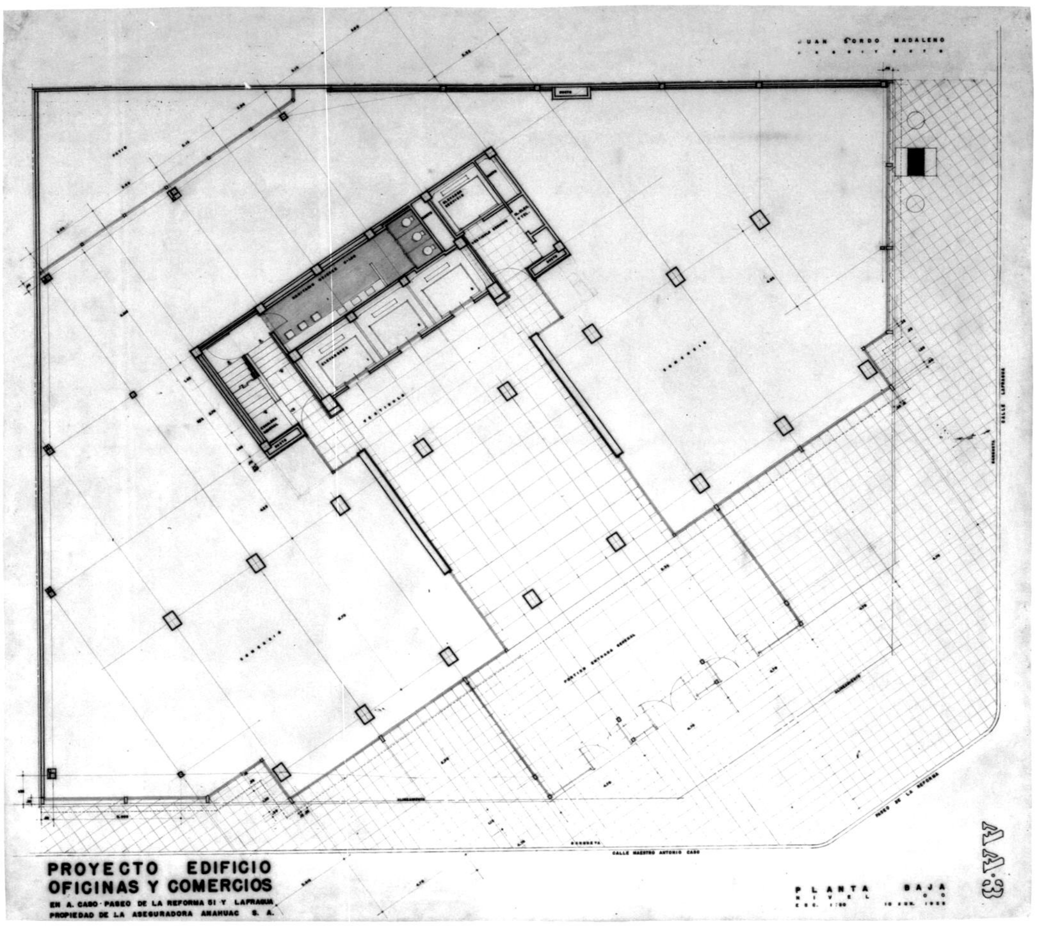

Above: typical office floor. Below: plan of ground floor.

Above: exterior view of the lobby. Below: interior view of the same space.

1963
DM NACIONAL

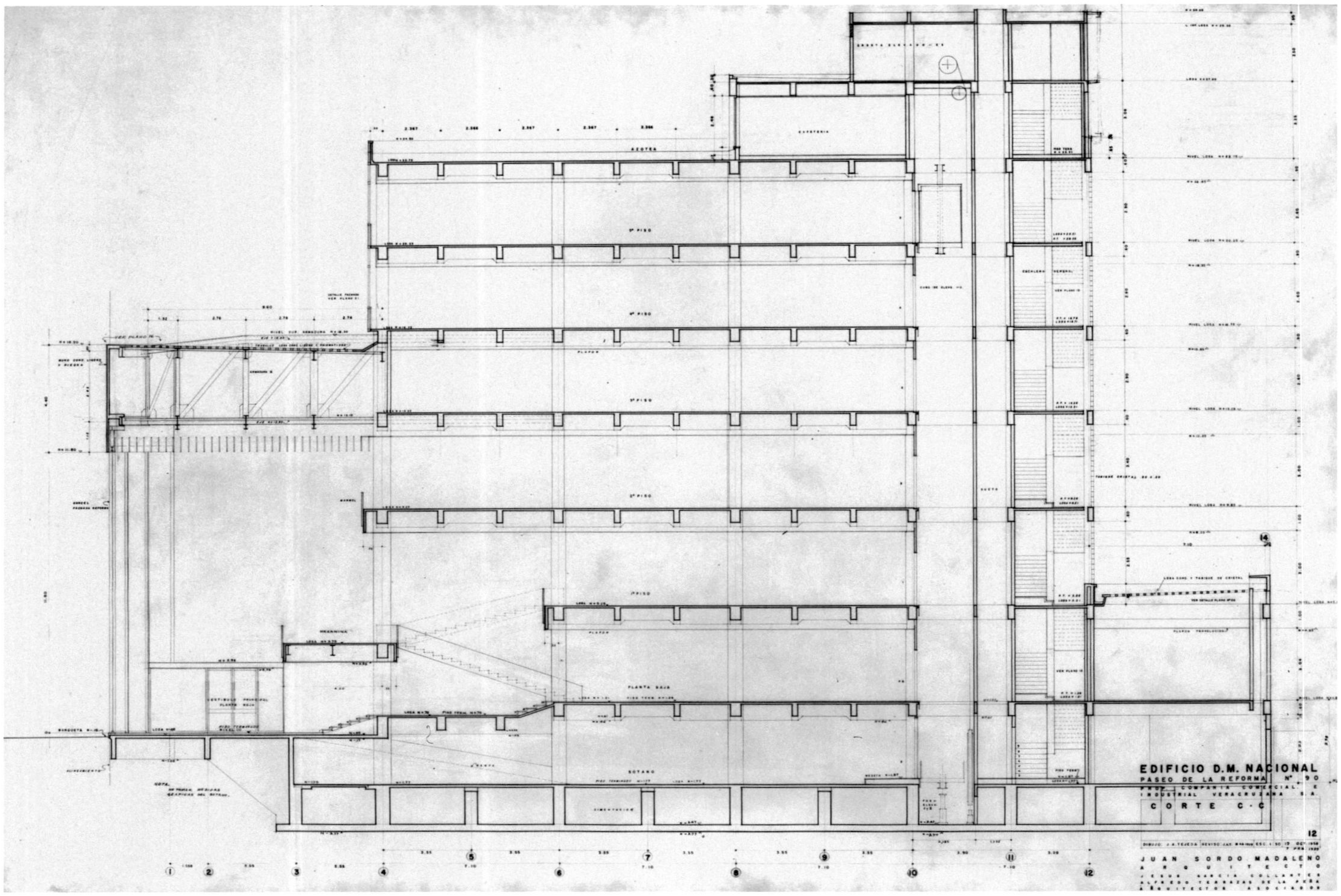

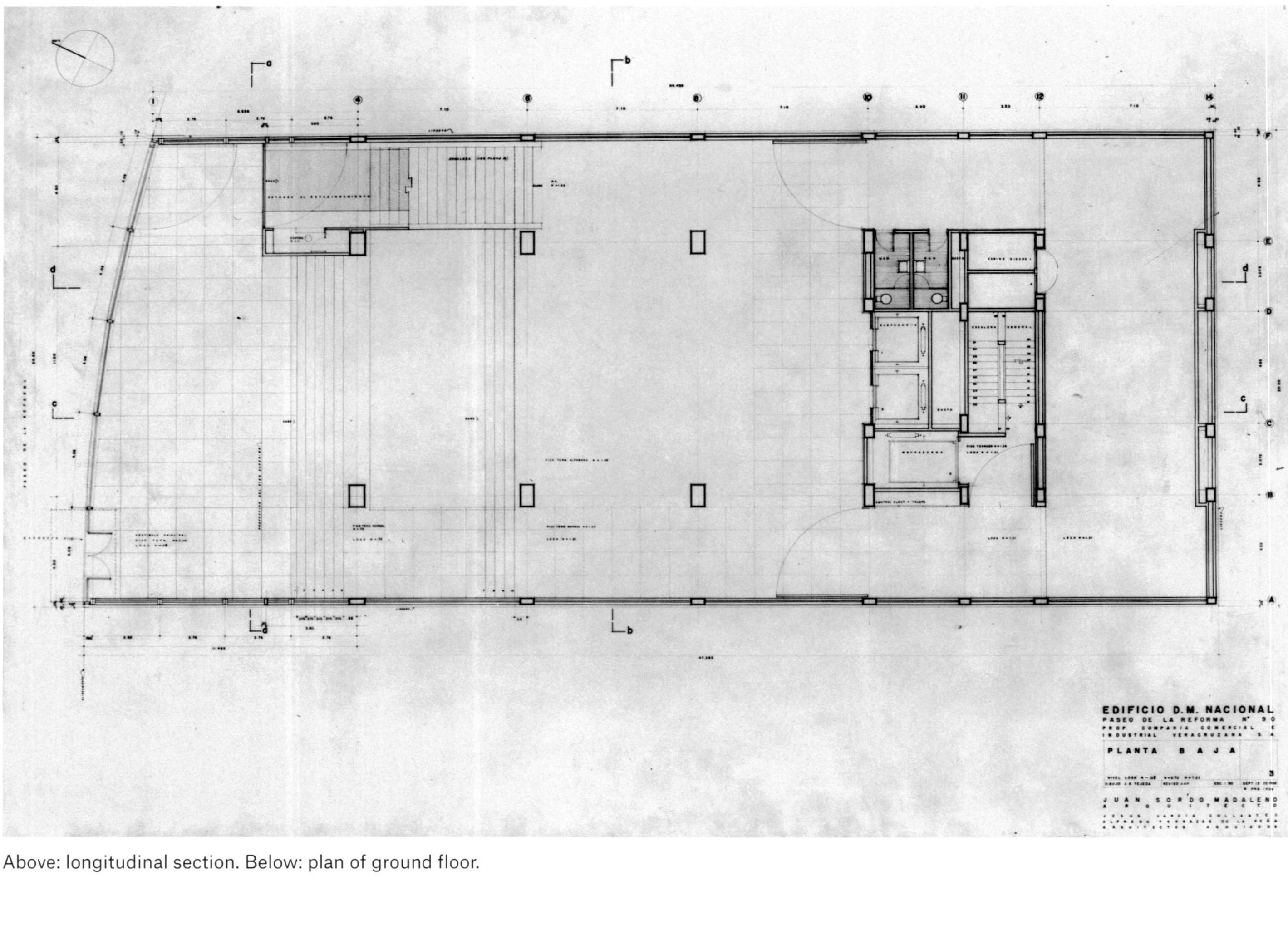

Above: longitudinal section. Below: plan of ground floor.

Above: interior view of the quadruple height, with the facade as an exterior exhibition showroom.

Below: interior view of the showroom.

3.

THE CITY THAT MOVES

JUAN JOSÉ KOCHEN

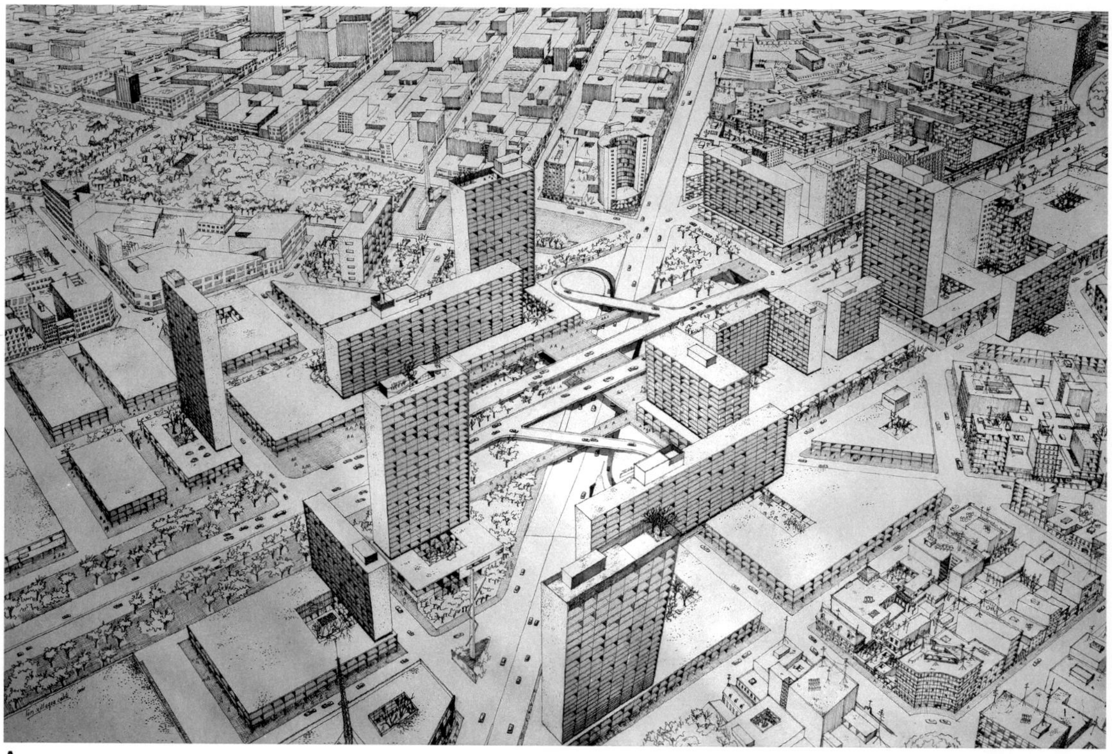

A

A Juan Sordo Madaleno, perspective of the urban plan at the intersection of Reforma and Insurgentes, Mexico City, 1954.

I.

In 1954, Juan Sordo Madaleno designed the Reforma and Insurgentes Complex (A) within the urban setting of Glorieta de la Palma, whose epicenter is at the intersection of Mexico City's two most important avenues. Models and plans show a development of five towers and eight horizontal buildings with ground-floor pavilions for commercial use. Unrealized, this complex was to include esplanades, plazas, walkways, and ramps that would have provided an ideal of the public potential of urban space.

Juan Sordo Madaleno's first designs with a sense of urban context and architectural rigor helped to define central nodes for Mexico City during its first stages of modernization. The city was preparing itself for growth and consequently its imminent internationalization. The exponential increase in population went hand in hand with urban change and requirements for infrastructure. In four decades, the Mexican capital went from one million inhabitants in 1930 to three in 1950, four in 1960, and seven in 1970. In the 1960s, there was a vast increase in the number of state construction projects that were to be indispensable for the country's future as it passed from nationalization to progress and from stabilizing development to the "Mexican miracle."

In issue number 100 of the magazine *Arquitectura México* (1968),[1] the cover of which featured Mario Pani's Nonoalco-Tlatelolco Urban Complex, the panorama of Mexican architecture of the era is defined through its leading practitioners. Interviews of the following fourteen architects were featured in the publication, by order of appearance: Augusto Álvarez, Luis Barragán, Félix Candela, Enrique Carral, Ricardo Legorreta, Héctor Mestre, Enrique del Moral, Juan O'Gorman, Mario Pani, Pedro Ramírez Vázquez, Ricardo de Robina, Juan Sordo Madaleno, José Villagrán, and Enrique Yáñez. With a small portrait and pictures of his works from 1953 to 1960, the section devoted to Sordo Madaleno was based on an interview that constituted a personal and professional portrait. The narrative hinted at a change in materiality and scale with respect to his first works:

> Luis Barragán and I try to combine urbanism and vista in such a way that people can live pleasurably. The streets should remain free of nearly all wheeled transport. The streets are for playing, walking, and conversing, not for obstacle races where you put your life at risk and breathe exhaust fumes. Families can live in small groups, understanding and developing the quality of good neighborliness. We shall continue with schools, offices, churches, shopping centers, clinics, and perhaps even universities.[2]

By then, Juan Sordo Madaleno had already designed many of these kinds of spaces; many other projects were firmly committed to and would be starting soon. After this brief introduction, Sordo Madaleno responded to the five standard questions sent to the architects selected for the edition, highlighting:

> The worldwide demographic explosion, technical advances, and the urgent need to resolve problems of habitation and social benefit directly related to construction, which oblige architects to work

1. "Juan Sordo Madaleno," *Arquitectura México*, April-June, no. 100 (1968): 79–83.
2. "Madaleno," 80.

B

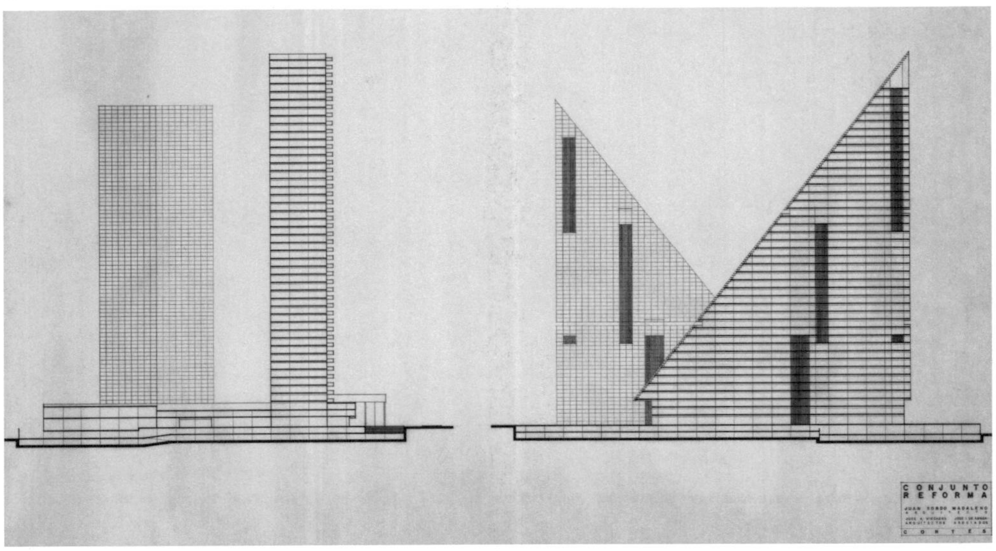

C

B Juan Sordo Madaleno, perspective of the Reforma Complex, Mexico City, 1969.
C Views of Reforma Complex, circa 1969.

D Montage of masterplan at the intersection of Reforma and Insurgentes from aerial view, Mexico City, circa 1954.

> more intensely and receive a more technical training… Our architecture, and I am referring to the last fifty years, has enthusiastically followed the current of renovation, and is distinguished from international architectures by its Mexicanness.[3]

While Sordo Madaleno's work spans designing notable houses, factories, churches, public institutions, hotels, shopping centers, and offices, his urban conscience was to be a constant in the reinvention of his legacy. Both the above-mentioned project on Paseo de la Reforma and Avenida Insurgentes (1954) and two others on Glorieta Reforma Colón, Río Ródano and Atoyac (1947), display a vision of a city with vertical buildings, open courts, covered traffic, horizontal bases, and civic plazas.

Shared uses are a constant in these incursions, a decision leading to the dissolution of the block and the rigor of the single typology. These buildings were mixed public and private ventures, often the result of multidisciplinary associations, such as Cine Ermita (1951), the UNAM Universidad Complex
(1952), Reforma and Lieja (1956), the Dirección de Policía y 346, 48
Tránsito (1956), the Merck, Sharp & Dohme pharmaceutical 52
complex (1960), the María Isabel Hotel (1961), Plaza Universi- 58
dad (1969), the Palacio de Justicia (law courts, 1964), Plaza 64, 190
Satélite (1971), 555 Palmas (1975), the Centro Operativo Ban- 348, 352
comer (1976), and Perisur (1980).

Two other unrealized projects from the 1960s confirm his firm interest in the optimum balance between density and civic qualities and that establish a blend of uses. These are the complexes on Reforma (B, C) (between Avenida Ejército Nacional, Manuel de Cervantes Saavedra, and the Anillo Periférico) and Universidad (corner of Avenida Universidad and Insurgentes), both of which include dwellings, cinema, club, offices, restaurant, sports facilities, and hotel.

3. "Madaleno," 82.

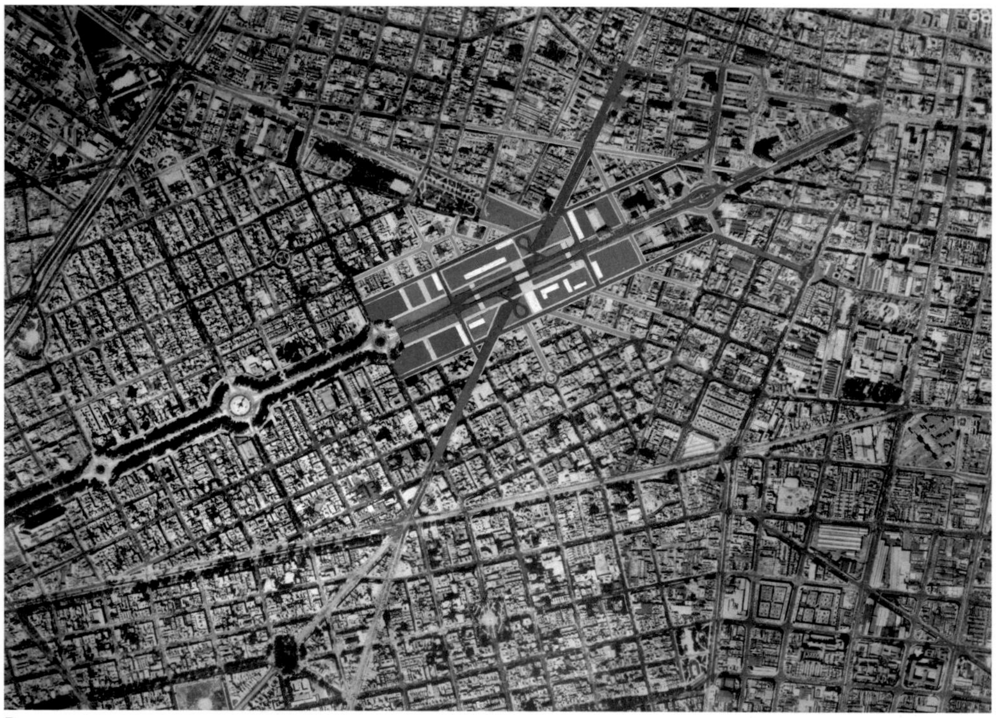

D

In a top-down progress from master plans to industrial zones, the drawings, models, and plans created for the works listed above prioritize their planning from a bird's eye view, with the project mounted onto photographs taken from above (D). In accord with other urban developments of the Modern movement, the architecture visualized tended toward the skyscraper. With modernization in full swing, these works reinforced the country's indisputable ambition to make the city a world capital.

At the same time, a bottom-up urban design also emerged. Its principal focus on insertion and appropriation at sidewalk level followed the collective ideal of Jane Jacobs together with the regional vision voiced by Lewis Mumford. The open and active ground floors, the set-back fronts, the esplanades, the courts, the walkways, the "civic hearts," the porticoes, the thresholds, and plastic integration all denote a clear stance toward the relationship of architecture with the city. These early works manage to soften the urban order, its flows and its concentrations, yet still achieving specific architectural projects and programs. Precise geometry, arranged and determined, accommodates the impulses of an emergent public dimension.

Sordo Madaleno would develop a singular amalgam of the "superblocks" of Mario Pani and the gardens of Luis Barragán. This idea was not an appeal to a concept of the superlative but to an accumulation of interactions and relations between the parts. The inhabitable cells designed by Mario Pani's studio (José Luis Cuevas, Domingo García Ramos, and Homero Martínez de Hoyos, among others) were represented through diagrams and centripetal flows with equipment, services, green space, and dwellings in the same place. That is, an extended multifamily block or a center converted into an urban complex (E). At the same time, the art of making gardens promoted by Barragán, principally in residences and on sublots, made outstanding use of organic panoramas without framed landscapes, resulting in a fluidity evocative of Parisian delicacy or the lines of Ferdinand Bac.

The two ideals of city and landscape converge in the first urban complexes of Juan Sordo Madaleno, who designed cities within the city with intersections and communication between neighborhoods, adding a variety of dwellings, mixed typologies, and flexible commercial premises. This was the start of a large-scale project whose model transcended architectural unity. It was a hybrid that would not only create new forms of habitation but would also have the size and versatility to bond together new ways of moving about in and connecting with the city.

II.

Also in the 1960s, David Harvey formulated theories, laws, and models in his *Explanation in Geography*[4] to support his thesis regarding the "geographies of capitalist accumulation" in modern cities and their growth to the point of overflowing. In his later book *Rebel Cities*,[5] Harvey focuses on the movement "from the right to the city to the urban revolution," as the book is subtitled, looking at the possibility of urban plans and vicissitudes with the citizens at the center, prioritized over other players with a stake in the city. This gives rise to political ideas about the public condition and social movements to

4. David Harvey, *Explanation in Geography* (New York: St. Martin's Press, 1969).
5. David Harvey, *Rebel Cities: From the Right to the City to the Urban Revolution* (London: Verso, 2012).

E Aerial photograph of the Modelo Housing Unit, Iztapalapa. Mario Pani and Félix Sánchez Baylón's concept of super-blocks, Mexico City, 1952.

F Luis Barragán, Carlos Contreras, José Alberto and Luis Bustamante, Jardines del Pedregal in San Ángel, Mexico City, 1945–1952.

E

F

change and rethink the metropolis in accordance with collective wishes: "To claim the right to the city is, in effect, to claim a right to something that no longer exists; [...] reinventing the city inevitably depends upon the exercise of a collective power over the processes of urbanization."[6]

David Harvey agrees with Saskia Sassen[7] on the need for social accumulation in the city to renew the bases of infrastructure and so enable complementary processes on a different scale. Besides stressing the community value, Harvey's position situates the debate in the public agenda on collective space.[8] The right to the city is thus the way to restore the sense of urbanity, a scenario whereby the populace comes together for the construction of the common. As regards this positive relationship with cities, Deyan Sudjic agrees on the regeneration of urban areas and their planning when he asks: "What can we really do to tackle what might be described as the general urban panorama so as to transform it and achieve positive effects? Are urban transformations possible right now? Or should we avoid the after-effects of running risks and limit ourselves instead to taking small, gradual steps?"[9] In *The Language of Cities*, Sudjic describes how capital and knowledge have been invested in an optimum future for cities, but reaffirms the unviability of a single source for all answers on the way we live.

This change from master plans to sutures on a different scale has proved an unequivocal virtue in the projects of Sordo Madaleno Arquitectos. The changing generations at the firm—the firm which until recently was headed by Javier Sordo Madaleno Bringas and now by his sons Javier, José Juan and Fernando Sordo Madaleno de Haro—have continued this architectural movement back and forth, reinforcing it with solid urban roots. Over forty years, every handover in the family has proved even more felicitous and well-calibrated than the last.

"We feel attracted to cities in part because they offer us the possibility of finding people and things we did not know existed, and which we did not know we wanted until we went there. A city offers the opportunity of social encounters and places

6. Harvey, 2012.
7. Saskia Sassen, *The Global City: New York, London, Tokyo* (New York: Princeton Architectural Press, 1991).
8. Dissertations on the analysis and future of cities, their utopia, entropy, and dystopia, have given rise to several incisive critiques and manifestos since the 1960s. Besides the collective projects of Archigram, Archizoom, and Superstudio, Kevin Lynch (*The Image of the City*, 1960), Jane Jacobs (*The Death and Life of Great American Cities*, 1961), Tom Wolfe (*The Kandy-Kolored Tangerine-Flake Streamline Baby*, 1965), Aldo Rossi (*L'architettura della Città*, 1966), Robert Venturi (*Complexity and Contradiction in Architecture*, 1966), Lewis Mumford (*The City in History*, 1968), Robert Venturi, Denise Scott Brown and Steven Izenour (*Learning from Las Vegas*, 1972), and Manuel Castells (*La cuestión urbana*, 1974) have all questioned the layout, living habits, and spontaneous transformations of architecture and the metropolis through signs, symbols, and typologies in their broadest version. While Rem Koolhaas (*Exodus, or the Voluntary Prisoners of Architecture: The Strip (Aerial Perspective)*, 1972, and *Delirious New York*, 1978) and Yoshiharu Tsukamoto (*Made in Tokyo*, 2001) have continued with this type of research, urban complexity requires constant scrutiny in step with planning innovation.
9. Deyan Sudjic, *The Language of Cities* (Harmondsworth: Penguin, 2016).

where new lives are formed. We have to give ourselves the chance to find them," Sudjic concludes.[10] This could stand as an excellent description of the strategies and aims of today's Sordo Madaleno. A commitment to upholding agreements has achieved unique strategic projects that reinvent typologies. It is not only a question of sustainable resilience but also of an innovation in perspective.

Interior design is resolved with the same skill as metropolitan urban planning, while at the same time engineering, finance, and commercial development complete a virtuous
116 circle of shared experiences and visible collectives. Antara
173 (2006–2014) and Artz Pedregal (2018), in Mexico City, Angeló-
polis (1998) and Luxury Hall (2010), in Puebla, Antea (2013), in
202 Querétaro, Toreo Parque Central (2014), in the State of Mexico,
130 and Andares (2009–2017), in Jalisco, are exemplary for their architecture and above all for their urban potential. In every case, the context of the site is catalyzed. These are lodestones whose magnetic fields encourage other developments, other encounters, and other ways of balancing permanence with transformation in the city, with formal gestures that include shopping arcades, walkways, porticoes, lattices, thresholds, radial plazas, mullions, and terraces.

The intention behind the project rests on the fundamental idea of reinhabiting a pre-existing site. As Teodoro González de León points out in *Arquitectura y ciudad*, working on "urban permanencies" demands a combination of chance, design, time, and memory: "An urban plasticity, very specific, configured not only by the spaces of streets, plazas, and parks, and by the variety of forms and surfaces of buildings and monuments, but also by all the objects that inhabit those spaces: posts, wires, adverts, vehicles."[11] These four dimensions occur with exercises of investigation, local "situationism," and architectural design on the basis of territorial reconnaissance, diagnosis, and analysis. In this manner, Sordo Madaleno embarks on projects involving modern buildings and historic centers, edges and peripheries, industry, and equipment. In the prologue of *This is Hybrid*, Steven Holl notes: "The concentration of many social activities dilates and warps the pure building type. If they were examined in the light of current theoretical concerns, some associations of forms, formerly abandoned, would be attached to the modern city to generate buildings that could be erected as an anti-typology."[12]

Holl assumes a hybrid definition, emphasizing the nature of the urban complexes incubated in twenty-first-century cities as containers of collective space, multifaceted social condensers, programmatic juxtapositions, sectional dynamics, sustainable architectures, and, principally, compositional liberties. Much of Sordo Madaleno's recent work upholds these principles. Reforma Colón (2022–2027) adopts this position as a hybrid whose epicenter reforms the idea of Paseo de la Reforma. All along its length, the avenue is identified by the multiple events, personalities, and constructions that have become associated with it, and its planning from east to west constitutes a foundational history of contemporary architecture in Mexico City. Its course today cuts across and connects the metropolis, imposing an urban geography that detached itself from spatial parameters and boundaries to reveal others of a temporal nature, those laid out for urban catharsis and civic demonstration. The modern buildings have become events, and their architecture dense with experiment.

Full of social (mis)encounters with shared spaces and pieces of city at sidewalk level, the origin of the avenue lies in the persistent notion of an integration with history and its frozen time. Juan Villoro's *Horizontal Vertigo*[13] converges on it, since it forms an essential hinge for transit westwards towards Chapultepec and Las Lomas, and eastwards through the *colonias* of San Rafael, Tabacalera, Bucareli, Centro Histórico, Guerrero, Lagunilla, Tlatelolco, and Peralvillo. This makes it Mexico City's most dynamic and vibrant corridor. Diverse and divergent, inclusive and including, it is a boulevard in constant reformation, and Sordo Madaleno has understood and studied it for decades.

Sordo Madaleno supervises, manages, designs, invests, administers, operates, rents, organizes, and revalues works that are transcendent for the city. Returning to the origin, the unrealized project by the architect who founded the group now coincides in its goal of retrieving the memory of the city and its illustrious passage through time. An elective affinity, a diagonal force, or a conversation between generations.[14]

---

10. Sudjic, 2016.

11. Teodoro González de León, *Arquitectura y ciudad*, speech given on induction to El Colegio Nacional (Mexico City: El Colegio Nacional, 1988). Author's translation.

12. Steven Holl, *This is Hybrid: An Analysis of Mixed-use Buildings* (Vitoria-Gasteiz: a+t, 2014).

13. Juan Villoro (2019), *El vértigo horizontal* (Mexico City: Almadía, 2019).

14. Johann W. von Goethe, *Elective Affinities* (Harmondsworth: Penguin, 1971); Hanna Arendt, *Between Past and Future: Eight Exercises in Political Thought* (New York: The Viking Press, 1961); Louis I. Kahn, *Conversations with Students* (New York: Princeton Architectural Press, 1998).

2006, 2013, 2017, +2024
ANTARA MASTERPLAN

Before
Above: General Motors plant of 1955, land currently occupied by Antara Masterplan. View from the easternmost point.

After
Below: Antara Masterplan, 2021. Aerial view from the easternmost point.

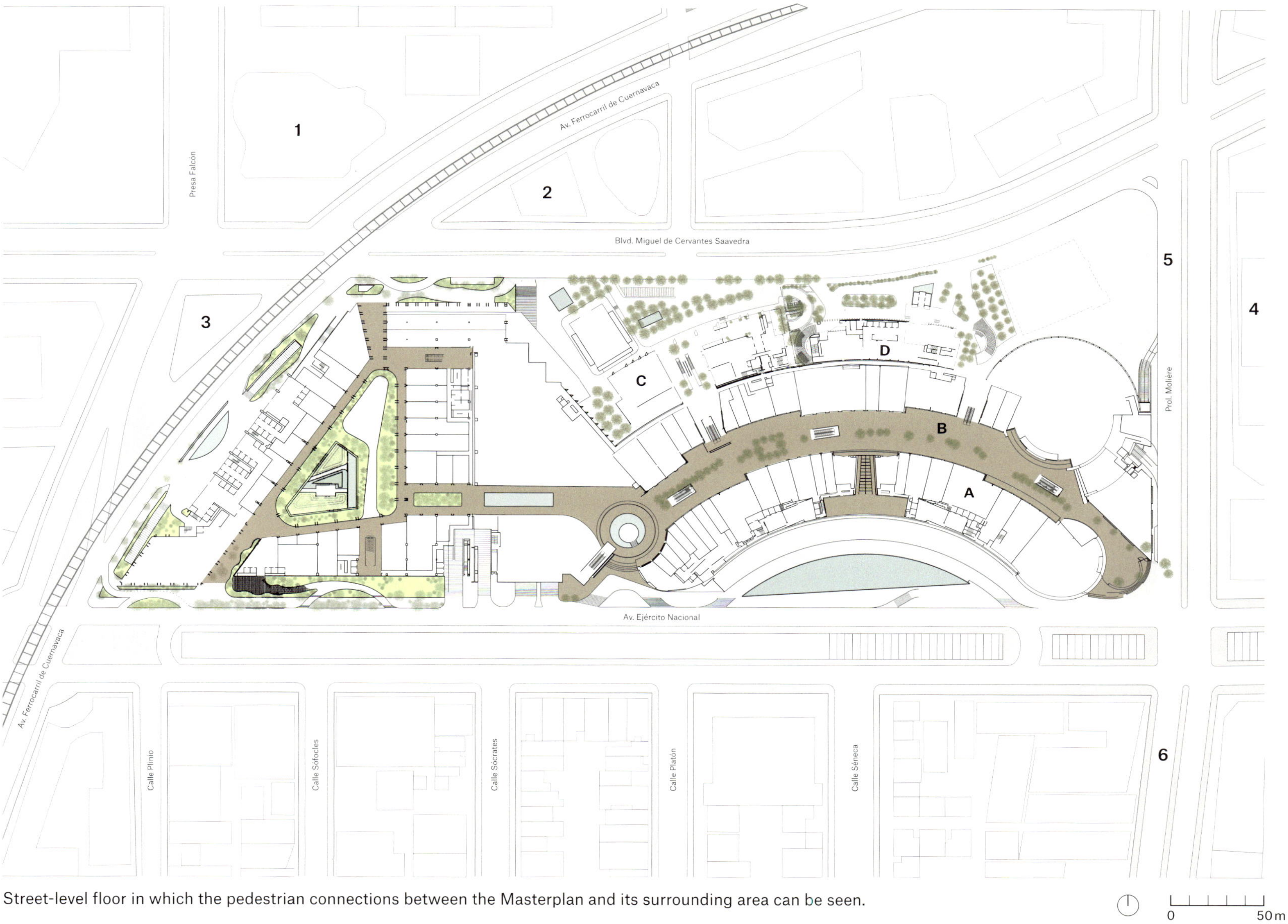

Street-level floor in which the pedestrian connections between the Masterplan and its surrounding area can be seen.

A. Paseo Tower
B. Comercial Corridor
C. Antara Corporate I
D. Antara Corporate II

1. Soumaya Museum
2. Jumex Museum
3. Inbursa Aquarium
4. Miyana
5. Colonia Granada
6. Colonia Polanco

Left hand page, above: main access plaza on Ejército Nacional. Below: motor lobby and Paseo Tower from Ejército Nacional.

Right hand page: Antara Corporate II in the foreground and Antara Corporate I in the background, from Miguel de Cervantes Saavedra.

GM

Left hand page: Apple Store and Antara Corporate I from Miguel de Cervantes Saavedra.

Right hand page, above: access plaza on Miguel de Cervantes Saavedra. Below: main access tunnel to commercial corridor from the traffic island on Ejército Nacional.

JULIO
BOSS

Cross-section in perspective.

Left hand page: interior view of the open-air commercial corridor from the second floor. From left side, Antara Corporate II and from the right side Paseo Tower.

Right hand page, right: access to ground floor from the underground parking lots.

NAUTICA
NoL & RoD
ALDO
ALDO

SPA

Left hand page, above: interior facade of Paseo Tower and its relation with the commercial corridor. Below: interior view from the ground floor of the open-air commercial corridor with restaurants and plants.

Right hand page: interior view of the commercial corridor from the first level.

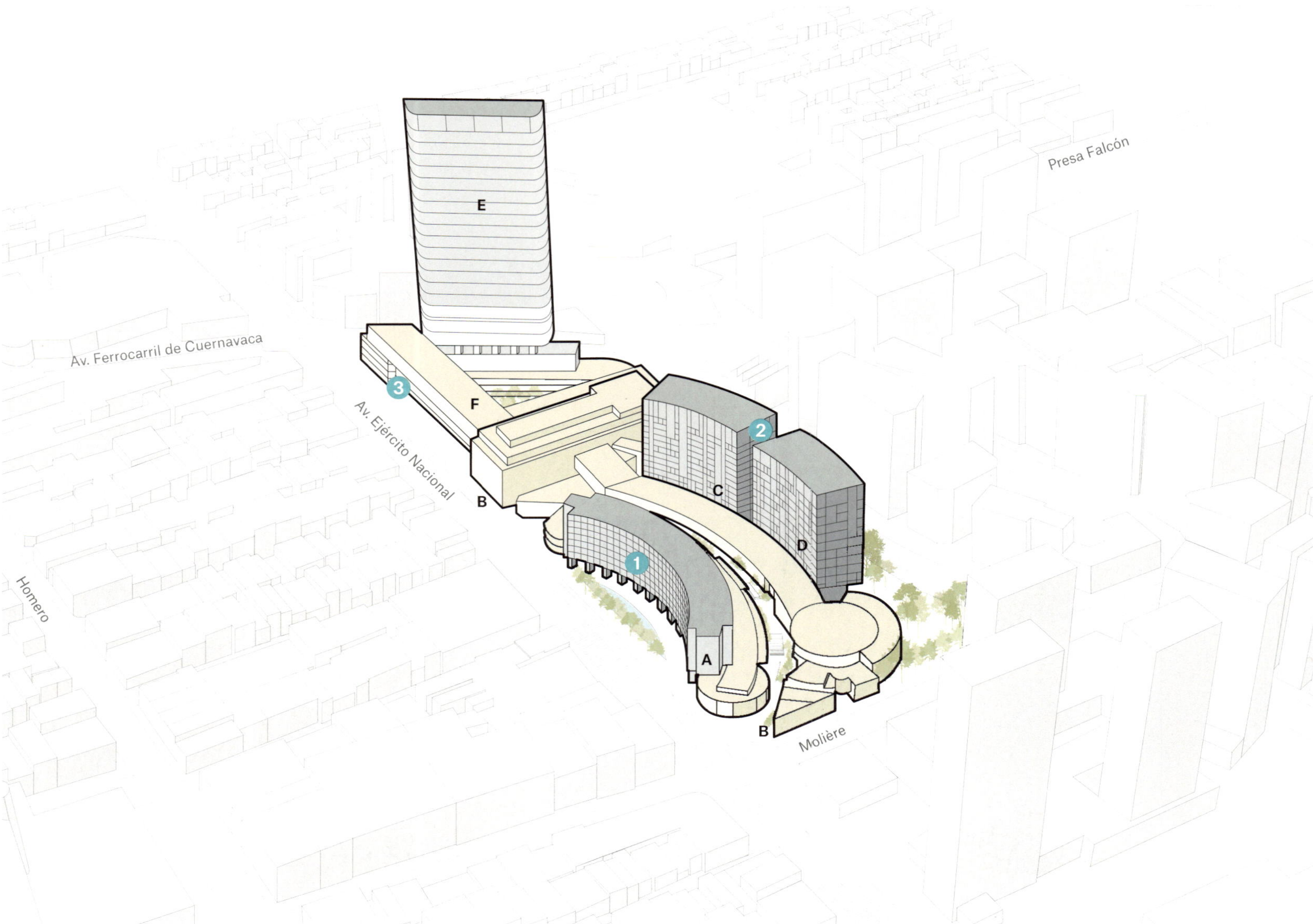

Diagram of phases and uses.

A. Paseo Tower, 2006
B. Commercial Corridor, 2006
C. Antara Corporate I, 2013
D. Antara Corporate II, 2017
E. Hotel and Corporate, +2024
F. Commercial Corridor and Art Gallery, +2024

Above: exterior view of the Antara Expansion from the north. Below: exterior view of the Antara Expansion from street level.

2009, 2017
ANDARES MASTERPLAN

HYATT REGENCY
Liverpool
cinépolis
banamex
Palacio de Hierro

Street view from the Andares Masterplan plaza.

Aerial view of the Andares Masterplan from The Landmark, mixed-use projects.

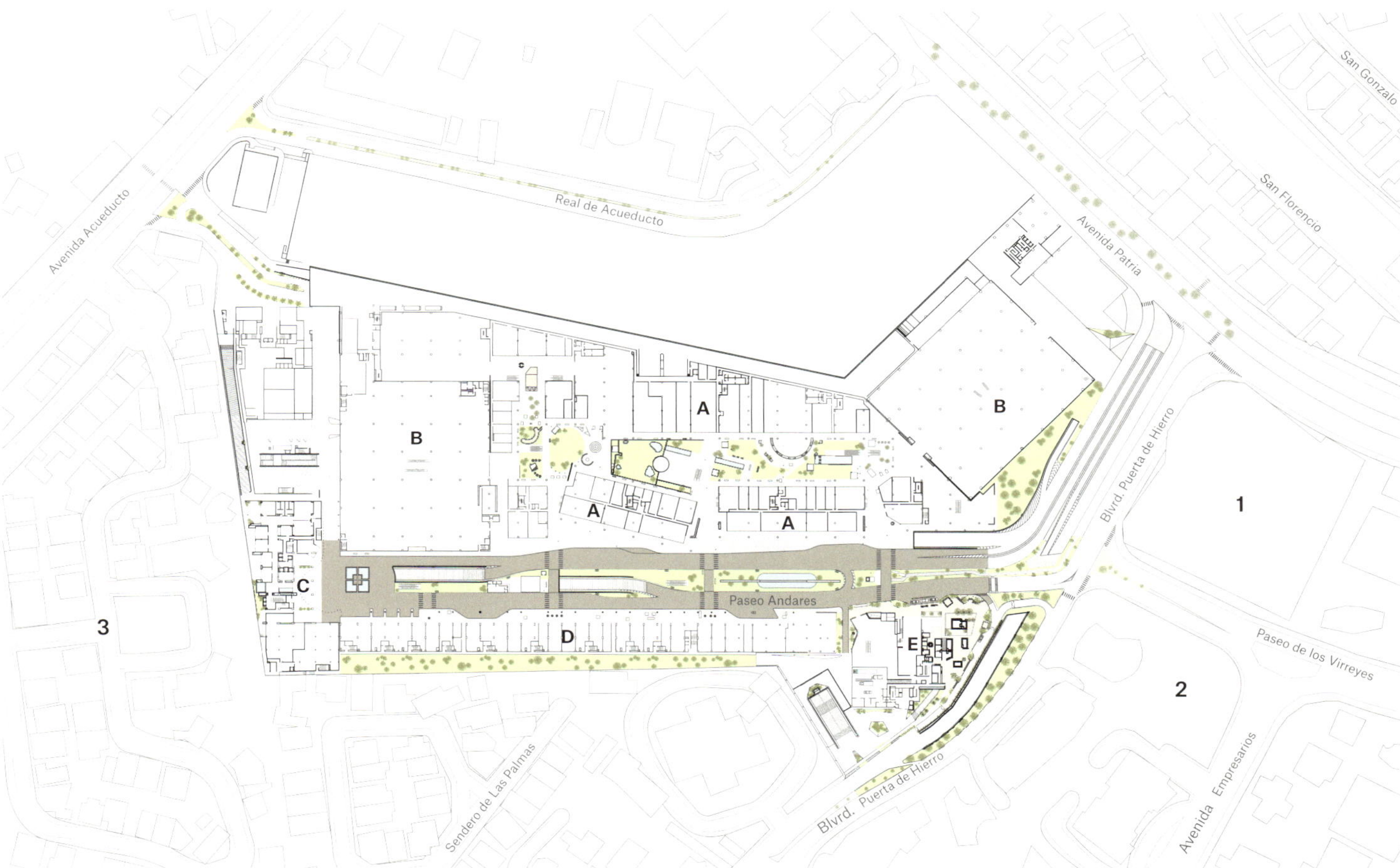

Ground floor of the Masterplan, with pedestrian corridors and vehicle connections.

0 100 m

A. Commercial
B. Department Store
C. Hotel Tower and Residencies
D. Residential Building
E. Market and Corporate Building

1. The Landmark
2. Legacy Tower
3. Pontevedra Residencies

A. Commercial, 2009
B. Residential, 2009
C. Hotel and residences, 2017
D. Corporate, 2017

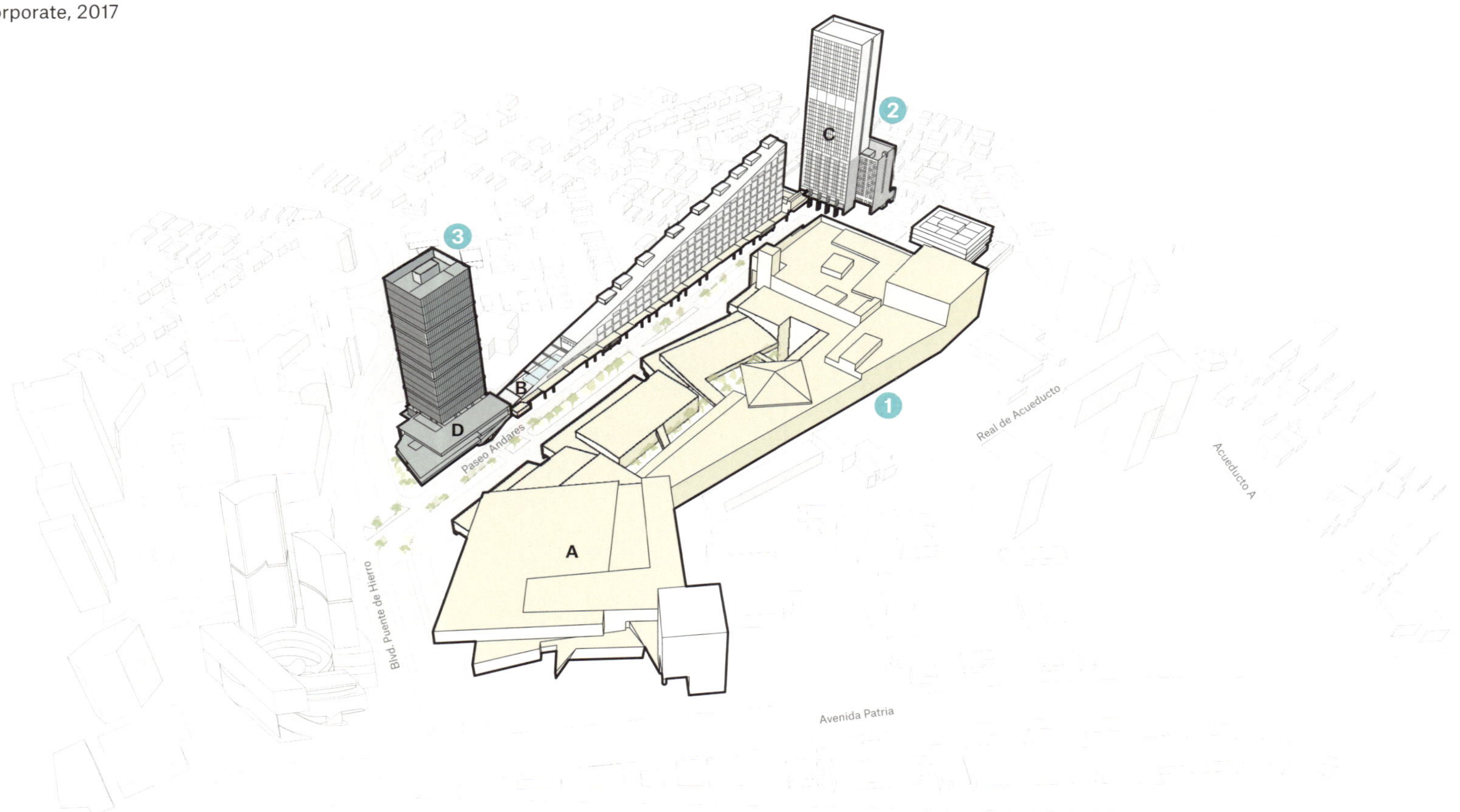

Diagram of phases and uses.

Left hand page, below: street view of interior Andares Masterplan. In the foreground, foundation and corporate tower. In the background, Andares Hyatt Regency.

Right hand page, above: interior view of the commercial complex with inner corridors guided by plants. In the background, the triangular volume of the housing. Below: view of the amenities of the apartment building. In the background, Andares Hyatt Regency.

HYATT REGENCY

4.

REFORMA COLÓN: REGENERATING THE CITY

ROSALBA ROJAS CHÁVEZ

A Aerial photograph of the Tabacalera-Juárez quadrant, Mexico City, 2021.

A

It's a small city inside the city.

Javier Sordo Madaleno Bringas

90

Precedents of a historic plaza

The famous Glorieta de Colón, the roundabout that until recently contained a monument to Christopher Columbus,[1] is located on one of the main avenues of Mexico City, Paseo de la Reforma. In Mexico's modern period of 1940–1970, this *glorieta*—a traffic circle embellished with a monument and small park at its center—was a landmark and a cosmopolitan urban referent, seen as a demonstration of the country's rise and international competitiveness. This "Mexican miracle"—also referred to as a "stabilizing development"—was the result of the economic boom the country was then experiencing. The architecture of the *glorieta* reflected the image of that period, as well as the greatness of its avenue and the economy and lifestyle of the surrounding area. A unique urban assembly was formed on the plaza, where several well-known architects designed buildings. These included Mexico City's first skyscrapers[2] and five buildings designed by the founder of Sordo Madaleno Arquitectos (SMA), Juan Sordo Madaleno, who came to develop great sensitivity and familiarity with Paseo de la Reforma, and especially with this *glorieta*. He designed some of these buildings in collaboration with other architects, a very common practice at the time: Reforma and Morelos (1946),

1. On October 10, 2020, the Mexico City government removed the statue of Columbus in response to the call by the anti-monument movement to take it down and, on September 5, 2021, announced that a sculpture by Pedro Reyes would be placed there as a monument to indigenous women. At the end of the same month, feminist activists unveiled the silhouette of a woman with her fist raised and declared the site the Traffic Circle of the Women's Struggle. Then, on October 12, 2021, the head of the Mexico City government announced that a replica of a young Amajac woman, a recently-discovered sculpture of Huastec origin, would be installed in the space in honor of Mexican indigenous women. *El Financiero*, October 12, 2021, https://www.elfinanciero.com.mx/cdmx/2021/10/12/escultura-de-la-joven-de-amajac-ocupara-glorieta-de-colon-anuncia-sheinbaum/.
2. Felipe Leal (Felipe Leal Difusión), *Programa ciudad de ciudades. Reforma, primera parte*, YouTube, video, 2013, https://www.youtube.com/watch?v=ZUI5AuWy5tE.

B Aerial view of Reforma Colón west to east from Reforma.

B

Barceló

Reforma and Versalles (1954), Cine París (1954), Anáhuac Tower (1958), and DM Nacional (1963), all now demolished except for the Anáhuac Tower, which has sadly been modified.

Originally, the development of this *glorieta* set a course for growth and advanced city planning. Living, working, or walking in this area became an aspiration. Years later, the area decayed owing to factors that persist today, as discussed in other essays in this volume.[3] The Glorieta de Colón still has the potential, however, to become a cultural, economic, public, commercial, and gastronomic hub as it was in the middle of the last century.

Reforma Colón at Sordo Madaleno Arquitectos

SMA is currently working on some 80 projects of different types and scales, and in different phases of development, among which Reforma Colón stands out for its special importance for the firm and the whole country. Naturally, some names, facts, or descriptions will change, since the design has been evolving over eight years in a creative process that integrates improvements and new considerations, although true to the original vision. This account was compiled through interviews with those in charge of the Sordo Madaleno project to provide a full overview of its characteristics.

Reforma Colón is expected to be the most important private project in Latin America this decade. In the Mexican context, it will result in some 3,500 direct jobs during its construction, 1,500 for its operation and a total of 10,000 indirect jobs, with an investment of 20,000 million pesos for its first phase. One of the most ambitious city development projects, it is intended to provide an economic boost at a regional and national level. It is vote of confidence in the country and in an area once emblematic of Mexico City, morphologically and typologically evincing its material transformation over time. And it is an urban vision that proposes the reinvention of Mexico City through a new analysis of the components and densities located in the center of the metropolis. In the words of the architect Javier Sordo Madaleno Bringas, the chairman of SMA: "Reforma Colón is not merely one more project on Reforma but will positively change the city. It will be the pioneer for the city's future developments."

Javier Sordo Madaleno Bringas and his three sons, Javier, José Juan, and Fernando Sordo Madaleno de Haro, work together daily, and Reforma Colón is part of this highly collaborative relationship between father and sons. The vision of different generations is important in the collaborative construction of large-scale projects with a major urban impact, 98, 94, 100
and they are all therefore closely involved with the design pro- 106
cess, management, and development of Reforma Colón.

Theirs is a horizontal collaboration that sets up a permanent creative network with the partners and various interdisciplinary teams at each stage of the project. Javier Sordo Madaleno de Haro, the director of Architecture at SMA, remarks that "it has required not only architectural creativity but also financial creativity, vision, strategic relations, and a great deal of patience. It's a project in which my father and my brothers have played a very important role."[4]

The complexity of Reforma Colón goes beyond formal architecture, as it creates both city and neighborhood through urban regeneration. Making this project a reality requires the convergence of many disciplines: urbanism, sociology, engineering, geotechnics, urban management, financial management, works administration, construction technologies, art, sciences, and a variety of requisites that must be perfectly coordinated to ensure success. Reforma Colón is a project designed and developed by Sordo Madaleno, and it is no novelty that the same hand should be responsible for both the design and the development. Indeed, this characterizes the firm's control of processes and quality, and its balance between architectural design and real estate development.

It would be difficult to visualize this project without Sordo Madaleno's 85-year career in architecture and more than 50 years in real estate development. It is the knowledge accumulated over three generations that gives such a broad perspective to this project located in a central area of Mexico City (A).

Urban regeneration

Major renovation and regeneration projects hold out the promise of making run-down neighborhoods vibrant and attractive again and offer an opportunity to find new purposes for underused or abandoned sites. According to Javier Sordo Madaleno de Haro, "regeneration takes time, usually a lot, but a clear, shared vision is vital to achieve it." All together, Mexico City and its metropolitan area constitute one of the largest

3. See the essay by Eduardo Alarcón Azuela in this volume, pp. 84–109.
4. "Interview with Javier Sordo Madaleno de Haro," *designboom*, April 25, 2017, https://www.designboom.com/architecture/javier-sordo-madaleno-de-haro-interview-sma-arquitectos-04-25-2017.

c Diagram of the location of the building lots that make up the Reforma Colón project, situated in Colonia Juárez.

urban developments in the world, and its urban expansion in recent decades has concentrated services in the central areas, creating a disconnected and unequal city.

Mexico City is in a process of constant change in many respects, which has meant recognizing both its deficiencies and its potential for improvement. The opportunity is an invaluable one for generating a new vision of the city. It is in this new context, under the focus of integral development, that the Reforma Colón project is presented as a catalyst for urban regeneration where the buildings are some of the most underutilized in Mexico City, renewing the existing urban fabric through a compact city model that will improve the quality of life for all.

As a result of various urban and social phenomena, the population of the Alcaldía Cuauhtémoc municipality has fluctuated, declining over the last three decades and only recently slowly starting to recover. Nevertheless, the population growth in the districts or *colonias* near Reforma Colón—even Colonia Juárez, which has good access to services and public transport and a wide range of cultural activity—fell short of 2008 estimates for the year 2020.[5] In this respect, Fernando Sordo Madaleno de Haro, director of Architecture at SMA, stresses that

c

"creating a city used to mean developing new urban areas; now it's regenerating what we already have with all its potential, unique on a worldwide scale. Regeneration is the future of Mexico City."

Major projects and investments in recent years have been focused on Paseo de la Reforma, nearly all of them on the area between Insurgentes and the Bosque de Chapultepec. The master plan for Reforma Colón aspires to promote the regeneration and densification of the city center and its surrounding areas as a new engine for economic growth and social integration. The urban infrastructure immediately around the project is very solid and has more than twenty-five points of interest and urban and social facilities. However, there are also around 550 underutilized plots,[6] presenting a great opportunity for the densification and regeneration of the area. Reforma Colón proposes a regenerative urbanism based on four principal lines of action to be implemented through various strategic projects:

- Society: through the building of community ties among the inhabitants.
- Quality of life: through the improvement of mobility infrastructure, access, safety, and public space.
- Recovery of heritage: by integrating and respecting the architectural identity of the area.
- Sustainability: by implementing ecotechnologies to reduce the carbon footprint and interventions to improve environmental conditions.

In the words of Jorge Gerini, urban director at SMA, "Reforma Colón, a project involving many years of effort, is born with a grand vision of urban regeneration, and will no doubt become a referent in the rescue of our heritage and our understanding of the city's historical memory."

---

5. Gobierno de la Ciudad de México, Programa Delegacional de Desarrollo Urbano Cuauhtémoc, *Gaceta Oficial del Distrito Federal*, 29 September 2008, 14, http://www.data.seduvi.cdmx.gob.mx/portal/docs/programas/PDDU_Gacetas/2015/PDDU-CU-AUHT%C3%89MOC.pdf; and study carried out internally with the consultant Maggi Hellary Franco Pineda on demographic dynamics of the area, Mexico City, 2019.
6. Study carried out internally with the consultant Maggi Hellary Franco Pineda on use, facilities, and underutilization of the area, Mexico City, 2019.

D Schematic/volumetric diagram of typologies and phases of the components of Reforma Colón.
E Ground floor Reforma Colón.
F Elevation of Reforma Colón in relation to its urban profile and the height of its surroundings.

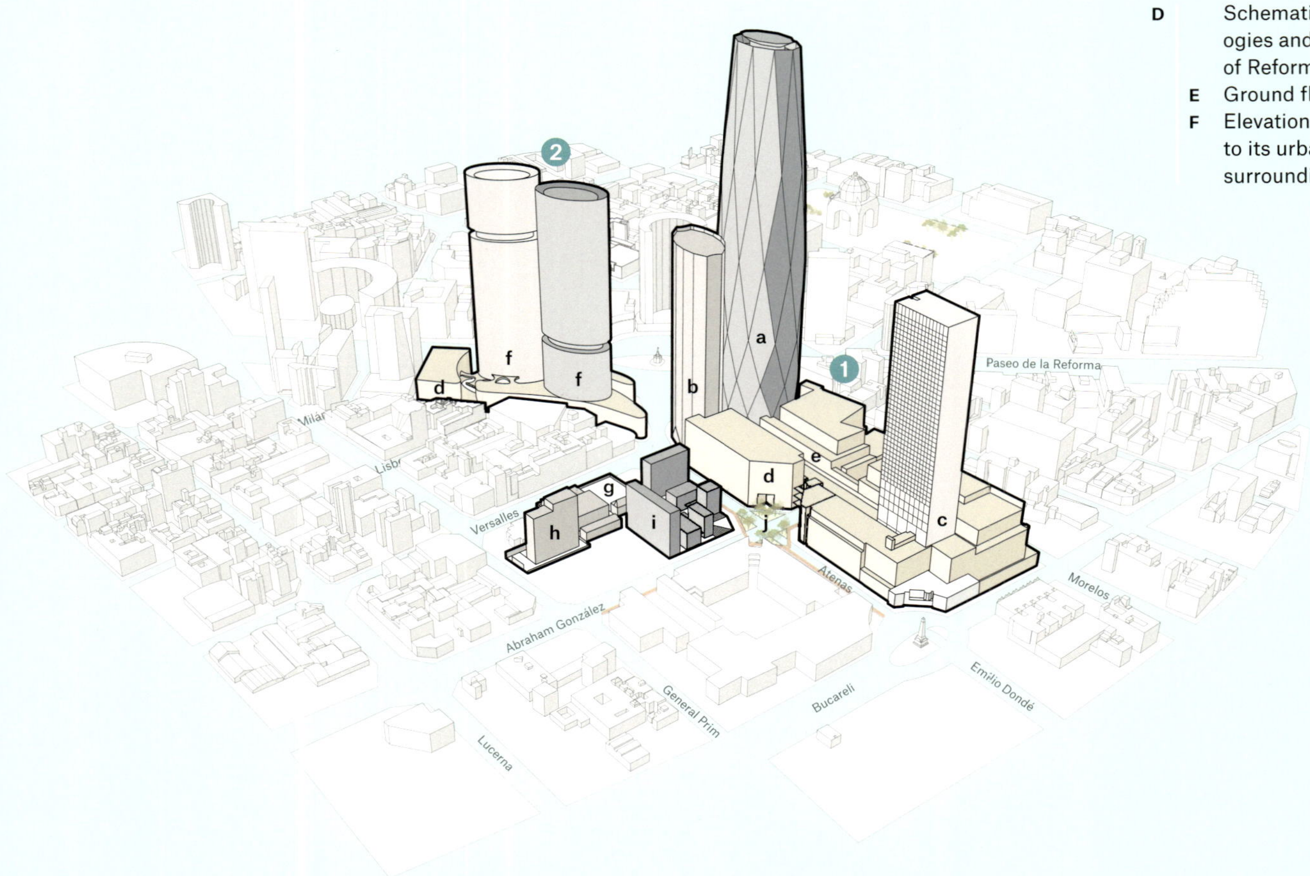

D

The masterplan

Reforma Colón changes the dynamism of the area and the whole city. It is a project for a minutely designed, compact, and connected city with a flexible structure that relates all its parts to one another and to the whole. In a clear articulation of space, it assembles different neighborhoods and close communities, reconnecting their inhabitants with their city.

The same plots of land—and several more—which contained the five buildings designed by the founder, Juan Sordo Madaleno, are to be newly reimagined for high-density mixed uses on a grand scale. The site of approximately 50,000 m² on Paseo de la Reforma almost completely occupies four blocks in the second *cuadro* of the Historic Center of Mexico City. It is the result of an enormous effort to acquire thirty-one plots, one by one, over a period of ten years (2010–2020), in order to merge them for construction in various phases (C). On these plots are three beautiful historic buildings listed by the National Institute of Fine Arts and Literature—two mansions from the era of Porfirio Díaz and a set of six residences from the same period—which are to be restored and reused, establishing them as the guiding principles for the design and its urban integration.

A project of these dimensions in an urban context with profound social and historical significance must ensure regeneration is carried out as amicably as possible. To this end, SMA has studied, researched, and taken into consideration cultural, architectural, and social questions, mobility, all in collaboration with various specialized agencies including direct consultation with local people. "The creative process has been particularly interesting because of the contextual research carried out, which has constantly fed our decisions on the design," says Fernando Sordo Madaleno de Haro.

Included in these contextual studies was the investigation, analysis, and recreation of the facades that once existed in the area and their link with today's-built context—to design new facades and views open toward both the interior of the project and the neighboring areas or exterior streets. The eight outward-facing facades were designed to provide continuity for the pre-existing heights, galleries, and rhythms of openings and closures of the surrounding buildings. Upper floors are thus set back up to ten meters above the second floor. This design decision envisions great urban permeability and an architectural insertion that is easy on a pedestrian level, sensitive to the context and respectful of local history, and generates a pleasant and humanized atmosphere in the street with activity in cafés, restaurants, and shops. Architect Luis Hernández, the project's director, explains "The city is rich, and the facades must be too."

---

7. Institute for Transportation & Development Policy (TOD), "TOD Standard," https://www.itdp.org/2017/06/23/tod-standard.

a. Reforma Colón
b. Hotel Tower
c. Residential Tower
d. Public Plaza and Commercial Esplanade
e. Historic Complex of Six Houses
f. Corporate and Residential Towers
g. Soho House Club
h. Soho House Hotel
i. Abraham González
j. Proposal of Urban Plaza

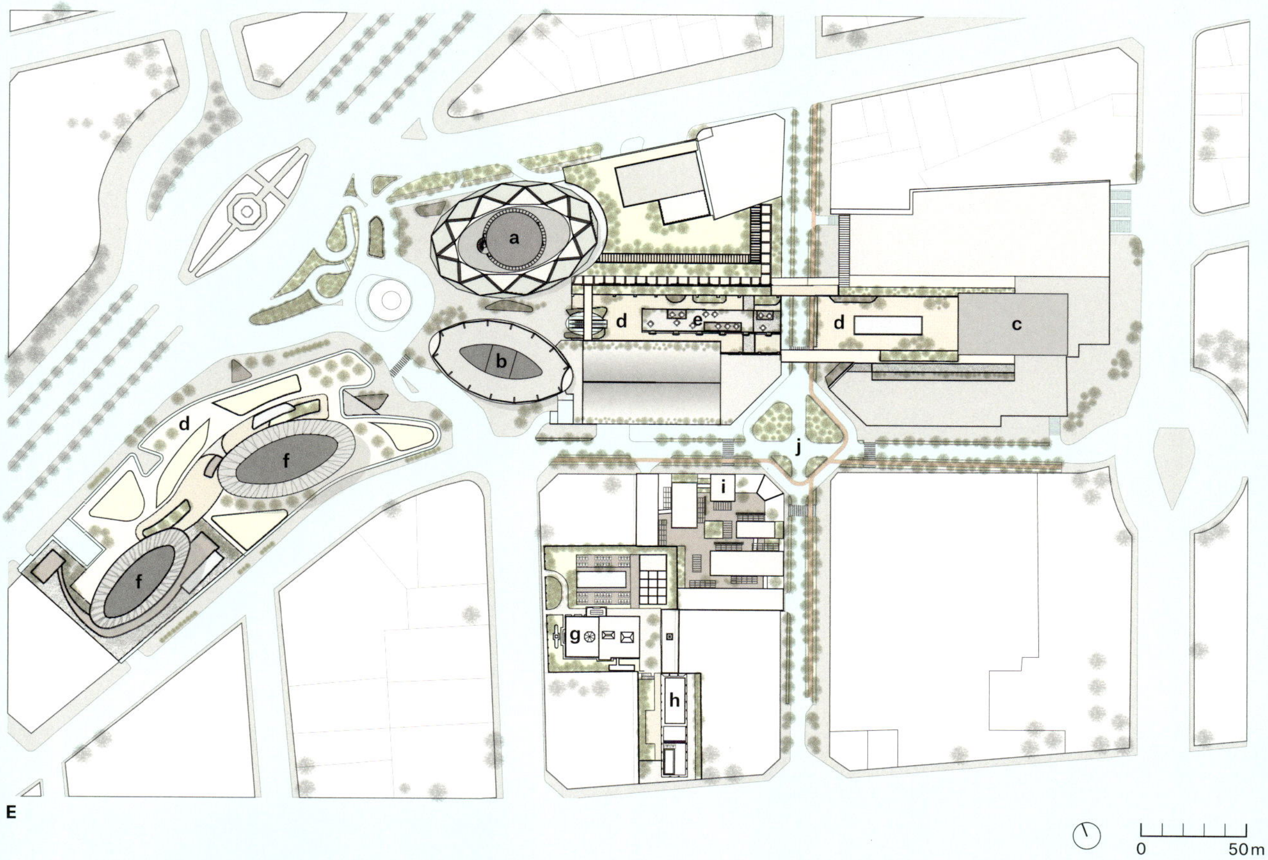

E

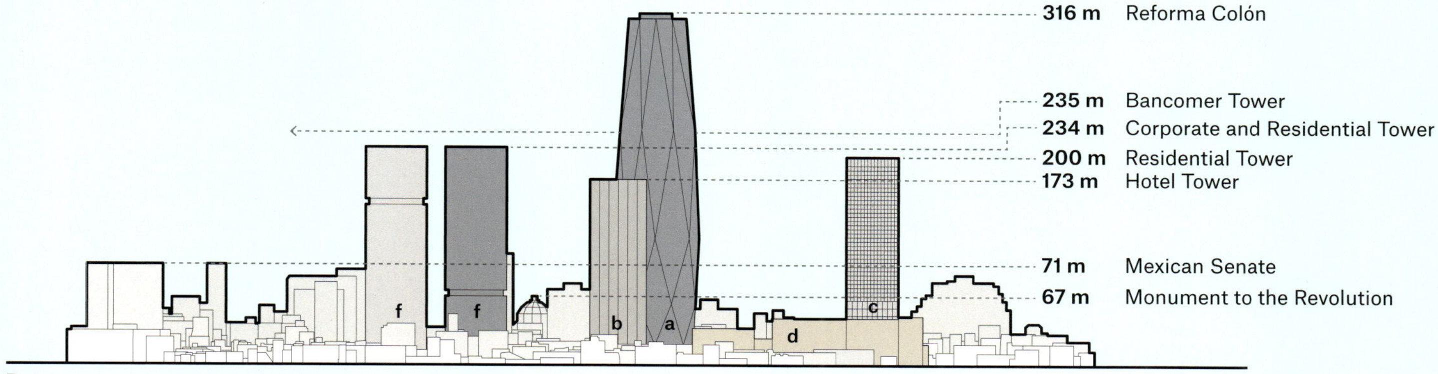

F

The focus lies on three aspects central to SMA's urban design projects: mobility, public space, and sustainability. Mobility is ensured with a vision that goes beyond "transit-oriented development"[7] to emphasize the experience of living and moving through the city via urban activation. In this way, special attention has been paid to the creation of pedestrian corridors and the promotion of sustainable mobility as well as the implementation of public transport. The plan foresees redesigned streets, walkways, and traffic lights, repaving, enlarged sidewalks, safe crossings, the incorporation of cycle lanes, and the creation and renovation of public plazas and pedestrian streets throughout the development. It offers a variety of activities for those passing through and includes small spaces for relaxation or exhibitions.

In this way, the city is kept vibrant, and life is allowed to develop organically. The city is understood to be focused on people and the way they experience it. The project promotes other types of mobility like walking, cycling, skateboards, public transport, and so on. After an in-depth mobility analysis in collaboration with specialists and the relevant government departments, a master plan for urban mitigation was proposed that includes corridors with the characteristics mentioned

G Ground floor lobby of Reforma Colón, with a triple-height space supported by exoskeleton columns.

H Structural System Abstraction of Reforma Colón.

I Aerial view of Reforma towards the east, with Reforma Colón and the hotel tower in the foreground.

G

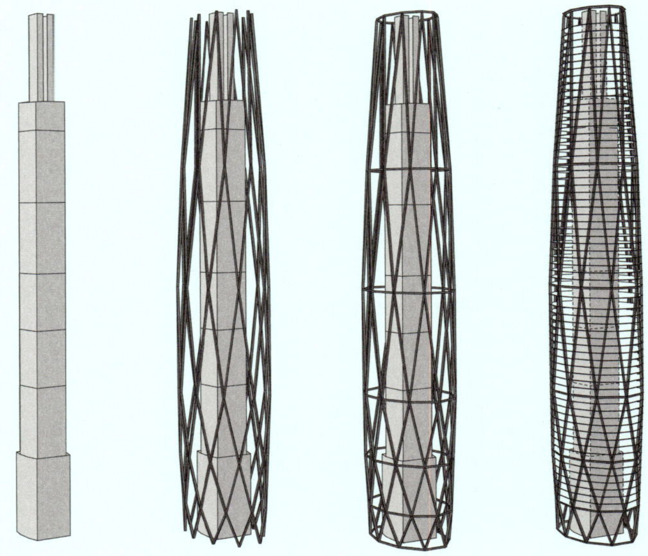

H

above, integration within the cycle lane network, and an increase in useful public space which in its turn will connect areas of the city that are currently isolated. Added to these strategies is a vision of landscape based on sustainability, with a proposal to renew the urban environment by integrating greenery through infiltration raingardens, low vegetation, and trees, to diminish the heat island effect, to capture carbon dioxide, and to permit the infiltration of water to the subsoil. These are integral solutions that increase resilience to flooding and help aquifers to recover. In the words of Javier Sordo Madaleno de Haro, "the process of design and team management has been highly demanding owing to the scale of the project and the enormous responsibility it brings with it."

Distribution and phases

The layout of the five towers that make up the project was planned based on in-depth analyses of different forms of occupation. The buildings will finally be positioned in such a way as to prioritize urban accessibility and permeability, quality of life, exposure to sunlight, mitigation of wind in pedestrian areas, and the privacy and comfort of users, while taking full advantage of views and connectivity with the surrounding area (D).

The master plan lays out two phases of construction. The first will consist of three towers and a large public plaza surrounded by shops and restaurants. Its siting is determined principally by its urban integration with Glorieta de Colón on Paseo de la Reforma, and by the inclusion of the six historic low-rise dwellings (e) in the heart of the commercial esplanade. The Reforma Colón Tower (a) is destined for corporate use, the second tower is a hotel (b) and the third will be residential (c). The base between the three towers is occupied by the commercial area (d), which runs around a large public plaza and forms a neighborhood pedestrian connection from Paseo de la Reforma to Calle de Bucareli.

In the second phase, it is planned to expand the public plaza and the commercial esplanade (d) westwards to enable continuity with the first phase. Two towers (f) for corporate and residential use will be in the center. The Soho Club and House (g, h) and Abraham González (i) projects are independent of the two phases; although, they have close urban and pedestrian links with the project, both their plots of land and their planning are separate.

To be able to manage each phase of the project, collaboration with the authorities of Mexico City has been close and productive. The different players involved have enriched the project and shown a positive attitude from the start with a focus on collaboration and commitment that the project will bring benefits for the community including inhabitants of the city center. "Reforma Colón will be the result of a global vision of the city which, in tandem with the authorities, private initiative, and expert consultants on environmental aspects and mobility, will change Mexico City radically," says Andrés Cajiga, project director. The first phase started its construction in 2022 and will conclude in approximately 2027. The second phase is then due to be completed in 2030.

8. "Mexico City," Skyscraper City, https://www.skyscrapercity.com/forums/ciudad-de-m%C3%A9xico.521/.

J View of the lower floors of Reforma Colón and the hotel tower from Reforma.

K View from the Chinese Clock plaza on Bucareli. In the foreground, the residential tower within the complex.

J

K

L Aerial view from the public plaza of the residential tower's western facade.

L

***Reforma Colón Tower* (a)**

The Reforma Colón Tower seeks verticality. It stands out imposingly as the tallest tower in the complex with a height of 316 m and a built area of 150,000 m². The tower will rise above the Mexico City skyline; its graceful figure will probably be the tallest skyscraper in Latin America (F).[8]

It rises on an oval plan and features a three-story space enclosed only by the ten V-shaped columns of the structural exoskeleton. This opening or spatial permeability integrates it directly into public life (G).

Sordo Madaleno Arquitectos designed its geometry in accordance with certain architectural concepts aimed at the expression of structural efficiency. The facade is the result of a fertile collaboration with the engineering firm SOM (Skidmore, Owings & Merrill) of San Francisco, California, which achieved structural solutions without altering SMA's artistic vision. The structure enables the building to be highly efficient and operationally versatile with a plan free of intermediate columns; instead, there is a central core for vertical circulation that is steadily reduced as it climbs. In all, a balance was found between form and function, and between the exoskeleton of the facade and the vertical core (H).

***Hotel tower* (b)**

The hotel has 44 floors and approximately 800 rooms with a built area of 60,000 m². The Reforma Colón Tower and the new hotel share the same design and type of structure at the base and up to the third level. Further up, the facades share similar materials that make for a homogeneous reading, but each tower preserves its own identity (I, J).

***Residential tower* (c)**

Toward the eastern end of the complex, a residential tower is to be built with a rectangular floor plan, 50 stories, a built area of approximately 54,000 m², and several *unités d'habitation* in different configurations. The tower is the visual culmination of the public plaza. Its main access is in Calle Bucareli. An early nineteenth-century mansion will serve as the linking element. Two of the mansion's seven original galleries are preserved. They will be restored and integrated into the project by the reinterpretation the facades in the new construction on Bucareli (K).

The residential tower can also be accessed from inside the complex, as its base is a contained three-story space where the public plaza enters and fuses with the eye-catching structure of the tower (L).

M Previous status of landmark preservation of the complex of six horizontal homes built in 1910. Southern facade. Mexico City, 2021.

N O Interior view of the public plaza set within a commercial building; in the center, the restoration of the original complex of six horizontal homes.

M

***Public plaza and commercial building* (d)**
From the ground floor to the third level, a commercial wing runs from east to west, providing a connection between the towers while forming a public plaza in the interior, permanently open and permeable to the city. The compositional axis is marked by the original location of a set of six low-rise dwellings (e) built in 1910 and known as "Corazón de Manzana" (heart of the block). This architectural heritage is to be respected, rescued, and transformed into a major feature of the complex (N, O).

The commercial building is located in the complex itself, links everything in its three levels, and gives internal access to the towers, despite these being separate structures. Inside, the public plaza creates paths across ample terraces, vast areas of greenspace, bodies of water, contemporary art, changing materials and visual keynotes, all in safety and in the open air. Such walks bring unity to the project and to the experience and quality of life of its users. The commercial building also establishes an agreeable scale for the pedestrian while permitting urban permeability in the area through a series of bridges, entrances, crossings, and meeting points—fronts on both the interior and the exterior of the project to integrate it smoothly with the city.

The principal material used throughout the commercial building, the public plaza, and the residential tower is concrete pigmented in a beige tone, with a rocky quality that relates it to the natural stone of the context, mostly the tufa known as *cantera*.

***Corporate and residential towers* (f)**
As of now, the use and design of these two towers are tentative. Although it is still too early to know the details of these two projects, they will be integrated harmoniously into the second phase of the master plan.

***Soho House* (g, h) *and Abraham González* (i)**
This independent, mixed-use complex is a parallel project closely connected on a pedestrian, architectural, and urban level with the development of Reforma Colón. It is a tangible

N

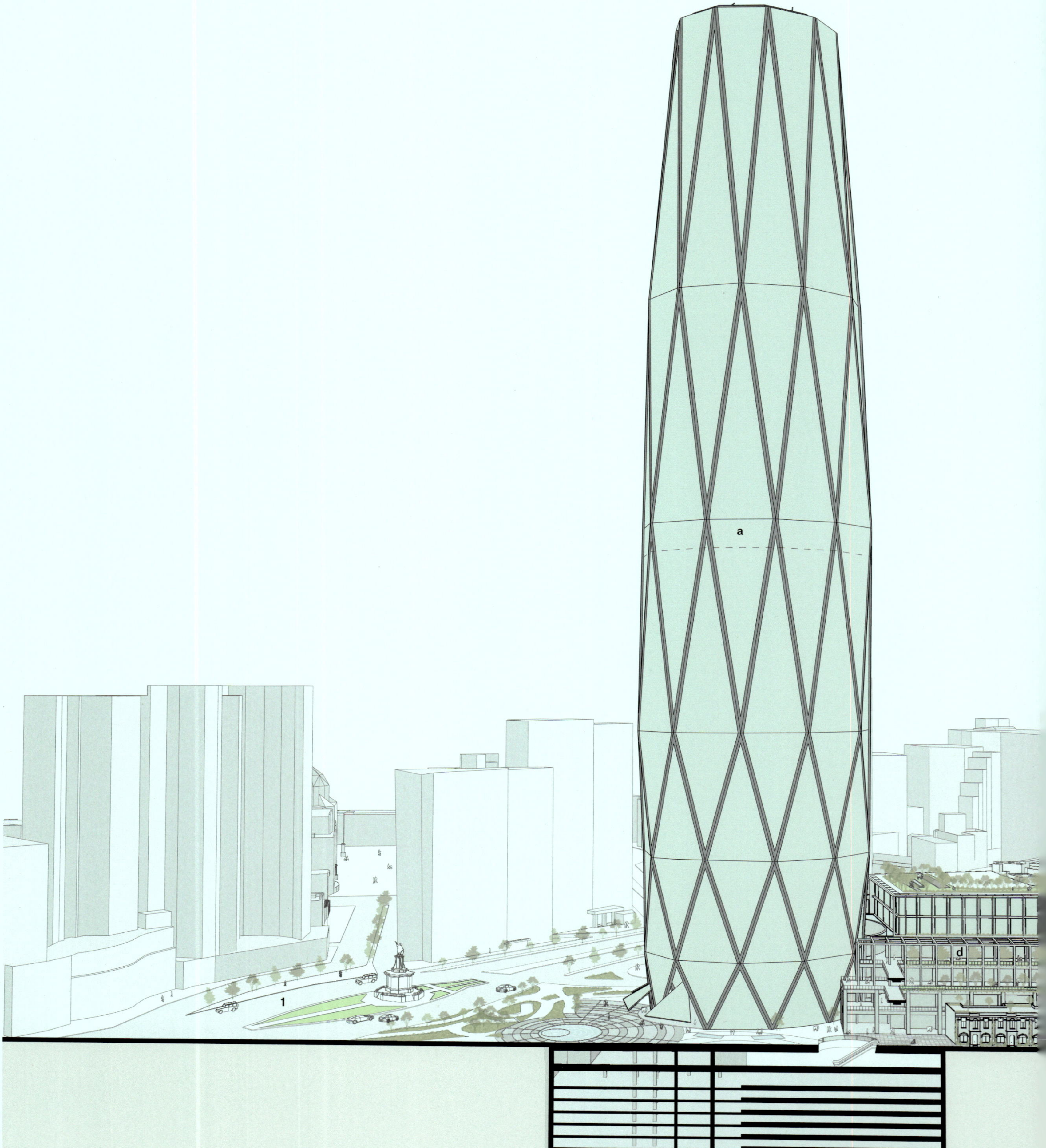
a
d
1

P Longitudinal section in perspective.

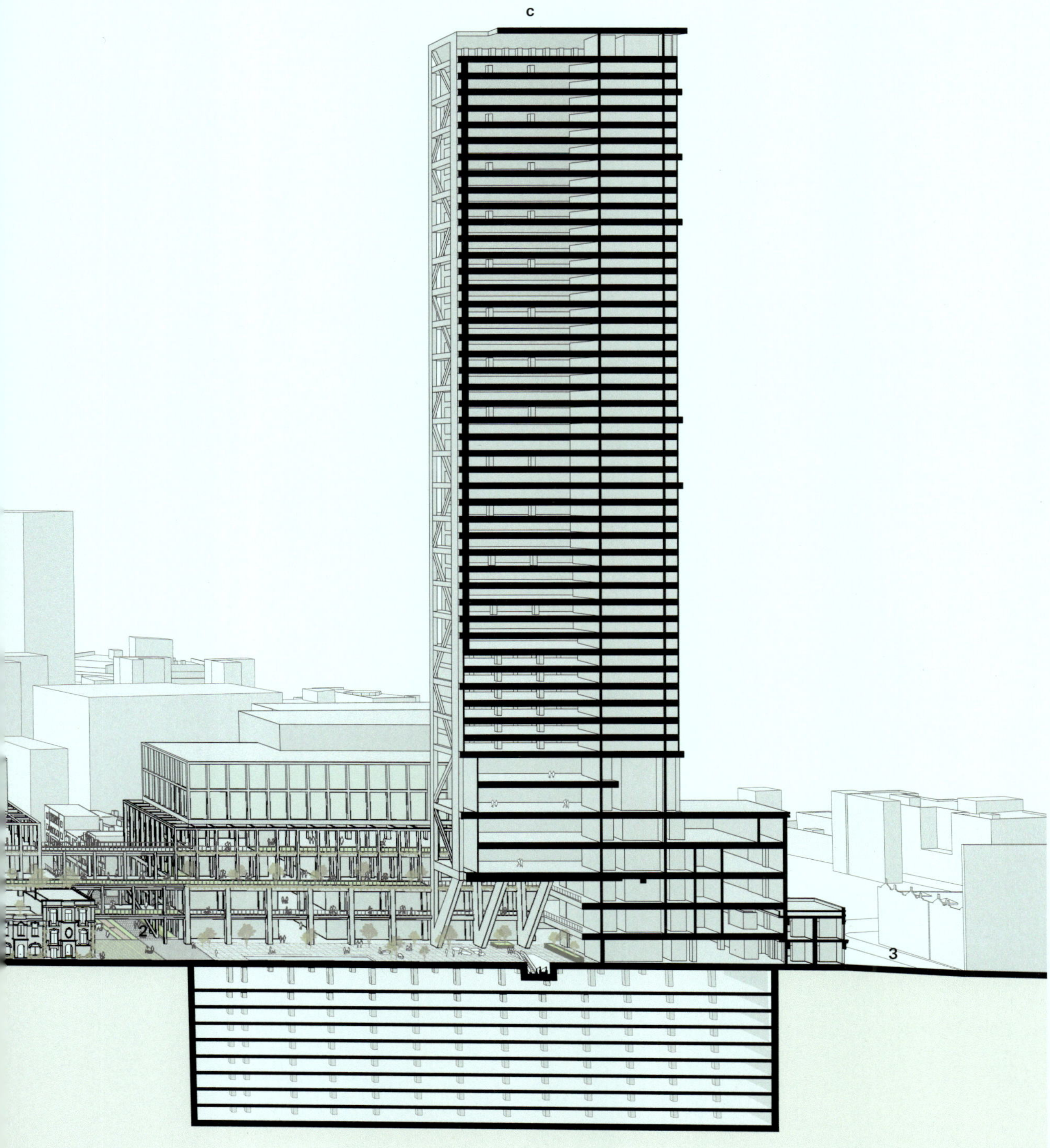

a. Reforma Colón
c. Residential Tower
d. Public Plaza and Commercial Esplanade
e. Original Complex of Six Homes

1. Reforma
2. Abraham González
3. Bucareli

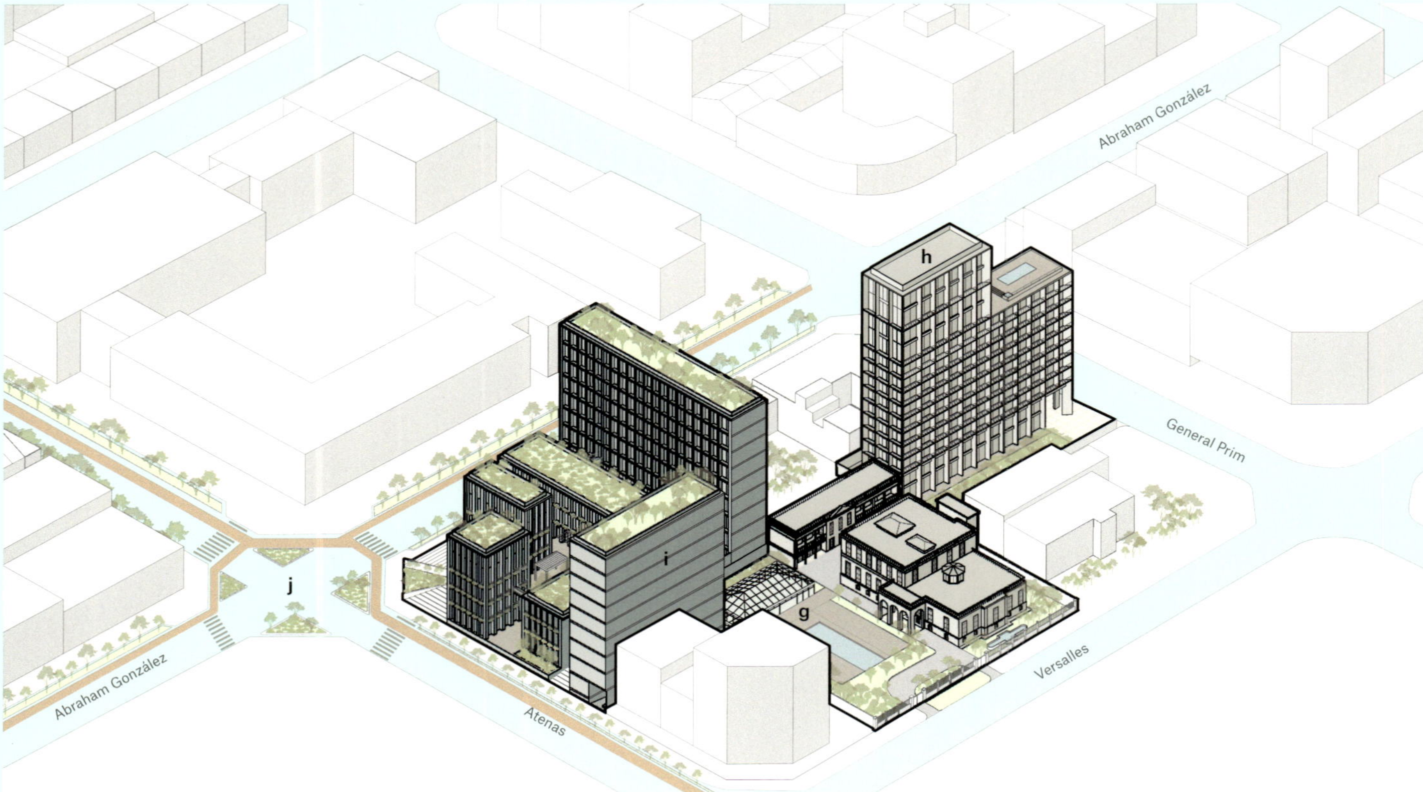

g. Soho House Club
h. Soho House Hotel
i. Abraham González
j. Proposal for Urban Plaza

Q

example of what can happen in Colonia Juárez if it is rehabilitated through smaller projects with strong cultural components that gradually reinforce the identity of the district. The complex covers 9,000 m² on seven merged plots in the block bound by the streets Atenas, Abraham González, General Prim, and Versalles, creating an irregular interior polygon accessed from the four adjoining streets. Its various uses include shops and plentiful restaurants, offices dedicated principally to the artistic community, art galleries, and the Soho House hotel and club.

This project is composed of two virtually complementary parts: the Soho House project, and the project temporarily named Abraham González, both internally connected and functioning in symbiosis (Q). The main entrance is at the intersection of Atenas and Abraham González, whose relationship is replanned and extended through a new urban plaza in front of the well-known chamfered corner (j), creating connectivity, openness, and above all urban permeability in the direction of Reforma Colón. In the words of Javier Sordo Madaleno de Haro, "the cultural importance of the place creates an ideal environment for fostering community through art."

The famous international hospitality chain Soho House seeks architecture, style, and urban life for its members—figures of the international creative community—and so decided to join the project with its club and hotel. The Soho House Club (g) is housed in an architectural gem on Calle de Versalles, a mansion of 1909 that was the home of General Diego Redo de la Vega. Typical of the area, it has an eclectic architectural style with strong French influences, typical of the years under Porfirio Díaz (R). The house provides the guiding concept for the interior design, where the priority is the recovery of its heritage. Inside are restaurants, cafés, bars, a gym, amenities, a pool house (S), communal areas, and four suites.

The Soho House Hotel (h) is being built on the southwest side, with direct access from the club or access for vehicles and pedestrians via General Prim. It is a graceful fourteen-story building housing some 60 rooms. The design is a modular grid that respects the rhythms and heights of the area, with which it engages in dialogue. At the same time, this grid of green-tinted exposed concrete is a structural facade, designed with a geometry of columns that ensures open plans for the interior distribution.

Abraham González (i, U) is a very peculiar urban concept of cultural and culinary spaces that complement and cater to the artistic community of Soho House. It consists of six

Q Diagram of the Soho House Club and Hotel and of the Abraham González project, Mexico City.
R General Diego Redo de la Vega Mansion, Mexico City, 1907.
S Front view of the Soho House Club pool house.

R

S

T Proposal for the new urban plaza at the intersection of Atenas and Abraham González.

elegant buildings rising from two to ten stories, with the ground floor and first level of each block destined for restaurants, cafés, and terraces that create a friendly, casual, and open atmosphere. The second level will house art galleries linked by bridges between the blocks. The adjoining six-story buildings are the tallest and will contain studios for the creative community. Unity of the interior and exterior facades is maintained through the rhythmic use of columns, differing heights, and plentiful vegetation (U). Pedestrian access can occur through any of the voids resulting from the separation between the blocks. Urban integration is also achieved through the proposal of an urban plaza on the intersection of Atenas and Abraham González (j), but also through the architectural design, which emphasizes openness to the city. Andrés Muñoz, project director of Soho House and Abraham González, clearly sums up the intervention: "The negative of the built goes flagrantly in search of a relationship with the city; it's the area which fuses with the public space."

Construction

One of the greatest challenges for the construction of the Reforma Colón project was the design of the foundations, since the subsoil is mostly wet clay. This is a well-known situation in the center of Mexico City, where buildings are constantly sinking in a lingering memory of the former Lake of Texcoco.

T

U View of the Abraham González Project from the intersection of Atenas and Abraham González.

U

v General aerial view of the Reforma Colón complex from east to west.

To tackle the soil conditions existing in foundation elements like the diaphragm wall and the deep foundations, pre-injection was necessary first to stabilize the terrain and improve the conditions. The selection of the technology and the design of the construction systems were dictated by the conditions of the terrain. Still other seismic solutions for the project are based on the design, not the system, meaning that while the construction technology is not unique, the design characteristics are. All seismic solutions comply with local Mexican code. In the opinion of Greg Miller, director of construction at SMA, "the greatest challenge during construction was the definition of the technologies owing to the condition of the soil."

The foundations and substructure system will be constructed by the very interesting "top-down" process, so called because construction begins at sidewalk level and works down to the deepest basement. It is the opposite of what is traditionally seen, when the whole plot is excavated and then built up from the lowermost basement to the sidewalk level. This type of procedure makes it possible to start building above street level when the basements have yet to be completed. For top-down foundations, the diaphragm wall is laid first together with all the foundation piles that will take the weight of the basements, the building, and the loads required on the scaffolding. These concrete piles extend from 54 to 80 meters deep, making this structure's foundations the deepest in Mexico City. It is then that the floors of each basement can be constructed from the top down since the pillars supporting them and each intermediate floor help to contain the diaphragm wall. The system is much slower than traditional ones, but it is more efficient owing to the quality of the soil. It bears pointing out that 72% of the concrete of the building is used below sidewalk level. The foundation structure was designed in collaboration with the engineering firm SOM at its U.S. offices in Los Angeles, San Francisco, and New York.

To achieve the highest levels of quality in the final project, SMA has used technologies that have never been seen before in Mexico. For example, the lens manufacturer, Leica, developed a very complex GPS system to confront the challenge of verticality control in buildings classified as "super tall"—a system used previously at the Burj Khalifa in Dubai. Another example is the so-called Plaxis 3D technology, which uses 3D modeling to analyze the behavior of the soil, calculating and monitoring the weight of the structure to study how it settles initially as against the projected long-term effect, and accounting for geotechnics, deformation, stability, and water flow. Additionally, criteria have been adopted from the start in favor of bioclimatic design with clean technologies to qualify for certification of sustainability and efficiency, like the LEED Gold in the case of the Reforma Colón Tower.

Reforma Colón regenerated

Mexico City always offers opportunities to those who know how to find them. It is considered one of the most important cultural and economic centers in Latin America, and projects carried out there are therefore likely to acquire prominence and attract growing international attention. This type of project requires the active participation of the community and the integration of various disciplines that contribute their respective skills and strengths to ensure a successful conclusion. The greatest ambition of this project is to generate an attractive and prosperous new pole of development for Mexico City and so encourage a return to the city center.

Reforma Colón's architects seek to make a positive impact on the surroundings by increasing the offering of different services in the area, complementing and balancing those already there. It casts out connecting nets toward the city that will lead to a physical and visual transformation on both the urban and the community levels. It will add value to the area and will increase safety and the sense of belonging of the inhabitants through urban improvements, adopting new models of mobility and displacement in a bid for a clear reorganization of public space and the appropriation of the project by local users and visitors.

The economy of the area will grow naturally and organically, reconnecting with the essence of the place and recalling its heyday in the middle of the last century through different interventions that involve urban design, architecture, and landscape. The goal is thus to construct a place where people will live, work, and enjoy the city through Reforma Colón. We must ask ourselves what kind of city we want. What is the change we are looking for? With Reforma Colón, the answer is clear: it represents a desire to reinvent the city at its heart.

V

W Skyline of Reforma including the Reforma Colón complex.

W

5.

THE POST-INDUSTRIAL CITY IN MEXICO AND THE WORLD

FELIPE CORREA

A Aerial photograph of La Rive Gauche development, Paris, France, 2011.

Throughout the second half of the twentieth century, major metropolitan areas witnessed the systematic transformation of vacant inner-city land. The disappearance of industry due to the gradual shift from manufacturing to service-based economies in city centers, along with the closure and relocation of large-scale urban infrastructures—cargo ports, city-locked airports, landfills—produced a new urban geography in urgent need of redefinition. By the early 1990s, most major metropolitan areas across the globe confronted large tracts of inner-city derelict urban land. The early photographic work of Edward Burtynsky in Canada and the decaying industrial spaces in the American northeast captured by the lens of Camilo José Vergara are two examples of the many artistic explorations that brought these spaces to light, giving them a cultural value that would later be monetized through real estate operations. Generally labeled as derelict or postindustrial land, by the late 1980s large parcels with defunct industries became ubiquitous in the urban landscape. Most, if not all, major metropolitan areas have had to envision a future for fallow land.

Examples of abandoned industrial land are abundant across the globe. An area like Pudong in Shanghai—a time-honored nodal point between Chinese industrial production and global markets—experienced the rapid migration of manufacturing enterprises upriver, opening a large tract of industrial heritage sites that became an integral component of the *Pudong Development Zone* in the 1990s, an ambitious urban operation that transformed Shanghai into a major twenty-first-century financial center.[1] Similarly, the city of Paris set forth the *Paris Rive Gauche* urban redevelopment project. Spearheaded in the mid-1990s, the project reclaimed 130 hectares of former industrial land and transformed it into a series of inner-city mixed-use districts.[2]

A

In Latin America, projects like Puerto Madero in Buenos Aires pioneered efforts to rethink postindustrial land. Today, large cities like São Paulo are examining the future of their vacant inner-city land. Mexico City has not been exempted from this process. The gradual shift of industrial clusters from Mexico City to the adjacent city of Toluca left behind large areas of fallow land within the city limits.

Post-logistical spaces have also been at the epicenter of urban agendas in metropolitan regions for the past three decades. The closure of maritime ports, airports, and landfills, among many other large-scale elements of logistical infrastructure have played a pivotal role in urban transformation in the late twentieth and early twenty-first century. For example, in Amsterdam, once the cargo port moved further west to be better connected with rail infrastructure in the 1970s, the city was confronted with large tracts of vacant waterfront land open for redevelopment. Similarly, the 1952 closure of Croydon Airport in London and the decommissioning of Berlin's Tempelhof Airport in the late 2000s, followed by their transformation into large urban parks, opened the possibility of re-imagining utilitarian infrastructures that had traditionally been walled off from the life of the city, into new public spaces that became an integral part of urban life.

The term "postindustrial land" has been used to define large quantities of derelict urban land within metropolitan regions all over the world. Yet, the language defines a present condition based on its previous functions, offering no hint as to what these spaces might become. The ambiguity in terminology has provided fertile ground for architecture, landscape architecture, and the design disciplines affiliated with

1. Yi-Fan Yu, Kong-San Li and Sheng-Lan Shu, *Preservation and Reuse of Industrial Heritage along the Banks of the Huangpu River in Shanghai* (Beijing: National Science Foundation of China, 2012), 3.
2. Ernek Benoit, "Paris Rive Gauche Project: (Re) developing the City in the City," *Journal of Land, Housing and Urban Affairs* July (2014): 123–129.

city making at large to envision alternative futures that can give derelict landscape a new lease on life. The scale and civic scope of these projects foreground the importance of design expertise in redefining the urban. Among the many tasks that come into play in the transformation of post-industrial landscapes, three seem to be common across most projects. One is the careful examination of contaminated landscapes and the ecological processes that can remediate them. The evolution of urban ecology as a science, and the study of the flora and fauna endemic to these urban sites has played a pivotal role in how we reimagine nature within the city. Two, paying close attention to the heritage of former industrial landscapes and a careful assessment of how their history should be interpreted and preserved in these contexts. Three, the strategic alignment of a spatial vision with economic development plans that can guarantee the project's viability over time.

While the specific design strategies used to intervene in the transformation of postindustrial land are both site specific and varied, there are two design approaches that throughout the last thirty years have set the stage for transforming postindustrial wastelands. These can be defined in two broadly conceived types. First, urban projects that restructure formerly industrial districts into mixed-use districts. Second, projects that envision ways to reincorporate large, formerly industrial, or logistical, landscapes as open space. Cities such as Amsterdam, Berlin, New York, and Paris have implemented inventive projects of urban transformation that have later been used as models in many other contexts.

Paris and Amsterdam

Paris was one of the first cities to examine the legacy and future transformation of its postindustrial and post logistical heritage. The *Paris Rive Gauche* project was one of the most high-profile initiatives to address this condition. Conceived in the late 1980s, the project gives a new identity to approximately 130 hectares of former industrial land on the left bank of the Seine toward the eastern edge of the city. Mostly warehouses, these structures were originally located in this area to store goods in transit from the docks of Paris along the Seine to the Gare d'Austerlitz on the western edge of the district. As new mobility networks rendered the area's boat to rail link obsolete, the demand for warehouse spaces declined, leaving a large empty quarter within central Paris. In 1985 the city established SEMAPA (Société d'Économie Mixte d'Aménagement de Paris), a public development corporation which along with SNCF (Société Nationale des Chemins de Fer Français), the national train company, was tasked with conceptualizing and administering the area's urban transformation.[3]

Paris Rive Gauche (A) involved a larger urban vision composed of seven smaller urban projects of approximately twenty to twenty-eight hectares, each led by a different coordinating architect. Districts such as Austerlitz Nord, Tolbiac Nord, Massena Nord, and Massena Chevaleret focused on the introduction of new block typologies that could gradually rescale an area mostly composed of long-span industrial buildings into new mixed-use blocks, introducing much-needed new housing stock into the area. Massena Nord, conceived by Christian de Portzamparc in 1995, stands out as a compelling example. In this case, Portzamparc developed a new block morphology that brought together the traditional Parisian perimeter block with the objectlike qualities of the modernist slab. Conceived as *l'îlot ouvert* or "the open block" model, the plan proposes a morphology that guarantees continuity of open space across multiple scales, while also providing a clear definition of public zones, privately owned collective areas, and private outdoor space.[4] Conceptualized as an urban project that defines the broader morphology of the block without defining the specificity of the architecture, the block type has been interpreted by multiple architects, who over time have consolidated the area through the construction of individual buildings. Furthermore, the conservation of select historic buildings that would house programs of metropolitan importance paired with the decision to place the new Bibliothèque nationale de France designed by Dominique Perrault at the center of the district, endowed the urban operation with international visibility. Gradually implemented over the course of thirty years, this project has been the largest pole of urban development inside of Paris's Périphérique, drastically changing the physical and experiential identity of the eastern area of the left bank.

In the late 1990s the Eastern Docklands in Amsterdam witnessed a similar transformation (B). In this case, the aggregation of smaller-scale urban projects was also the main mechanism to set forth a larger urban operation tasked with

3. Benoit, 123–129.
4. Joan Busquets and Felipe Correa, *Cities X Lines: A New Lens for the Urbanistic Project* (Rovereto: Nicolodi Editore, 2006), 170–171.

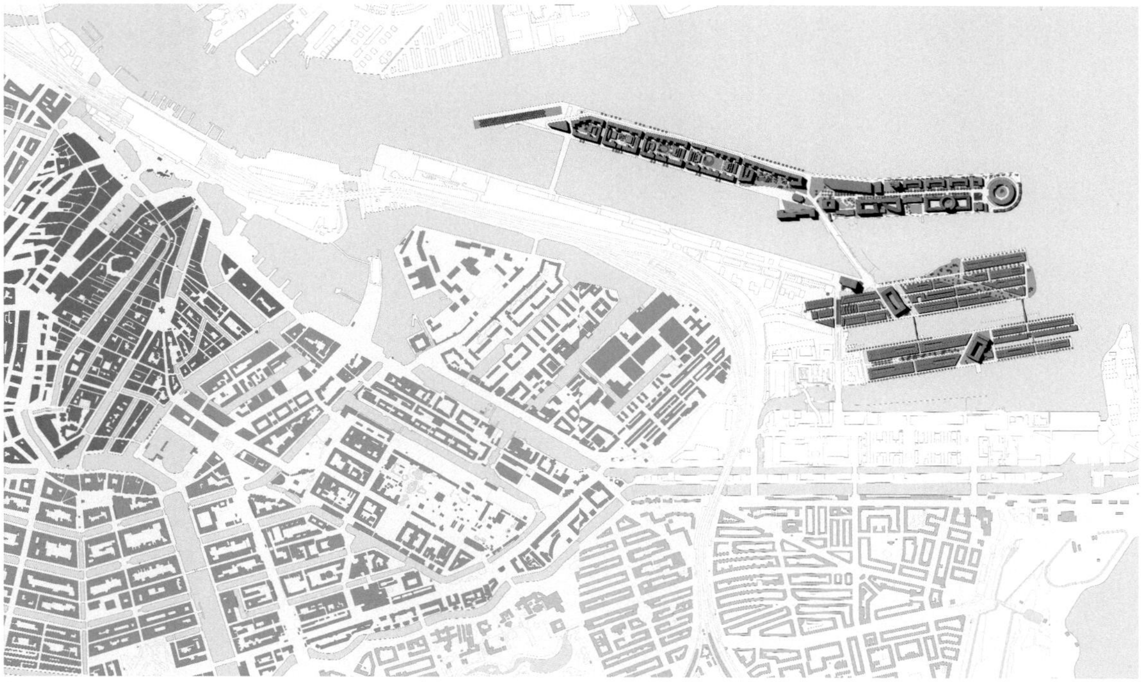

B

B Map of the Amsterdam Docklands, Netherlands, 1990-2000.

transforming the old port. The main strategy was to rezone the entire area as residential and assign it a gross floor-to-area ratio (FAR) of one. Then, three distinct design teams would each take a smaller portion of land and conceive a new urban quarter that responded to the established gross FAR but had the freedom to sculpt urban density and open space in multiple configurations.[5] For the first district, KNSM Island, Jo Coenen Architects envisioned a series of oversized courtyard buildings, each making up one block and designed by a different architect appointed by Coenen. The second urban project, coordinated by architect Sjoerd Soeters, relied on a variety of building types that get repeated based on a system of rules along a central green space. This resulted in a block morphology that seems randomly constructed but that follows a clear set of urban rules. The third and most well-known project, Borneo-Sporenburg, designed by the Adriaan Geuze and his landscape architecture firm West 8, relied on a carefully calibrated parcel strategy that accommodates a broad range of housing typologies, from single-family townhouses to larger residential building. The multiplicity of housing typologies offers variety in residential lifestyles. The three projects come together in a larger landscape strategy that reconnects the docklands back to the city center.

Urban projects where a set of rules define the general morphology without defining the specifics of its architecture, like those implemented in Paris and Amsterdam, have become popular in the restructuring of many postindustrial zones. Other cities like Copenhagen and Shanghai have implemented projects that follow a similar strategy.

New York City and Berlin

The rescaling and transformation of formerly industrial and logistical landscapes into mixed-use districts has become common practice in the last thirty years. Another equally important approach involves the environmental remediation and gradual transformation of these sites into large-scale parks and open space networks of metropolitan importance. In general, this approach addresses the reorganization of early and mid-twentieth-century urban infrastructure, originally placed at the periphery of the city, that today has been surrounded by urban growth. Airports, landfills, and wholesale markets are some of the most common spaces that have gradually been transformed into parks once their original use is decommissioned. While the design operations for these spaces tends to be specific to each case, one can find two principles that are consistent. First is the reconceptualization of the role of natural processes as integral to the dynamics of the twenty-first-century city. The second involves the experiential identity of these sites, specifically addressing how spaces that historically existed to serve the public but were generally inaccessible are transformed into a "new commons" open to all.

Across the Atlantic, the closure of New York City's Fresh Kills landfill in the early 2000s marked a major shift in how cities envisioned decommissioned industrial and logistical sites in metropolitan regions. Covering approximately 900 hectares, the landfill sited in the borough of Staten Island, south of Manhattan, had been in operation since 1948 and was the largest landfill in the world until its closure in 2001.[6] Once closed, New York City launched a major competition to rethink the future of Fresh Kills. Central to the competition brief, and evident in the winning entry by James Corner/Field Operations, was an attitude that moved beyond the divide between

5. Busquets and Correa, 171–172.
6. Martin V. Melosi, "Fresh Kills: The Making and Unmaking of a Wastescape," *RCC Perspectives* no. 1 (2016): 63.

dichotomies like nature and culture to achieve a space where humans and non-humans coauthor space. In the same manner that environmental historian William Cronon argued for wildness instead of wilderness, the project by Field Operations embraces the evolution of wildness over time.[7] Through a vision plan that unfolds over the course of thirty years, the project relies on a spatial/temporal diagram that brings together remediated waste mounds, new ecological habitats, and recreational infrastructure, crafting a new image of the landfill in the collective memory of New Yorkers. The implementation of the thirty-year plan began in 2008, and over time, parts and pieces of the park are gradually being opened to the public.

Seven years after the decommissioning of Fresh Kills, the highly controversial closing of Tempelhof Airport in Berlin also offers important lessons on how cities can give derelict lands a new lease on life. One of four major airports serving the city at the time of its closure, Tempelhof played a crucial role in the urban history of Berlin. Opened in 1923 and sited south of the city center, Tempelhof served as parade grounds for Prussian troops, an epicenter of military activity during Nazi Germany, and later an American military base.[8] Beyond its utilitarian purpose as an airfield, the site has a storied history ever present in the mind of Berliners.

Many years prior to its closing, a series of conflicting opinions fueled the debate about the future of Tempelhof. Some wanted it to continue operating as an airport given its proximity to the city center. Stakeholders with real-estate interests wanted to dissolve the figure of the field into lucrative urban blocks. Other voices argued for its preservation and transformation into an urban park. In 2010, only two years after its official closure and with minimal interventions to guarantee safety, the city opened Templehof's gates to the public, turning the field into a ready-made park where bikers could cycle down the runway and families could have a picnic sitting on the terminal's apron. The opening of the park prior to the implementation of a grand plan offered visitors the opportunity to experience a space that until then had always been mediated through the window of an airplane. The novelty of the experience incentivized the public to preserve the figure of the airfield and not erase the geometries defined by its previous use. Shortly after the opening, the Berlin Senate launched an international competition for the transformation of the park. The winning entry, submitted by the Edinburgh-based landscape architecture firm Gross.Max. builds on the ethos of preserving the figure of the airfield, yet adapts it by adding facilities and dissolving the inherited harsh edges between field and city.

Fresh Kills and Tempelhof have offered valuable lessons, not only through the implementation of each specific project, but also in the drawings and images produced by Field Operations and Gross.Max. Widely published in trade journals and the popular press, these two cases have been widely consumed all over the world.

Latin America and Mexico City

While cities in Latin America hold significant amounts of post-industrial inner-city land, urban projects that have guided a comprehensive transformation are few and are primarily located in Argentina and Mexico. The transformation of Puerto Madero in Buenos Aires is an early example of a new model of urban development for South America, one that coupled the public and private sectors to establish a real estate-driven urban operation. A plan drafted in 1990 by Catalan architect Joan Busquets spearheaded the process. Conceived as a new urban district on the northern side of the docks, the project proposed a new mixed-use block morphology with taller commercial buildings along the edges, while also offering large amounts of midrise high-density housing within the block's interior. Met with significant opposition by local constituencies, the original plan was revisited and redrawn by multiple stakeholders, and a rudimentary strategy that paid little attention to design was implemented throughout the second half of the 1990s.

Similarly, Mexico City was not exempt from the footprint of industry in the shaping of its urban form. The rapid urbanization from the 1940s onward was partially catapulted by an emerging industrial sector strategically connected to regional and national mobility infrastructure. Municipalities like Azcapotzalco, Gustavo A. Madero, Álvaro Obregón, and Miguel Hidalgo—considered part of the urban periphery at the time—accommodated a large amount of industry serving city and

7. William Cronon, ed., *Uncommon Ground: Rethinking the Human Place in Nature* (New York: W. W. Norton & Co., 1995), 69–90.
8. Michael Dumiak, "Up in the Air," *Landscape Architecture* 104, no. 3 (2014): 137.
9. Felipe Correa and Carlos Garciavelez Alfaro, *Mexico City: Between Geometry and Geography* (Cambridge: Applied Research and Design, 2015), 159–191.

C

116

D

C Aerial photograph of the Pemex Azcapotzalco Refinery, Mexico City, 1945.
D Urban Design Group, Mario Schjetnan, Bicentennial Park, Mexico City, 2010.

countrywide markets. As these areas were surrounded by urban expansions, industries migrated further from the city center, releasing large parcels of postindustrial land proximal to the city center and other burgeoning neighborhoods in central Mexico City.[9] While many of these sites still await intervention, Parque Bicentenario and Nuevo Polanco are two key projects that have set the stage for new models for transforming fallow land in Mexico City.

Bicentenario involved the transformation of the former Azcapotzalco oil refinery into a beautiful twenty-first-century park (C, D). More than a decade after the closure of the refinery in the late 1990s, due to extreme soil contamination, Petróleos Mexicanos (Pemex) transferred the property to the national government. Shortly thereafter, world-renowned Mexican landscape architect Mario Schjetnan, along with a team of international consultants, started the remediation process, conceiving the design of an ecological park that recreates through 55 hectares seven ecological zones from across the Mexican landscape. The park opened to the public in 2010, providing important lessons to the city on how highly contaminated land can be remediated and over time turned into a vessel for new forms of urban nature.

The second project involves the conversion of former automotive factories into what became the "Nuevo Polanco" mixed-use district. Adjacent to the Polanco neighborhood to the south, the Hospital Español to the east, and the right of way of the former Ferrocarril de Cuernavaca to the north and west, Nuevo Polanco has resulted from the transformation of several defunct automotive factories—General Tire, General Motors, and Chrysler—into a new commercial district. Implemented throughout the 2000s, the project brings retail, offices, cultural programs, and residential uses into this formerly industrial void. Nuevo Polanco established an important new centrality in the city. The project not only increases inner-city density but also provides many complementary urban programs to adjacent neighborhoods.

A key architectural project within the broader urban operation is the 2006 mixed-use complex Antara by Sordo Madaleno Arquitectos. The project revolves around a network of open and semi-enclosed collective spaces flanked with retail on the lower floors and office space above. Taking advantage of Mexico City's temperate climate, Antara translates the main elements of a shopping mall into an exterior collective space that, while not being inherently public, engenders public life. In doing so, the project becomes a destination that works at a metropolitan scale and defines a central space of the urban project. The participation of Sordo Madaleno Arquitectos in this project went beyond the boundaries of the fashion hall and included working with other partners and authorities to rezone the district and establish better connections with the adjacent areas. The hall itself served as a physical catalyst of a much larger urban operation.

Beyond Parque Bicentenario and Nuevo Polanco, Mexico City still has a great deal of derelict or soon-to-be derelict urban land awaiting intervention. The continually increasing cost of land near the city center paired with a general desire from the public to incorporate postindustrial land back into the life of the city opens up an entire new landscape for urban interventions across Mexico City. Additional inner-city Pemex sites, residual urban geometries created by the implementation of the "Anillo Periférico," and the reorganization of the Central de Abastos (the largest wholesale market in the world) are just a few examples of the complex postindustrial landscape that awaits transformation in Mexico City. Crucial to the restructuring of these grounds is the potential to reimagine them as spaces that can improve the overall quality of life for city dwellers. Envisioning them as sources for new models of inner-city affordable housing, spaces for a more equitable distribution

E **Before**
Aerial photograph of the old General Motors Plant, Colonias Granada, Ampliación Granada and Polanco, Mexico City, 1974.

E

F After

Aerial photograph of Nuevo Polanco with Antara Masterplan in the middle and the cultural district to the north, Mexico City, 2021.

F

G **Before**
Aerial photograph of the old General Motors plant, Colonia Granada, Mexico City, northeastern view, 1955.

H **After**
Aerial photograph of Nuevo Polanco, Mexico City, 2021. Northeastern view of Antara Masterplan.

I Diagram of the Anillo Periférico in relation to the urban landscape of the center of Mexico City.

G

H

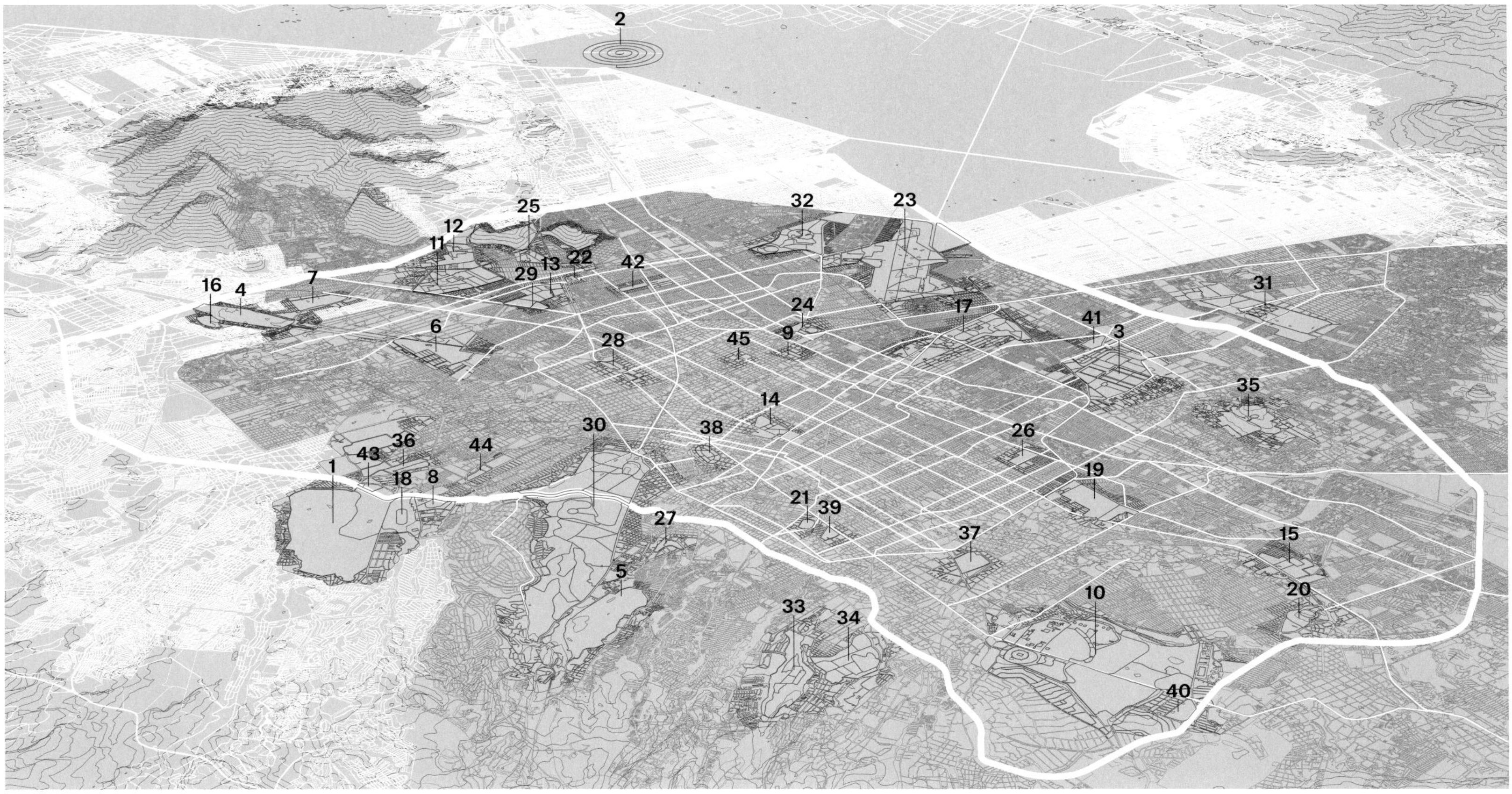

Logistics
1. Military Camp 1A
2. El Caracol
3. Central de Abastos Market
4. Train Patio
5. Industrias militares
6. Pantaco Station
7. Vaso Regulador Carretas
8. Military Camp 1K
9. La Merced Market

Culture-Health
10. Ciudad Universitaria, UNAM
11. Zacatenco Campus, Instituto Politécnico Nacional
12. Instituto Politécnico Nacional
13. Juárez Hospital
14. General Hospital
15. Valle de México University
16. Post-Graduate Faculty, Iztacala, UNAM

Recreational
17. Sports City
18. Las Américas Racetrack
19. Churubusco Country Club
20. Azteca Stadium
21. Azul Stadium
22. 18 de Marzo Sports Complex

Mobility
23. International Airport
24. Eastern Bus Passenger Terminal (TAPO)
25. Indios Verdes Station
26. Electric Transportation Deposit
27. Western Bus Central Terminal
28. Buenavista Station
29. North Bus Terminal

Public Spaces
30. Chapultepec Park
31. Meyehualco Park
32. Aragón Park
33. Tarango Park
34. Garden Cemetery
35. Cerro de la Estrella
36. Cemeteries
37. Coyoacán Park
38. Mexico Park
39. Hundido Park

Shopping Malls
40. Perisur
41. Plaza de Oriente
42. Plaza Tepeyac
43. Pericentro
44. Antara
45. Buenavista

of urban services, and areas where new conceptions of open space can materialize, can provide a new urban agenda for these spaces but also alleviate some of the most Mexico City's most pressing challenges.

Mexico City has been a crucible for SMA for eight decades. Through their thoughtful body of work, they have left an important legacy of built projects, helping Mexico City to evolve into a modern metropolis. Equally as important as this legacy is the broad-ranging expertise that Sordo Madaleno Arquitectos has consolidated over the years in Mexico City.

As the firm charts its path for the next decade, this expertise across multiple design scales is uniquely positioned to continue examining and transforming the changing urban landscape of the metropolis and in doing, continue to shape the Mexico City of the twenty-first century.

J **Before**
Aerial photograph of the old General Motors plant, Colonia Granada, Mexico City, 1949, northeastern view.

K **After**
Aerial photograph of Nuevo Polanco, Mexico City, 2021, northeastern view of Antara Masterplan and surroundings.

J

K

SORDO MADALENO AND THE CITY IN MINIATURE

KENNETH FRAMPTON

Within the universal placelessness of the megalopolis made up by an endless proliferation of ill-conceived and ill-related free-standing objects, the "city-in-miniature" proffers itself as a bounded domain having a permeable relationship with the city at large. Although the origins of this heterotopia are many and varied, ranging from the Middle Eastern souk to the quadrangle of a medieval university, there are two unique, but otherwise unrelated, antecedents of this paradigm in architectural history. The first of these is the Palais Royal in Paris (A) which emerged around 1780, as a "city-in-miniature" in that it comprised a defining perimeter of elite apartments raised above a peripheral enclosure of shopping arcades, selling luxury goods and given over here and there to restaurants, cafés, bookstores, casinos, and political clubs, plus two major theaters and the baroque confines of a royal house which even now continues to accommodate the offices of the state.

The second is the Rockefeller Center in New York (B), under construction from 1930 to 1940 and comprising a beautifully proportioned cluster of mid- to high-rise office structures, faced in stone and covering a comparable labyrinth of shops that sell luxury goods. During its heyday from the Second World War to the first half of the 1950s, it also featured two major auditoriums; a 3,500-seat luxury cinema, known as the Center Theater and the 6,200-seat Radio City Music Hall, dedicated to vaudeville and other forms of popular entertainment. These permeable, micro-urban spaces in Paris and in New York were exceptionally popular in their own way and in their own time; the one at the beginning of the nineteenth century, in the epoch of the *flâneur* and the other in the heyday of Manhattan in the 1930s as a mecca of modernity.

A

B

A defining characteristic of the Palais Royal was, above all, its paradoxical permeability given that it remained an elite enclave throughout its history. The fact that it remained open at all hours—day and night—ensured its popularity across time and class—particularly since, while dedicated to the conspicuous consumption of the elite during the day, at night it would be equally available after the shops closed when it would be casually occupied by citizens at large.

Although the Rockefeller Center, equally open at all hours to the citizens of Manhattan, would not be as indiscriminate as the Palais Royal, it was even more systematically populist in its devotion to midcult entertainment. Focused on a plaza, which serves as a café-terrace in summer and as a skating rink in winter, the art program of Radio City was the worldly celebration of supposedly egalitarian capitalism, ranging from a gilded statue of Prometheus on the central axis of the complex to the spectacular ornamentation of the Rockettes chorus line within the music hall. Such was its broad appeal that it would become, for the best part of the last century, the ultimate touristic mecca for the average American family.

Nothing of this civic spirit would be evident in Victor Gruen's 1954 invention of the suburban shopping center—countless examples of which he would realize all over the United States during the next two decades. Throughout his career, Gruen (discussed in a separate essay in this volume by Vera Simone Bader) seems to have been perplexed by the fact that the suburban shopping center—invariably marooned in a sea of cars—had no capacity whatsoever for engendering a sense of community. Only too aware of this alienating paradigm, Sordo Madaleno gravitated toward the idea of an urban enclave as a way of transcending both the non-place of the suburban shopping center and the reductive heterotopia of the gated community—wherein the elite are willing to forgo the cultural benefits of traditional civic life in the name of security.

Sordo Madaleno Arquitectos (SMA) have nonetheless recently returned to the paradigm of the "city within the city" to realize, first, in their Antara project (116). Built in the central Polanco district of Mexico City in 2006, it is a permeable enclave of luxury shops arranged around both sides of an elliptical plaza-cum-garden—a *hortus conclusus* (enclosed garden) flanked on its sides by mid-rise office buildings. SMA returned to a similar mixed-use paradigm with its Artz Pedregal project (C) realized in 2018, some fifteen kilometers away from the core of the city to which it remains linked only by the Anillo Periférico—the elevated autoroute that circumnavigates the greater urbanized region of Mexico City, in effect connecting it directly by car to the Reforma Colón area.

A | Palais Royal, Paris.
B | Rockefeller Center, New York.

C | Aerial view of Artz Pedregal, Mexico City, 2018.

C

D E

F G

D — Motor lobby with *De la rotonda de la fuente. Cinco colores para México* (The Fountain Circle: Five Colors for Mexico) by Daniel Buren.
E — Outer corridor near the park, second level.
F — Commercial corridor. Espacio Arte Abierto in the park, second level.
G — Inner street and corporate buildings.

H — Central park, second level; in the background, two of the four corporate buildings.

H

Built on top of a six-story parking garage and occupying the entire site, this shopping center is primarily accessed by a two-way, double-lane (G), ramped vehicle entry into its lowest level and culminating in a drop-off rotary that circulates around a cylindrical fountain piece by the distinguished French artist Daniel Buren (D). This point of arrival is flanked on one side by restaurants and on the other by a shopping esplanade which also affords access to the escalators and greenways leading into the core of the center and thus to the four tiers of set-back shopping galleries rising above (F). The fourth wall of this trapezoidal space is occupied by the first two of three projected high-rise office buildings. The lobbies of these two fourteen-story structures are accessed by a separate service road running along the northern boundary of the site. A similar short road gives access into the lobby of a fourth, free-standing, fourteen-story office tower situated at the southernmost corner of the site. The three high-rise office towers situated to the north of the center are treated as if they were segments of a continuous glass wall, interrupted at mid-point by a two-story, curtain-walled bridge linking the three towers (H). The dynamic aestheticism permeating Artz Pedregal subtly announces itself at this juncture in the detailing of this three-part curtain wall wherein warped mullions rise to the midpoint after which the glazing is held in place by mullions set a standard width apart. This conceit is particularly evident in the combined elevation of the three tower blocks, which when viewed from the shopping galleries, appear to incline to the left as they rise to their full height, even though the basic structural frame carrying each tower remains normative throughout. On closer inspection one realizes that the apparent inclination of the curtain-walled towers is produced by an incremental “stepping-out” of floors toward the left at the western end of each tower with a corresponding “stepping-in” at their eastern ends (H, E). These graduated adjustments are achieved by increasing the cantilevered spans at the western end and decreasing them at the eastern end. In addition, the towers are also slightly skewed in plan and terminated by an accented cornice corresponding to the rhythmic spacing of the mullions beneath.

Equally anamorphic mannerisms prevail throughout this center, most notably in the detailing of the cladding, which is invariably cut at an angle and laid in place with exceptional precision. This angular revetment has a direct impact on the mass-forms from which the center is composed, producing a series of exaggerated kaleidoscopic perspectives that are only momentarily perceivable as such from a sequence of vantage points that constantly shift as one proceeds through the galleries. Thus, the visitor is always half aware of the visual inflections that propel one forward, through an ever-changing mise-en-scène. The net effect of the angular cladding combined with equally angular shifts in the orientation of the galleries make the overall space form seem bigger than it is. Part of this optical illusion stems from the fact that the constantly changing revetment makes one acutely aware of material as an end in itself. This is particularly the case where hardwood boarding is laid in short lengths and bonded as if it were stone and vice versa. By a similar token, this sensuous feeling for texture is particularly heightened where precisely laid stone and wooden flooring are laid side by side with nothing but a hairline joint between them (I). One is aware that none of this would have been possible without laser cutting and the control of the profile of every single numbered piece, combined with the digital resolution of the interaction between exceptionally complex geometries.

Similar sensitive refinements prevail throughout the landscaping of the center, which is enriched everywhere with plant material of varying scale, texture, and character, thereby passing from episodic, carefully tended lawns to unexpected mounds of unkempt grass and planters filled with exotic tropical succulents. All of which is interspersed with episodic stretches of water—the perceptual character of which changes depending on how it is framed—as one passes from the transparent presence of relatively still, deep water contained by thin, Corten steel tanks to shallow ornamental stretches of water bounded by stone curbs and animated by discreet fountains (J). The whole is imbued with a ludic theatricality which is heightened by the incidental placement of minimalist artworks, ranging from the gilded irony of Ai Weiwei's stacked bicycles to equally arresting pieces by Tania Candiani, plus here and there, minimalist rotating, brightly colored play devices, along with static set pieces such as one entitled *Measure Up* against which children of all ages may compare their respective heights. However much visitors may be diverted by their movement through a seemingly endless sequence of galleries as they rise up the complex to the fourth floor, one is constantly returned to a trapezoidal island in the compound's center, isolated by greenways from the terra firma of the galleries. Here, one's attention is repeatedly brought back to the angular parallelepiped of the art gallery suspended on top of a grassy mound and faced in mirror-glass on its sides (K, L). The paradoxical dematerialization of this form asserting the presence of something that is simultaneously present and absent evokes a sense of a metaphysical inaccessibility, recalling the atmosphere of the final frames of Stanley Kubrick's *2001: A Space Odyssey*. In this respect the art gallery remains an enigmatic *boîte à miracle* (miracle box)—to borrow Le Corbusier's felicitous phrase.

Anamorphosis is a relatively rare phenomenon in art let alone in architecture, particularly when the distortion becomes manifest as an all-embracing aesthetic, when no surface or mass is allowed to escape its formative obsession—as is the case of the Artz Pedregal—where it amounts to a totalizing mannerism. This raises the question as to what exactly was the underlying motivation that led the SMA design team, under the leadership of Javier Sordo Madaleno, to opt for this aesthetic stratagem and to carry it through to the very last detail. And while one cannot finally know the rationale behind the angular inflection throughout, nonetheless there is a sense of being caught in the web of an extremely sophisticated postmodern gesture testifying to the fact, however unconsciously, that a city-in-miniature, sealed off from all but nearby pedestrian access runs the risk of being a contradiction in terms.

As in the case of Rockefeller Center, the ultimate success of this diminutive "city within a city" depends on its cultural programming. In this regard, the development arm of the practice has envisaged and maintained the nonprofit Arte Abierto program dedicated to the creation and promotion of a wide range of art works, including an emphasis on interactive mixed-media performance art

I

J

I Restaurant in the central park, under the Espacio Arte Abierto.
J Commercial corridor on ground floor.

K Detail of fallow earth on the garden slope in the Espacio Arte Abierto.
L Central park and Espacio Arte Abierto.

K

L

involving as much audience participation as possible. In effect what they have achieved since the opening of Artz Pedregal in 2018 is a program of inclusive, interactive, multimedia events capable of enlightening the public in ways that transcend the passive perception of art in traditional galleries and museums. Arte Abierto is committed to the socially transformative power of art, which it aspires to achieve through the collective experience of a given event or performance. The aim is to constantly ring the changes over a wide range of expressive, interactive formats from workshops and seminars to theatrical events and musical performances.

It is just this activity that gives Artz Pedregal its cultural significance—going beyond its traditional role as a shopping center to influence the wider culture of the entire city. So far, I have yet to acknowledge the crucial role played by the presence of cinemas in both Antara and in Artz Pedregal, for although they are but pale gestures when compared to the theatrical spaces of the Palais Royal and Rockefeller Center, they are, nonetheless, spaces of public appearance. However, the most original aspect of the Arte Abierto foundation is that ample segments of the shopping space are transformed from time to time into temporary theatrical spaces, where since 2018, radical artistic groups, such as the Cocolab Collective and the Squidsoup Collective, stage spectacular participatory events, attracting audiences of up to 200,000 attendees. Since then, in 2019 Artz Pedregal hosted the Ambulante Documentary Film Festival and in February 2020 Arte Abierto opened "Espacio Arte Abierto" with *Latidos* (N), the third monographic exhibition of biometric artwork with digital and participatory media by Rafael Lozano-Hemmer. It is crucial that, by way of compensating for the consumption of the upper middle class, all these events have been open to the public free of charge.

M Longitudinal section in perspective.
N Above: *Latidos* (Heartbeats) exhibition by Rafael Lozano-Hemmer in the Espacio Arte Abierto, 2020.
Below: *Luz instante* (Instant Light) exhibition by Julia Carrillo, 2021.

M

a. Access to Offices
b. Offices
c. Restaurants
d. Motor lobby
e. Movie Theater
f. Art Gallery
g. Shops
h. Access Plaza
i. Parking Lot

0 40 m

II.

EVOLVING TYPOLOGIES

1.

RETAIL AND URBAN SHAPE

VERA SIMONE BADER

A

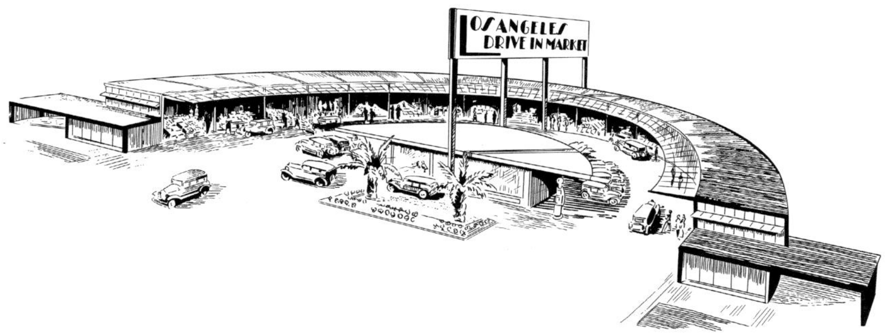

B

A Malcolm Smith, Ye Market Place (demolished), Los Angeles, California, USA, 1924.
B Richard Neutra, project for a drive-in shopping mall, Los Angeles, California, USA, 1928.

136 | Reforma Colón, the new large-scale project by Sordo Madaleno Arquitectos (SMA), scheduled for first-phase completion by 2025 along one of Mexico City's most famed boulevards, is scarcely what many consider to be a shopping mall. The complex incorporates diverse uses, including apartments, offices, and a hotel in its five tall, narrow towers, as well as shops and other commercial facilities in the shared podium that links them. This means that the entire residential and commercial district of this dense, multi-purpose place has been planned for effectiveness and efficiency by a "single hand." With its open and enclosed spaces, it will blend into the city's existing structures, make use of already existing infrastructure, and act as a stimulus for the development of a new economic motor that will push out and have an impact on the city—at least that's the plan. The influence of this highly concentrated range of facilities on their immediate vicinity is scarcely to be underestimated.

How did it come to pass that shopping centers, which primarily catered to the increased purchasing power of a growing middle class after the Second World War, developed from destinations outside city centers into major instruments for the regeneration of inner-city districts and their operators thus became veritable city builders? A look at the United States is necessary in this regard, as new models of urban shopping have emerged over the years and have been path-setting internationally. A brief overview of the various phases of that development will also help to classify the shopping centers that SMA has designed over the last fifty years.

From shopping centers to shopping malls

Shopping malls would never have come into existence without the rapid motorization of American society in the early twentieth century and the resulting expansion of the road network.[1] Even before World War II, there were several factors that stimulated key innovations in the retail sector in the United States. Retailers started thinking about geographically concentrated business models that made it easy for customers with cars to reach them and thus catered to a larger area. In the 1920s, the shopping mall was developed as a successful new building type that primarily offered food products, but might also include workshops and gas stations, particularly in southern California, close to the Mexican border. These malls were erected far away from city centers on busy arterial roads, with many created as the road network expanded. The buildings were L- or U-shaped, based on the layouts used for gas stations, as in the case of the Ye Market Place in Glendale, California, of 1924, which integrated a forecourt, where customers could park their cars—an absolute novelty at the time (A). To attract customers, Malcolm Smith, its architect, turned to Spanish colonial architecture as inspiration for a simple facade pierced by arcades, a stylistic decision that hinted at a shared Hispanic identity. Likewise, each of the shop units, despite their various tenants, were so arranged as to maintain the impression of overall unity.

As an entirely new building typology, the mall offered a unique opportunity for modern architects to engage with new concepts that became an important part of the urban fabric, and which took the automobile into account. In 1928, for example, Richard Neutra drew up designs for a "drive-in market," which would consist of an elegant frame of reinforced concrete and an extensive use of glass (B). Frank Lloyd Wright was also interested in this type of architecture, which was tailored to suit car drivers. In his suburban concept, Broadacre City, he defined his ideal of a city as a decentralized, self-sufficient

1. Richard Longstreth, *City Center to Regional Mall: Architecture, the Automobile, and Retailing in Los Angeles, 1920–1950* (Cambridge, Ma.: The MIT Press, 1998), 6.

C Victor Gruen, Milliron's Department Store, Westchester, California, USA, 1947.
D Victor Gruen, Southdale Center, Minnesota, USA, 1956.

C

D

region. A building complex, some twelve hectares in extent for shopping facilities would serve as a meeting point for the community.[2] In terms of function and scale, it was thus like the regional shopping malls that eventually developed in the USA after World War II.[3] The shopping mall became an international export success, readily accepted in Latin American countries, and above all in Mexico. As one of the first business models to focus on the car, its influence on the shopping habits of Americans and on metropolitan landscapes can hardly be underestimated.[4]

Another important trend was the further development of department stores, which had to adapt to the automotive age. Austrian architect Victor Gruen, who had emigrated to the United States after the expropriation of his architectural firm by the Nazis, built a complex for the Millirons department store in the Westchester section of Los Angeles, already in 1947. Here the sales area was concentrated on the ground floor.[5] The roof—accessible via two ramps—served as a parking lot (C). There was also a part of the building that was outfitted as an auditorium with a stage and a restaurant, which was open in the evenings and on Sundays and public holidays, making it an attractive area connected to the public spaces.[6] The radical urban restructuring brought about by the automotive era, which led to the explosion of suburbs in the United States, prompted Gruen in 1943 to publish in *Architectural Forum* his vision for the future: urban shopping protected from the growing volume of road traffic and housed under a single roof punctured by interior courtyards.[7] This shopping center would also offer a wide range of everyday services. He had the idea of a "shopping town," containing streets and open squares that were aligned with the "character and atmosphere" of European cities.[8] It was to serve as a new focal point for a community that lived in the sprawling suburbs, without direct access to everyday supply structures.

Gruen was given the opportunity to realize his ideas in 1954, when he planned the Northdale Center on the outskirts of Detroit. It was intended to act as a community center for the surrounding residential areas, whose inhabitants could reach it via both main roads and access roads. Parking lots would ring the single-story shopping center, strolling in open air to reach the shops. The Southdale Center, which Gruen built in Minnesota two years later, also pursued the idea of revitalizing the desolate outskirts of major American cities with a center of commerce, entertainment, and community institutions. It was the first enclosed, fully air-conditioned shopping mall that

---

2. Frank Lloyd Wright, *The Disappearing City* (New York: W. F. Payson, 1932).
3. Richard Longstreth, *The Drive-In, the Supermarket, and the Transformation of Commercial Space in Los Angeles* (Cambridge, Ma.: The MIT Press, 1999), 132.
4. Longstreth, 126.
5. Victor Gruen, "Der große Durchbruch," in *Victor Gruen: Shopping Town, Memoiren Eines Stadtplaners (1903–1980)*, ed. Anette Baldauf (Vienna: Bohlau Verlag, 2014), 180.
6. Gruen, 180.
7. Victor Gruen, "New Buildings for 194x: Shopping Centers," *Architectural Forum* 5, no. 78 (1943): 101–103. The magazine invited well-known architects, like Mies van der Rohe, to describe their visions of the future for American cities.
8. Victor Gruen, "Der große Durchbruch," 169.

E Juan Sordo Madaleno, University Plaza, Mexico City, 1969.
F Juan Sordo Madaleno, model for the University Plaza project, Mexico City, 1969.

E

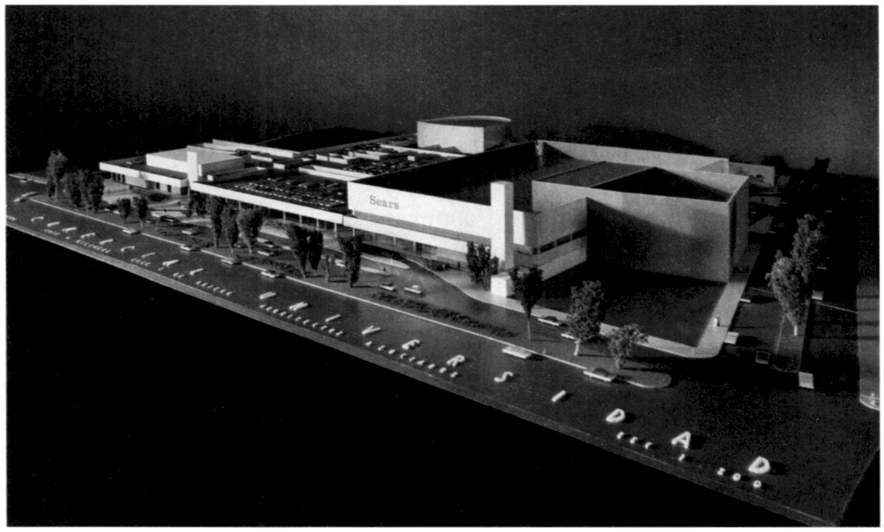

F

was focused entirely inward (D). The building type had thus taken on a form that countless other developers would adopt in the coming years, ultimately turning it into a monofunctional box.[9] This purely commercial model, exported to many other countries, has been criticized, down to this day, for having destroyed vibrant city centers.

In many ways, the first shopping mall designed by Juan Sordo Madaleno recalls Victor Gruen's initial concepts. In 1969 he designed an open-air shopping street for Plaza Universidad (E), Mexico City's first shopping mall, thus avoiding the concept of a completely artificial and—above all—fully air-conditioned environment.[10] The reason for this kind of structure and design is probably to be found in the climatic conditions, since Mexico City's climate is vastly different than that of the northern United States. Sordo Madaleno also banished the parking lots to the roof, allowing the building to better integrated into the urban environment (F). With daily opening times, the integration of local services and landscaped spaces, the shopping mall quickly became a focal meeting place for the local population. As a new landmark in the urban landscape, the mall took on urban functions, which Victor Gruen also promoted in his book *The Heart of our Cities*, published in 1964, in which he postulated "urbanity through density" and called for the creation of urban focal points in the form of multifunctional shopping centers.[11]

The heart of the city

It was no coincidence that Gruen titled his book with the same phrase used for the CIAM Congress held in England a decade earlier in 1951, which brought together avant-garde architects and urban planners.[12] Prominent international architects argued about the reorientation through urban and community centers, focusing among other things on the structural change toward a modern consumer and service society. The topic was not only of interest to those from the United States, but above all to Europeans, who were seeking new urban planning strategies for devastated cities in the wake of World War II. They saw the construction of new housing estates and satellite cities as solutions. A similar development occurred in Latin America, where architects and urban planners increasingly worked on problems of uncontrolled urban sprawl.[13]

During this development, Juan Sordo Madaleno and Luis Barragán presented an urban development project for Lomas Verdes in 1966.[14] Together, they proposed an independent

9. Alex Wall, "Southdale Shopping Center," in *Victor Gruen: From Urban Shop to New City*, (Barcelona: Actar, 2005), 18; Vera Simone Bader, "Die Architektur der Shopping Mall," in *World of Malls: Architekturen des Konsums, Architekturmuseum der TUM*, eds. Andres Lepik and Vera Simone Bader (Munich: Pinakothek der Moderne, 2014), 14.
10. Liliana De Simone, "The Latin American shopping centre," in *Acculturating the Shopping Centre*, eds. Janina Gosseye and Tom Avermaete (London: Routledge, 2019), 76.
11. Victor Gruen, *The Heart of Our Cities: The Urban Crisis, Diagnosis and Cure* (New York: Simon and Schuster, 1964).
12. Eric Mumford, *The CIAM Discourse on Urbanism, 1928–1960* (Cambridge, Ma.: The MIT Press, 2002), 201.
13. Mexico City grew rapidly in the '70s from 8 to 14 million people. See Mexico Megacity, eds. James Pick and Edgar Butler (New York: Routledge, 2018).
14. Juan Sordo Madaleno and Luis Barragán, "Proyecto Urbanístico Lomas Verdes, México," *Arquitectos de México*, no. 27 (1965): 30–43.

G

H

urban organism for precisely 100,000 residents, to the northwest of Mexico City. Their plan envisioned four zones with different types of housing and amenities for the population. Planned atop a hill, the shopping center was to be the highlight of the entire area, meeting the needs of the new development's residents as well as those of people in neighboring communities. Streets punctured by plazas radiated out from the mall, some of them lined by arcades which were to form the architectural heart of the new city and the focal point of urban life.[15] It is not for nothing that Sordo Madaleno and Barragán called this nucleus "the Heart of the City." In so doing, they made explicit reference to the book edited by Ernesto Nathan Rogers, José Luis Sert, and Jacqueline Tyrwhitt a year after the CIAM Congress in 1951. The proposed uses are comparable—apartments, doctors' offices, law firms, administrative offices, retail space and recreational facilities were to be brought together in a single place. Sordo Madaleno and Barragán's plans were never realized, but some of the ideas were implemented in Ciudad Satélite, which was built a decade later, and for which Mario Pani was responsible for the master plan. Sordo Madaleno, in turn, designed and developed Plaza Satélite, a shopping mall that would serve as a supply structure for the new, autonomous residential district and thus relieve pressure on the city center. Around fifty years later, Javier Sordo Madaleno took up the concept of "recreation" with his modernization measures that converted the parking lot of Plaza Satélite into a four-hectare public park, thus meeting the great need for green space in the mega-metropolis of Mexico City.

From megastructure to postmodernism

Building on the CIAM congresses of the 1950s, devoted to the theme of the human habitat, and in response to the extreme social and economic upheavals of the 1960s and 1970s, architects developed the idea of the megastructure. They designed scaleless residential machines that fulfilled multiple urban functions to be built in the middle of historic city centers, but very few of these gigantic structures were realized: The Cumbernauld New Town Centre (1967) near Glasgow and the Brunswick Centre (1972) in London are examples of these utopian ideas, as they combined technology, transport, and mobility with social, cultural, and commercial activities in a single complex (G).[16] In both of these projects, the mall played a prominent role alongside the residential space, but ultimately there was only a short window of five years during which such architectural solutions to urban problems were proposed and implemented. The interplay between architecture and the urban landscape only gained importance again around the turn of the millennium in the form of district centers, while in the 1980s and 1990s other trends took center stage.

190

The development of the building typology into larger and more complex facilities was also linked to the changing consumer behavior of society, which was increasingly seeking an experience, in addition to simply purchasing products. Postmodernism offered new opportunities, since architects used images for orientation and identification.[17] Horton Plaza in San Diego (H), built in 1985, is a clear example of these new formal and structural expressions. Jon Jerde's design was based on medieval Italian cities, opening up long streets and using

---

15. Vittorio Magnano Lampugnani, *Die Stadt im 20. Jahrhundert: Visionen, Entwürfe, Gebautes*, 2 (Berlin: Sachbuch, 2010), 556.
16. Reyner Banham, *The New Brutalism: Ethic or Aesthetic?* (London: The Architectural Press, 1966), 73.
17. Kevin Lynch, *The Image of the City* (Cambridge, Ma.: The MIT Press, 1960).

G Cumbernauld New Town Centre, Cumbernauld, Scotland, 1967.
H Jon Jerde, Horton Plaza, San Diego, California, USA, 1985.

balconies, towers, bridges and other architectural images to simulate a dense city fabric composed of historical fragments. It was also the first example of a new generation of malls: Jerde brought the entertainment center from the suburbs to the city core, hoping that it might revitalize the deserted center.[18] This development, which simulates an individual experience through means of identification in architecture, continues to be built to the present day and finds expression in the architectural design of streets and squares, in the specific shape of roofs, or in luxurious interior design.

202 | The Toreo Parque Central (2014) designed by Javier Sordo Madaleno Bringas, with its colossal, domed glass roof and a park on the top floor, reflects this approach, as do the Luxury Hall (2010) in Puebla, the Andamar (2014) in Veracruz, and
210 | Midtown (2019) in Jalisco, which the architect also shaped with elements from nature with water, wood, granite, and plants for a relaxing, refined ambience—a flair that is intended to appeal to a predominantly high-income clientele rushed by everyday
173 | 130 life. Artz Pedregal (2018), in Mexico City, also belongs in this category, since it combines the shopping experience with a sculpture park, an art gallery, and a cinema, as well as restaurants. The combination with other functions, such as an art gallery and an opera house, has enjoyed great popularity in recent years, as demonstrated by the K11 Art Mall in Shanghai (2013), the Ashiti Foundation in Beirut (2015), or the Opera Galleria in Muscat (2011).[19] However, the shopping centers developed by Javier Sordo Madaleno are usually much more than entertainment oases. Most of them are based on a mixed-use concept to create diversity not only in form but also in function.

The District Center

Since the turn of the millennium, there has been a reorientation in response to the increase in online shopping, which is widely blamed for the decline of those malls exclusively geared towards shopping.[20] Against this background, the ideas formulated in the mid-twentieth century to integrate the immediate human environment have gained increasing relevance. New building complexes that combine apartments, offices and leisure facilities with shops are being built around the
116 | world. For example, in building Antara—its first phase completed in 2006—Javier Sordo Madaleno was not just the architect, but also the developer and operator and could therefore decide on the formal design, the interior structure, the range of services offered, and the individual tenant communities. He thus assumed the task of the planner—as envisioned for megastructures. However, in this case, he created a highly controlled framework focused on economic efficiency for a wide range of activities.[21] As planner, he was able to develop a diversified urban building block from scratch. In the case of Antara, he decided against the conventional model of anchor tenants, which until recently ensured circulation in a mall by attracting visitors. Whereas in the past large tenants such as department stores were located in prominent parts of malls, they are today replaced by restaurants, cinemas, and offices, due to changes in customer behavior. In his concept for Antara, however, Sordo Madaleno goes a step further by connecting the curved mall to the urban infrastructure on both sides, transforming it into a sub-center of the city. This configuration is also gaining increasing importance for this type of facility in a digitized and increasingly virtual world. Instead of isolation, integration plays an important role in satisfying the need for a place that offers a concentrated spatial experience.

In this context, the mixed-use center Andares in Zapopan, which opened in 2009 and is similarly staged as an urban planning hub, is worthy of mention at the end. On the one hand, it is visually defined by the flat, upward-moving triangle, which, with its two towers, marks the transition from residential to commercial district; on the other hand, it is structurally positioned by a sophisticated network of paths that connects the two areas. Its function as a connecting link gives the entire building complex an outstanding significance within the urban structure.

---

18. Dietmar Steiner, "Der völlig normale Mensch. Jon Jerde, Prophet des neuen öffentlichen Raumes," *Die Zeitschrift der Kultur*, 63 (2003–2004), 30.
19. American department stores included art galleries until the end of the nineteenth century.
20. Franz Pesch, *Stadt-Center: Ein neues Handelsformat für die urbane Mitte* (Stuttgart: Rohn, 2013).
21. Regina Bittner, "Die vergangene Zukunft: Shopping Malls als Megastructure," in *World of Malls*, eds. Andres Lepik and Vera Simone Bader (Munich: Pinakothek der Moderne, 2014), 73.

1971, 1993, 2018, 2020
PLAZA SATÉLITE

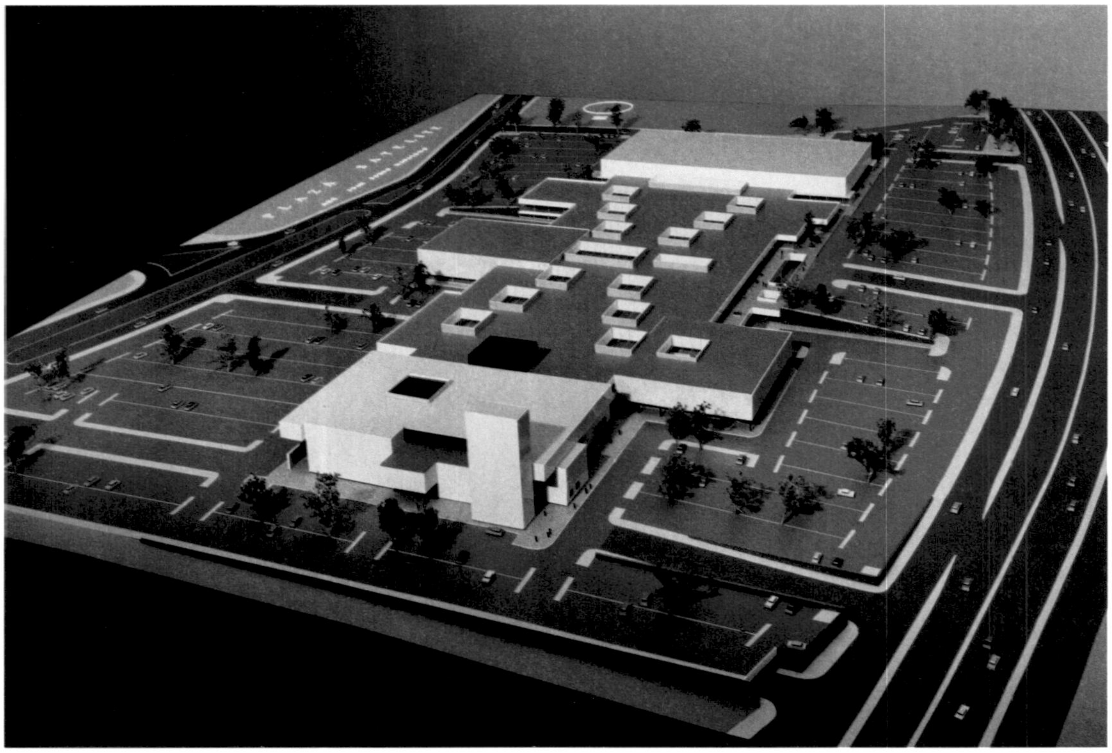

Left hand page, above: aerial view of Satélite city in 1958. Below: blueprint model.

Right hand page: aerial view of Ciudad Satélite, with Plaza Satélite in the center, circa 1971.

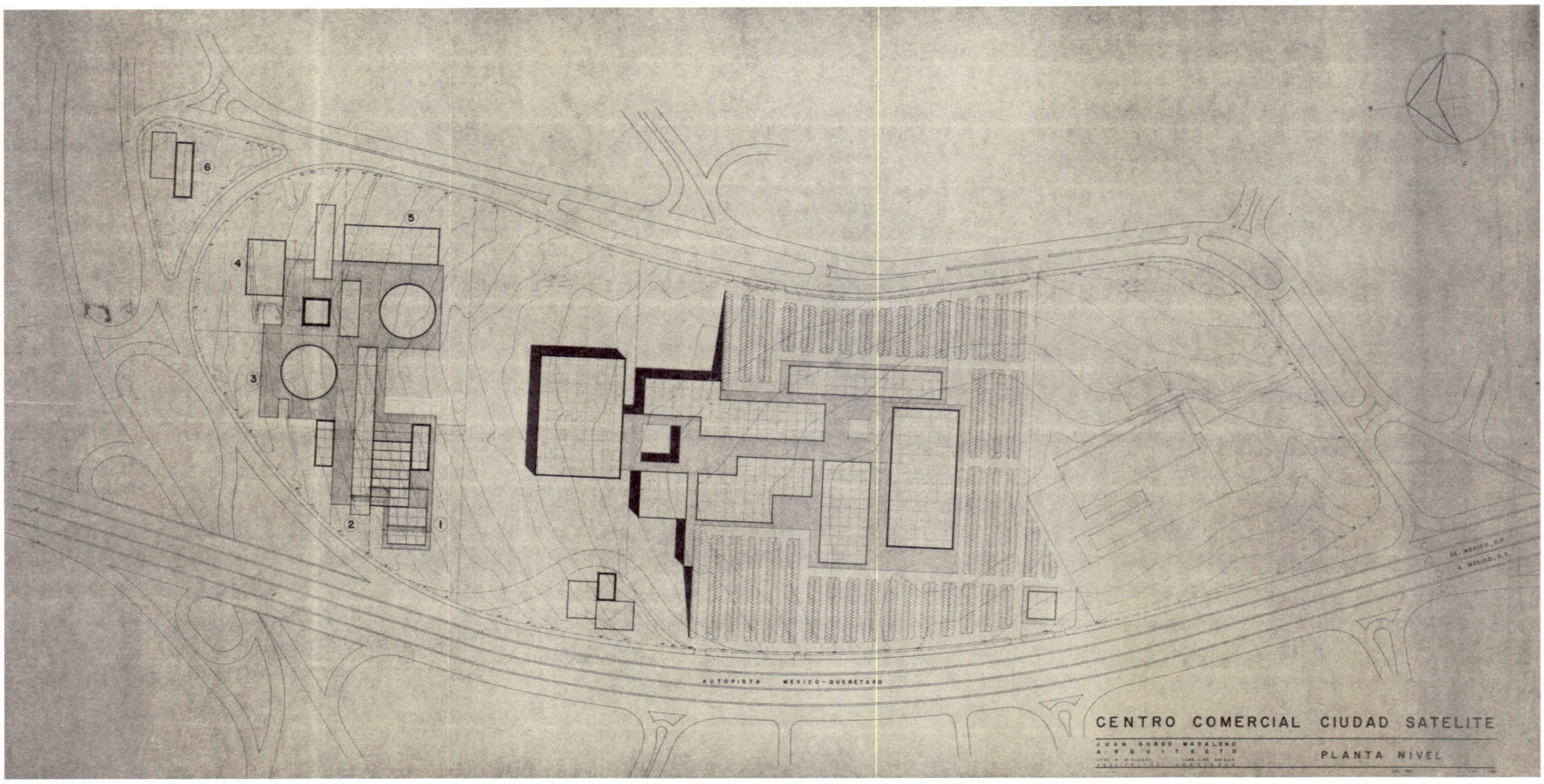

Preliminary plan of complex.

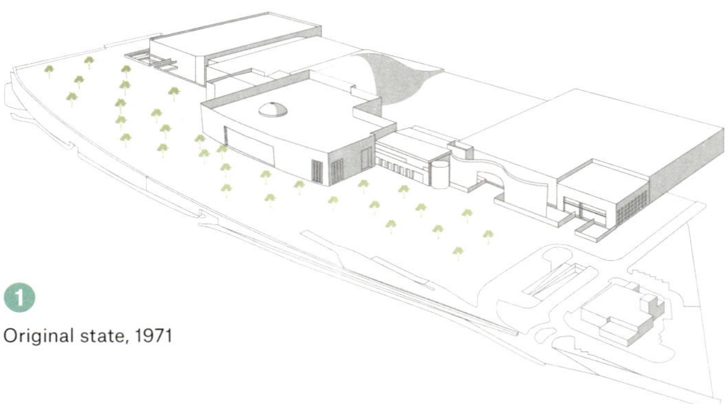

1 Original state, 1971

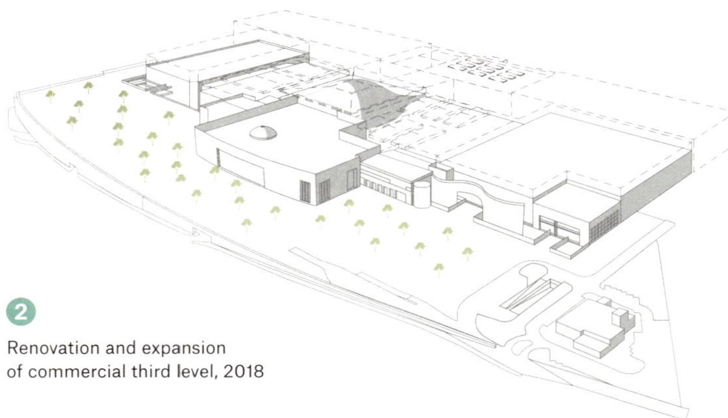

2 Renovation and expansion of commercial third level, 2018

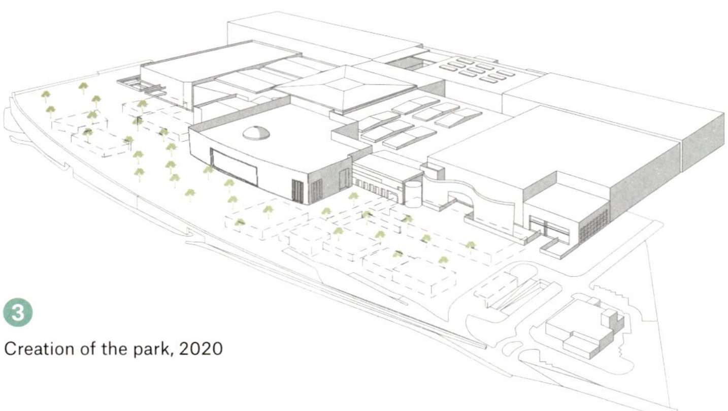

3 Creation of the park, 2020

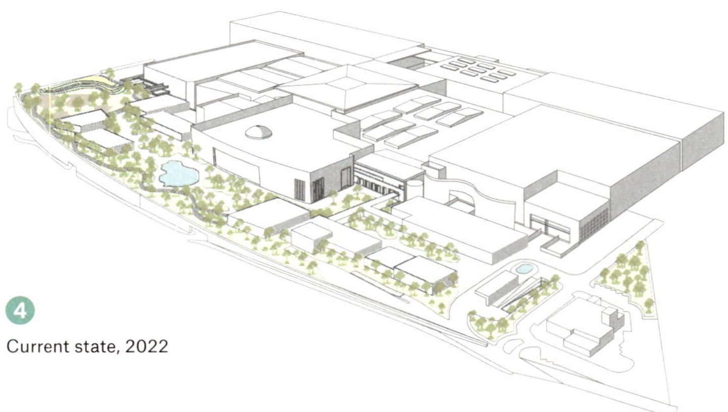

4 Current state, 2022

Diagram of the phases of Satélite Parque Plaza.

Before
Above: aerial view from the north side, circa 1970.

After
Below: aerial view from the north side, 2021.

Left hand page: three perspectives of interior renovation proposals of Satélite Parque Plaza at the beginning of the 1990s.

Right hand page: central plaza in the 2018 renovation seen from the ground floor.

Above: interior of the renovation and expansion of the third level in 2018.

Below: central plaza in the 2018 renovation.

Above: aerial view of the central part of Satélite Parque Plaza.

Below: aerial view of the amphitheater in Satélite Parque Plaza.

1997, 2015
MOLIÈRE DOS22

HERMÈS

Left hand page, above: photomontage of the aerial view of the first phase of the project. Below: perspective of the motor lobby and main access to the commercial area in the renovation and expansion, 2015.

Right hand page, above: night view of the gastronomic terrace in the commercial area, circa 1996.

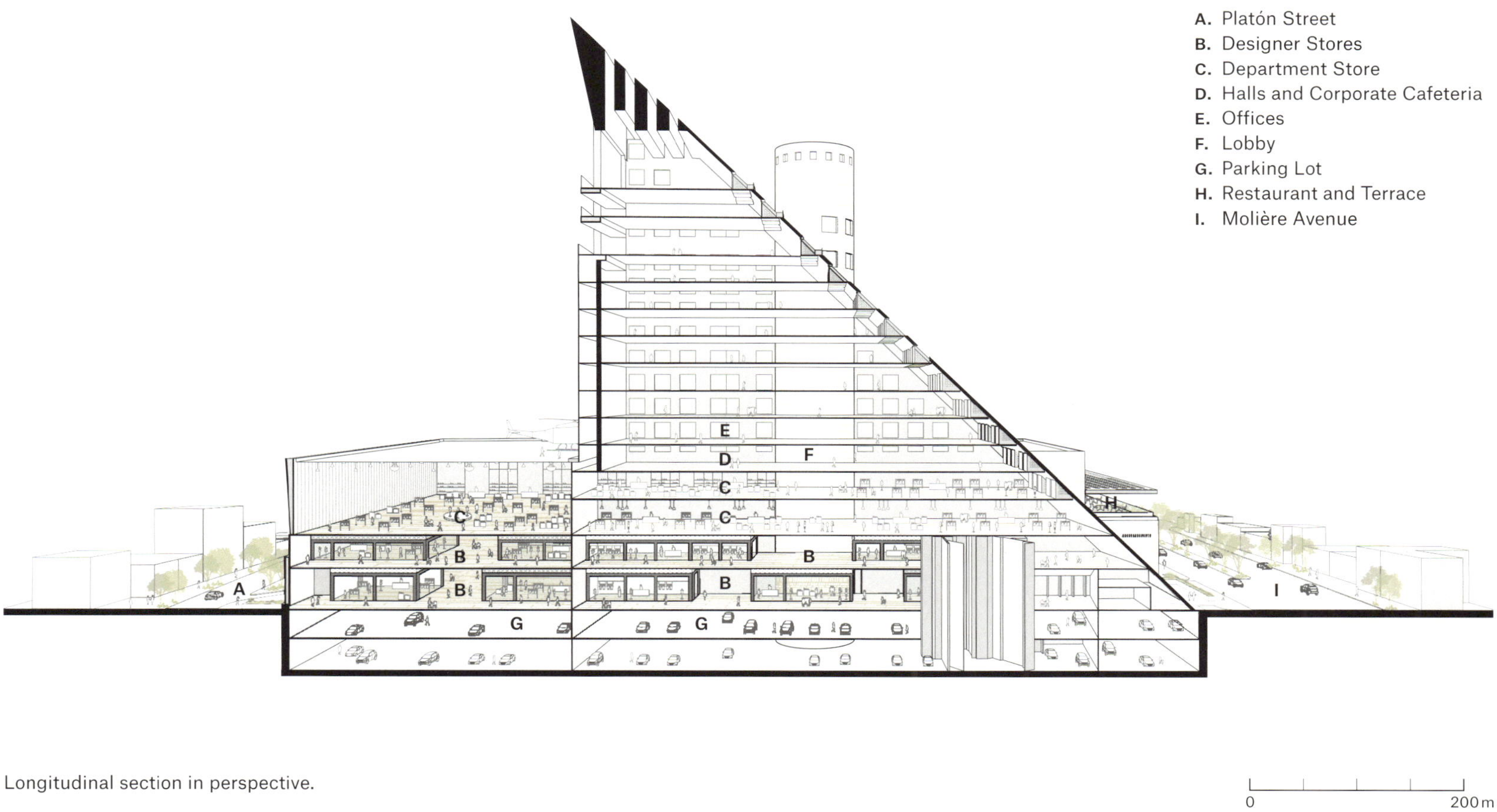

Longitudinal section in perspective.

2014
TOREO PARQUE CENTRAL

D' GALERI BY ENRIQUE

Before
Above: aerial view of Cuatro Caminos and the land now occupied by Toreo Parque Central in 1968, from the south side.

After
Below: current aerial view of the complex, from the south side.

Above: detail of the facade of the corporate towers.

Below, left: motor lobby on Parque de Chapultepec Avenue. In the background, the hotel tower. Right: detail of the corporate towers from Río San Joaquín Avenue.

A. Río San Joaquín Avenue
B. Parking for Offices
C. Corporate Towers
D. Commercial
E. Movie Theater
F. Supermarket
G. Park
H. Restaurants
I. Hotel
J. Department Store
K. Circunvalación Street

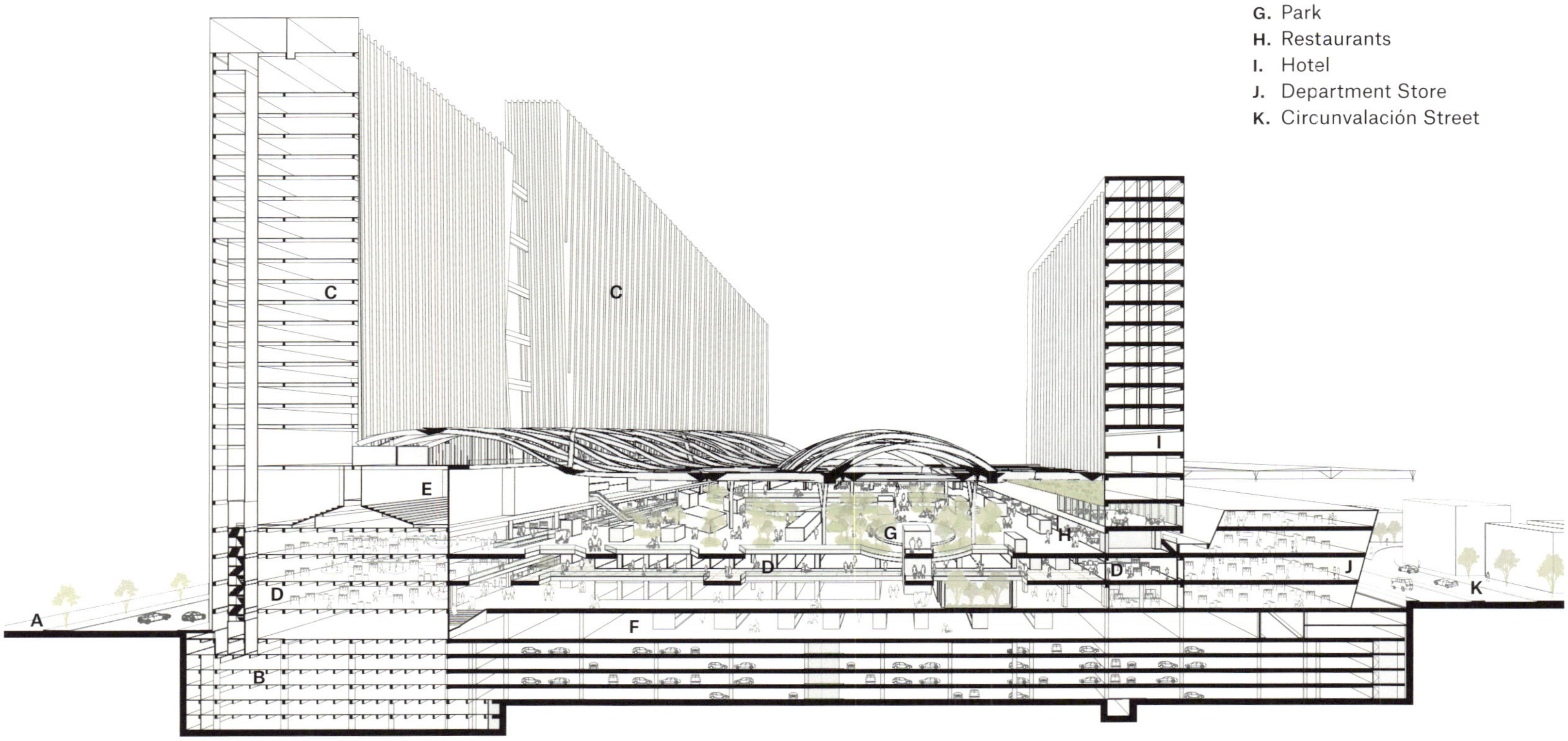

Longitudinal section in perspective.

0 50 m

Left hand page, below: interior view of the shopping center. In the center, the park inserted into the second level. Detail of the dome that references the old Cuatro Caminos bull ring.

Right hand page: interior view of the park and commercial levels from the third floor.

Cinépolis VIP

Left hand page: detail of the dome as part of the metallic roof that frames the park.

Right hand page: transit level between commercial levels and ground floor offices.

2019
MIDTOWN

Hilton
wework
Cinépolis VIP

AVIERCITOS

Left hand page and right hand page, below: gastronomic area on the second level under the semi-open roof, which allows for ventilation and controlled sunshine.

Right hand page, above, left: interior view of the commercial open-air passageway. Right: sculptural stairway as vertical circulation between the shopping mall levels and the lobby of the office tower.

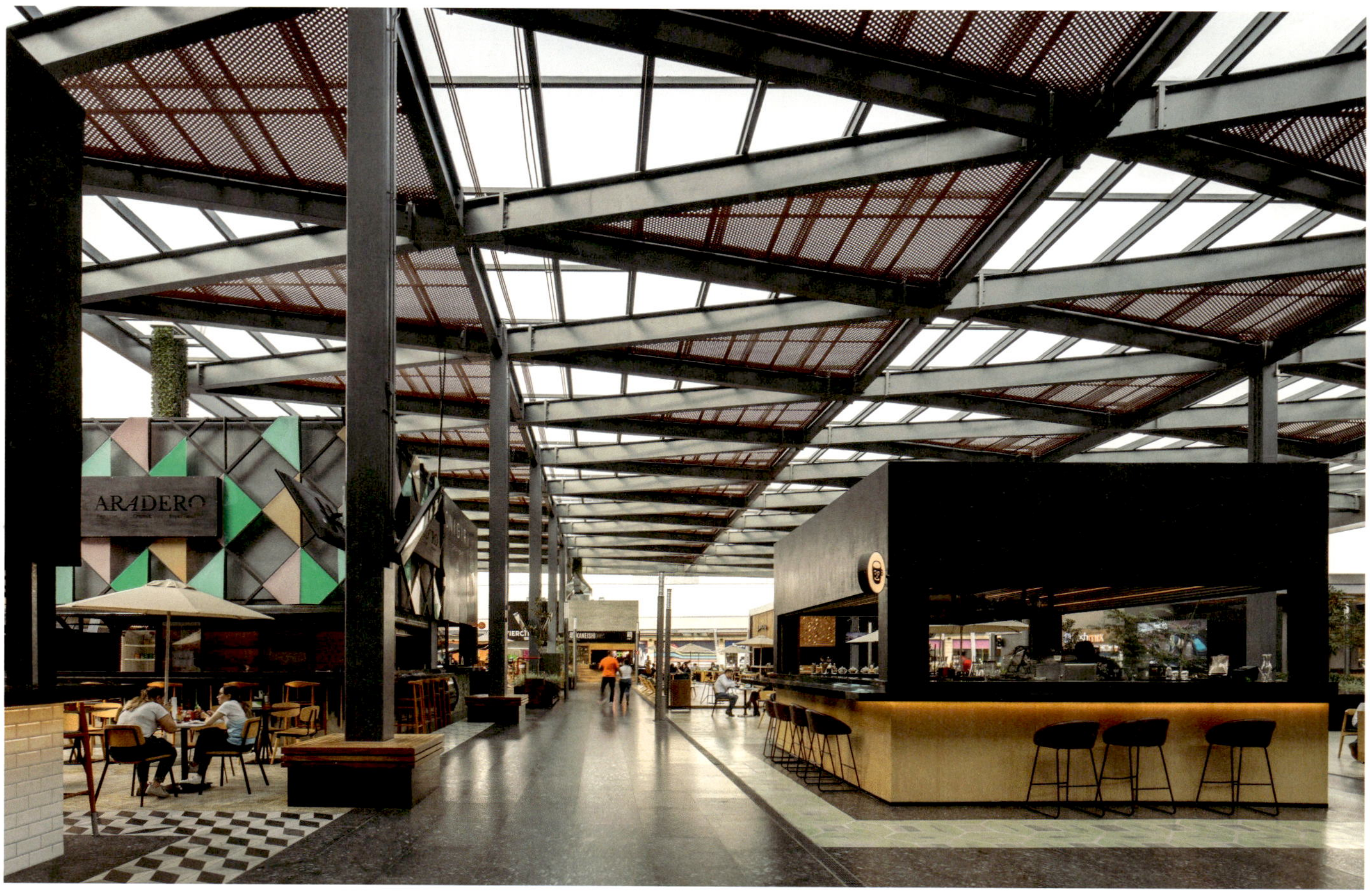

2.

HOTEL ARCHITECTURE ON THE MEXICAN COAST

CATHERINE R. ETTINGER

A Panamericana highway Laredo-México.
B California Apartments in Monterrey, tourist court-type lodging.

Introduction

As an architectural type, the hotel has received relatively little attention from historians of Mexican architecture despite its ubiquity and visibility as an urban landmark and its role in the formation of coastal developments. Architecturally, the hotel is particularly interesting because it must resolve the tension between the desire of visitors for modern amenities and the need at the same time to offer them an experience that genuinely differs from their everyday lives. In other words, hotel design responds not only to changes in the paradigms of tourism and the needs of different generations of guests, but also to how those guests imagine their destination: a highly sensitive topic in international tourism—one of special relevance in the case of Mexico.

In the 1920s, after the Revolution, Mexico tried to forge a new image of itself abroad, replacing its reputation as a land of adventurers and bandits by fostering an association with tradition, folklore, handicrafts, and the vestiges of pre-Hispanic cultures. The Summer School of the Autonomous National University of Mexico (UNAM) attracted expatriates who sympathized with the Revolution and helped to promote the country's muralism, handicrafts, and traditions. The policies of the Cárdenas government to boost tourism, which included the opening in 1936 of the first stretch of the Pan-American Highway from Laredo, Texas, to Mexico City and Acapulco, led to a significant flow of international tourism, mainly from the United States (A). In the six years under Cárdenas (1934–1940), the number of visitors to the country doubled, despite a fall in 1938 owing to the oil expropriation. The number of hotels also doubled.

A

B

During the six-year government of Manuel Ávila Camacho (1940–1946), the rise in tourism continued, in part because the Second World War made it impossible for North Americans to travel to Europe and turned them instead toward Latin American countries. Tourism grew more sharply after 1945, and sustained growth was achieved during Miguel Alemán's six-year term (1946–1952). The new generation of foreign tourists travelled Mexico's roads, mainly in search of recreation (fishing, hunting, or the seaside). This period of tourism by car along the new highway and its branch roads brought major changes to natural and urban landscapes. Some colonial sites were developed, and various types of accommodation and roadside services appeared. This gave rise to a precursor of the motel: the tourist court, replicating a common format in the United States that was generally built and staffed by the owners, where motorists and their cars were lodged in horizontal rows with plentiful greenspace, a restaurant, a gas station, and a garage for repairs (B). In Mexico, they tended to be built gradually over large terrains. There are some examples that simulate villages with cobbled streets and buildings with whitewashed walls, red tiled roofs, and wall tiles. By the 1950s, the growth of both domestic and international tourism and the development of Mexico's coasts pointed to a need for new solutions in hotel architecture.

Promoting a modern Mexico

During the Alemán administration, great importance was attached to the promotion of the image of modern Mexico. In the tourist sector, publicity was given to the notion of a cosmopolitan Mexico City with elegant nightlife and sophisticated hotels. The promotion of seaside destinations, Acapulco among them, was oriented toward new international tourism, which could enjoy modern facilities in idyllic surroundings, as well as the growing domestic tourism, driven by a burgeoning middle class. The architecture that arose was of a dual nature. While representing modernity and the expectation of attracting a national and international clientele, it also proposed exoticism,

C Juan Sordo Madaleno and José Adolfo Wiechers, aerial photograph of the Presidente Acapulco Hotel, Guerrero, 1961.

C

or at least references to Mexico as a place that ensured the experience of the "other" sought by the tourist.

This was the moment when the Presidente Acapulco Hotel (1958) (C–D) was built on the coast road, in a new zone of the tourist enclave. It was the first project by the firm Nacional Hotelera, of which Juan Sordo Madaleno was a founding partner, and an important antecedent of the large urban hotels the architect was to design later. A large canopy articulates the hotel's function as a mediator between the coast road and the sea, opening onto the lobby and the reception area. This mediating function is also manifest in the visual continuity achieved on the ground floor and in the gesture of framing the view of the sea. The solution found for the orientation of the large accommodation block with central circulation allowed practically all the rooms to have that same view. As in other works, Sordo Madaleno incorporated art in the project and worked with the furniture designer Clara Porset. *The Lovers*, a sculpture by Mathias Goeritz with figures wrought in bronze, was placed in front of a white wall where it cast its changing shadows. Clara Porset designed the dining-room chairs, made with wooden frames and woven seats and backs to amalgamate modern lines with traditional techniques. This was one of Porset's several collaborations with Juan Sordo Madaleno.

220

The focal point of the complex is the large square swimming pool, an important symbol of leisure and glamour in late-twentieth-century modernity. The hotel also incorporated commercial and entertainment areas to attract non-guests.

D Félix Candela, La Jacaranda nightclub in the Presidente Acapulco Hotel.

58

D

La Jacaranda (D) was a cabaret housed in a natural rock formation by the beach whose arrangement in terraces (for the restaurant and dance floor) and use of curved forms differentiate it from the strict modern geometry of the accommodation block and service areas. The roof of the night club, designed by Félix Candela, is a great concrete paraboloid that touches the ground at only three points, resulting in very light roofing for an airy space connected directly with the sea (D).

226 Ten years later, in the Presidente Cozumel Hotel (1969), Sordo Madaleno showed great sensitivity to the natural site with an architectural language whose refinement does not hide the fact that this is a hotel in Mexico. The entrance is a grand sculptural gesture, with walls that barely touch and a monumental canopy leading into the lobby, from which the views of the sea are directed and framed. The spatial distribution resumes previous experiments, but now the hotel is conceived as a set of independent structures, an extension of the landscape parallel to the sea, with a single-story wing of rooms to the north and a double-story one to the south. The pool, together with the service building (lobby, reception, offices, concessions, and restaurant), acts as the element articulating the different parts. The architects skillfully achieved continuity between the interior space, the exterior, and the individual private balconies.

Opening up to international capital

By the late 1950s, tourism was already one of the country's principal sources of foreign currency. The state tried to bolster the sector by improving the infrastructure and tourist facilities of cities like Tijuana, Ciudad Juárez, and Matamoros, as well
230 as locations in the center of the country. Several museums were opened, including the National Museum of Anthropology (1964), and archaeological sites were conditioned to receive visitors. Between 1958 and 1970, the number of foreign tourists nearly tripled, as did the corresponding economic outlay (E). This was the moment of the María Isabel Hotel in Mexico City (1961), designed by Juan Sordo Madaleno with José Villagrán, then the biggest hotel in Latin America.

A second shift in policies on tourism was oriented toward the development of coastal resorts. To this end, the Bank of Mexico created a special fund that boosted the creation of Cancún and Ixtapa, and later of Los Cabos, Loreto, and Huatulco. The idea was to increase both domestic and international tourism and at the same time attract the yachting fraternity by building marinas that would allow them to moor at different tourist destinations along the Pacific coast. The National Fund for Tourism (Fonatur), created in 1977, promoted the integral planning of the new destinations, including infrastructure and facilities like airports. Many of the new destinations had golf clubs, timeshare condominiums, and yachting facilities. The Fonatur policies encouraged the participation of foreign firms and capital through the figure of the trustee, which permitted the purchase of coastal property by foreigners. The reforms made to the Federal Tourism Law (1980) and the entry of Mexico in 1986 into the General Agreement on Tariffs and Trade (GATT) allowed greater private interests within a neoliberal pattern of state withdrawal.

In this framework, two processes took place simultaneously. The first was the arrival of international chains, mainly in large cities and coastal resorts, and the second was the development of local hotels in medium-sized cities. The international hotels followed company lines adapted to the local environment, with well-established patterns of rooms in vertical towers and communal areas laid out horizontally. Local hotel companies also emerged, among them the Camino Real hotel chain, whose architecture functioned outstandingly well as a representation of Mexico (F). At the same time, local hotels appeared in medium-sized cities around the country, generally with horizontal layouts around large gardens, pools, and tennis courts.

The creation of integral resorts

Within this scenario of opening up to foreign capital and new leisure concepts, the Westin Regina Hotels were designed by Javier Sordo Madaleno in Puerto Vallarta (1993) (G) and Los Cabos (1994). Both were large complexes aimed principally

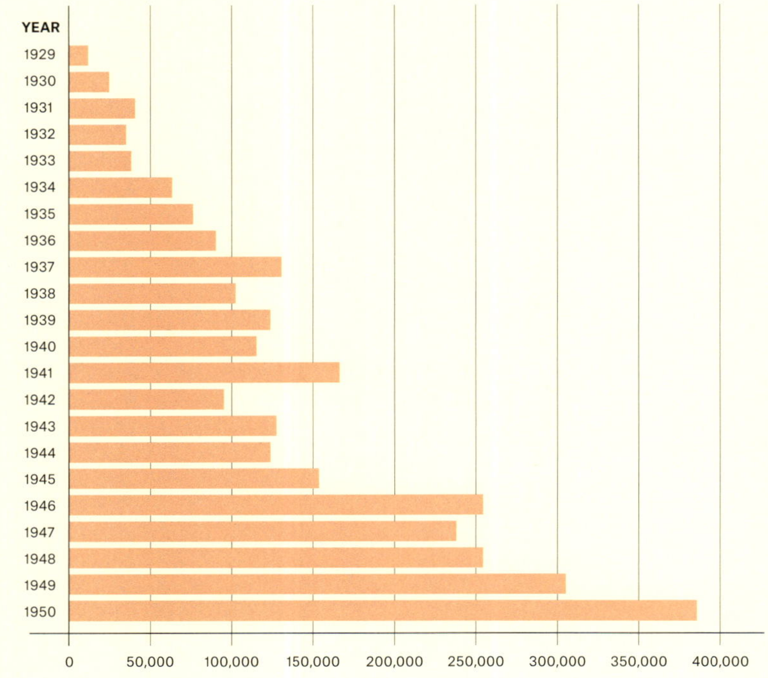

YEAR	QUANTITY OF TOURISTS
1929	13,892
1930	23,769
1931	41,271
1932	36,964
1933	39,541
1934	63,739
1935	75,432
1936	92,092
1937	130,091
1938	102,866
1939	127,822
1940	125,569
1941	165,627
1942	90,398
1943	126,905
1944	120,218
1945	156,550
1946	254,844
1947	239,756
1948	254,069
1949	306,065
1950	384,297

E

E "Arrival of Tourists in Mexico," taken from Dina Berger, *The Development of Mexico's Tourism Industry. Pyramids by Day, Martinis by Night*, New York, Palgrave MacMillan, 2006.

at international tourism with hotels, timeshare apartments, tennis courts, fitness centers, restaurants, bars, concessions, pools, and sun terraces. At the Westin Regina Puerto Vallarta—built in collaboration with José de Yturbe—respect for the local environment led on the one hand to the conservation of the palm groves—providing organic shade for the pools—and on the other hand to references from traditional Mexican architecture in the use of color and patterns of light and shadow projected by lattices and pergolas (G). The project at Los Cabos is based on a monumental, curved wall with openings to frame the views and create a protected area with tropical vegetation that contrasts with the surrounding desert. The colors, the sensitivity to light and shadow, and the use of large-scale volumes situate the tourist unmistakably in Mexico. This major development signaled an innovation in hotel architecture on the coast, with the emphasis now on monumental complexes with everything a visitor might need.

Two more recent complexes, the Grand Hyatt Playa del Carmen Hotel (2015) and the Solaz Los Cabos (2018), benefit from the Sordo Madaleno firm's experience in the field. From the Westin, the former borrowed the gesture of framing the view of the sea with the accommodation block but differed from it in its use of sober materials and colors to achieve integration with the landscape. The rooms are distributed in a "U" shape around the gardens and a central corridor whose lower level is occupied by a large spa area. A large artificial *cenote* (sinkhole) and a monumental flight of steps are clear references to Mexico, with no need to resort to the intense color that characterized the Mexican architecture of the last decades of the twentieth century. In the design of the Solaz Los Cabos, the preservation of the mangrove swamps on the site was a central concern. Integration with the natural environment was here achieved by means of a series of terraces, with the hotel and condominiums developed horizontally in an isolated area along the coast. The access building and several structures with rooms form a kind of fence that follows the coastline organically. Between these structures and the sea are three large terraces with rooms. Plants were arranged on the rooftops of these rooms so that the structure looks from a distance like a continuation of the desert landscape. All the rooms have spectacular sea views. Once again, new habits made the spa into an important component.

Representing Mexico

The changes in tourism policies and leisure concepts marked paths for innovation in the hotel architecture of the second half of the twentieth century. As air travel replaced car journeys and holidays of fifteen or twenty days were cut down to
little more than weekends, the hotel was forced to adapt. First, 234
the idea of a modern, clean, and cosmopolitan Mexico was 242
reflected in the hotel architecture of the fifties and sixties. Afterwards, the resort made its appearance, guaranteeing a restful stay in safe surroundings while catering to a sector that was not seeking a cultural experience but a few days' break. While this meant coming up with new proposals for the solution of environmental and functional aspects, it also brought changes in the hotels' function of representing Mexico to both national and foreign visitors. Small complexes made way for greater monumentality, with buildings that were clearly modern but employed formal resources that let guests know they were in Mexico. This recalls the development of the Hilton hotels into icons representing "a piece of America" in distant

F Ricardo Legorreta, Camino Real Hotel, Polanco, Mexico City, 1968. Latticework by Mathias Goeritz and Eternal Movement Fountain by Isamu Noguchi.

G Sordo Madaleno Arquitectos, Westin Regina Puerto Vallarta Hotel, Puerto Vallarta, Jalisco, 1993.

H Toro Ferrer, Caribe Hilton Hotel, Puerto Rico, 1949.

F

G

capitals besides functioning as representatives of the exotic cultures around them. The Caribe Hilton in Puerto Rico, an example that Juan Sordo Madaleno surely knew, was one of the first to attain this architectural duality of appearing both modern and international and, at the same time, local and exotic (H).

In the closing decades of the twentieth century, architects resorted to color as a way of representing the essence of Mexico, perhaps because of the international recognition won by Luis Barragán and Ricardo Legorreta and perhaps because of the promotion of such imagery within the country itself. In any case, it was almost certainly what tourists expected to find and what domestic travelers identified as their own. Besides colors and thick walls, another distinctive element of the country's hotel architecture is the use of local materials, especially wood and palm fibers. In recent decades, there has been a tendency toward enclosed resorts that guarantee international visitors a controlled, hygienic, and safe experience. The visitors of the twenty-first century want to share photographs of themselves in culturally exotic settings with spectacular natural scenery, but they do not wish to be disturbed or put at risk by the imperfections of this natural and social environment. In short, the desire to participate in an authentic experience of the "other" while retaining familiar comforts remains a central tension in hotel design.

H

1958
PRESIDENTE ACAPULCO

Perspective of the tower, phase 1.

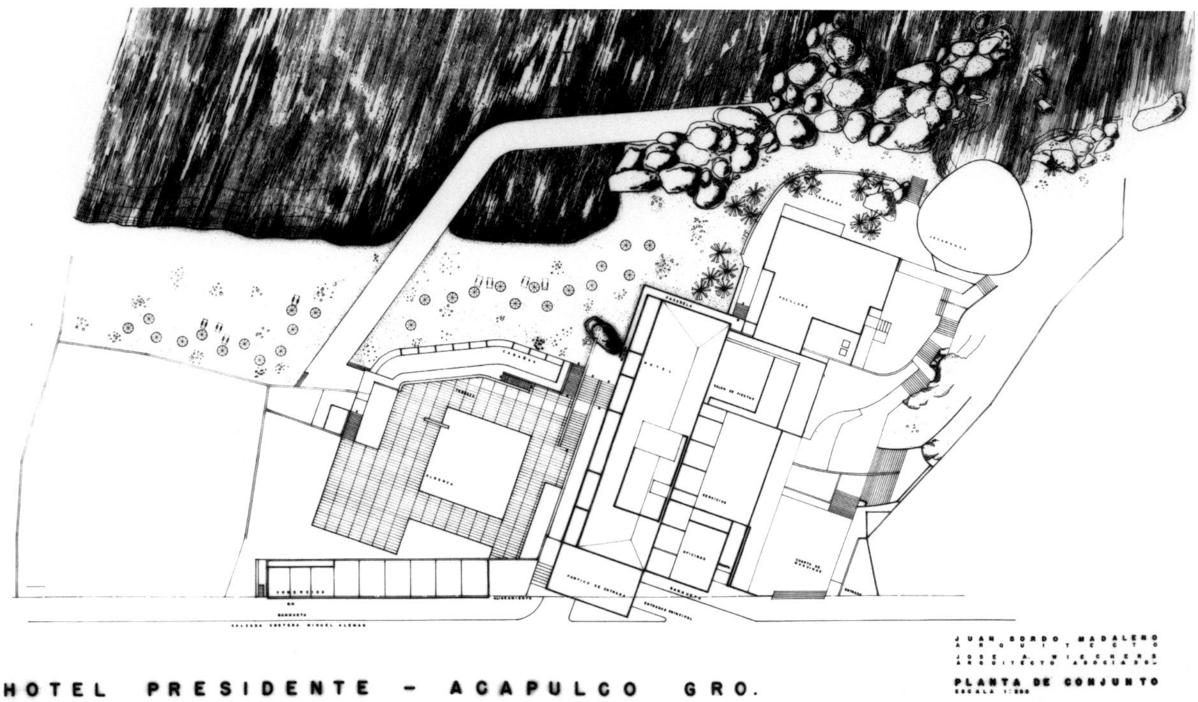

Above: plan of the complex, phase 1. Below: model of the original project in phases; phase 2 was not built.

Left hand page: view of the hotel facade and swimming pool.

Above: exterior passageway. Below: interior view of one of the rooms.

1969
PRESIDENTE COZUMEL

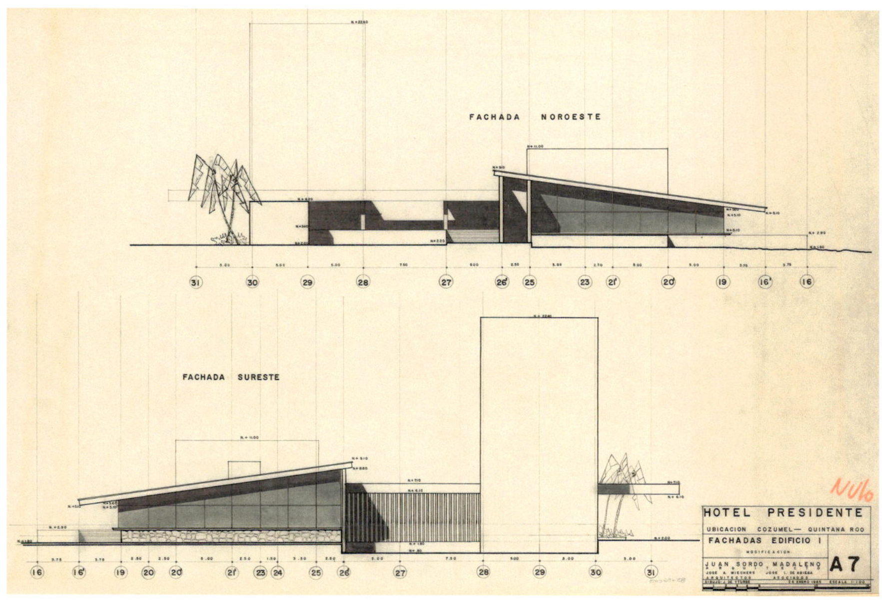

Below: facades.

Exterior view towards the swimming pool.

Two views of the main exterior hallway leading to the hotel rooms.

1994
WESTIN REGINA LOS CABOS

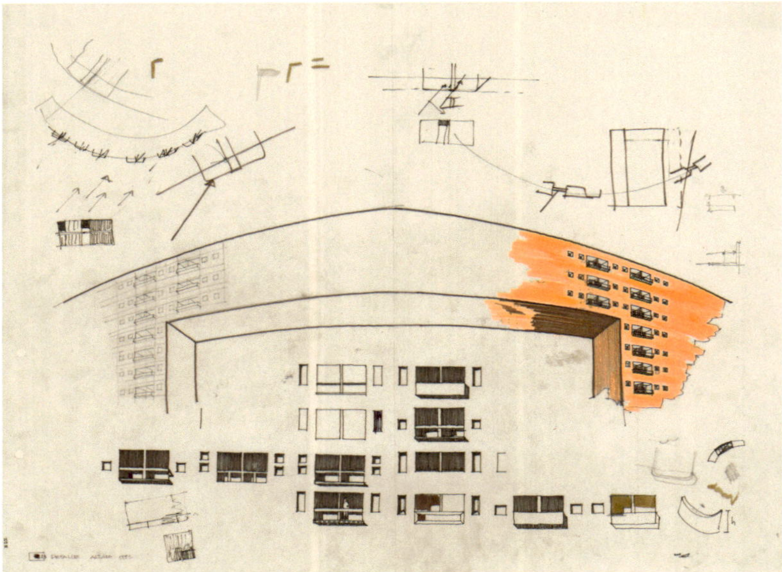

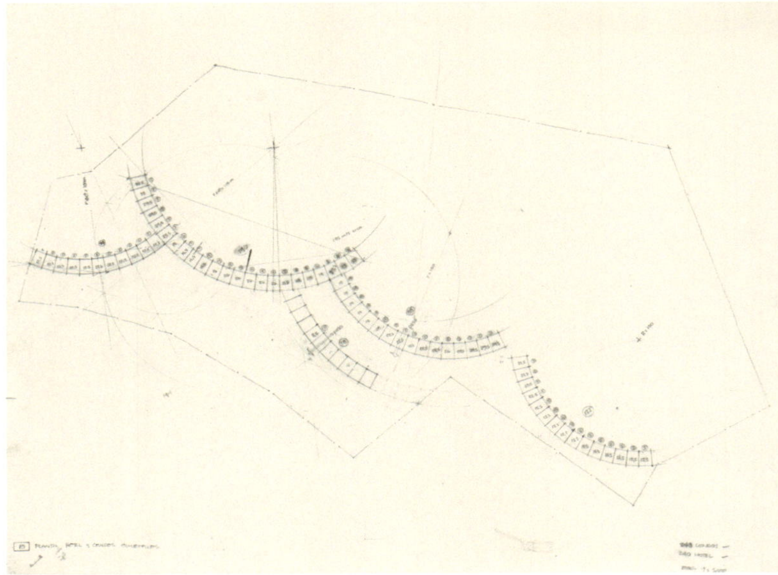

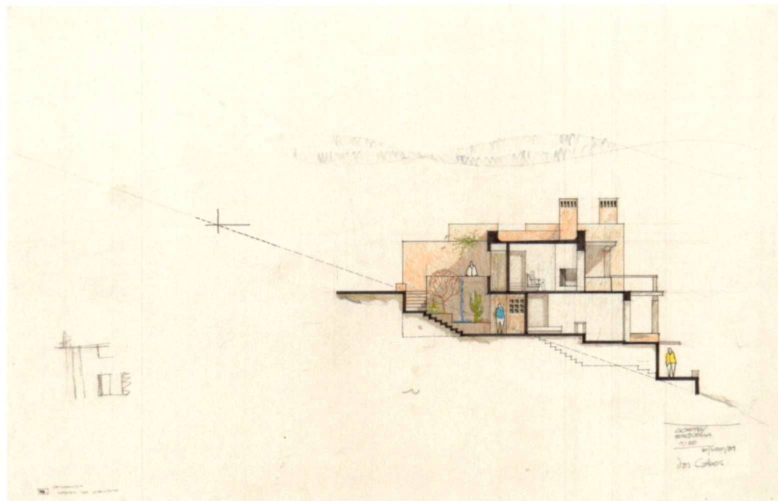

Above, left: study sketch of the windows.
Right: schematic drawing of layout.

Below, left: initial sketches.
Right: schematic drawing of the villas section.

Drawing of the main facade.

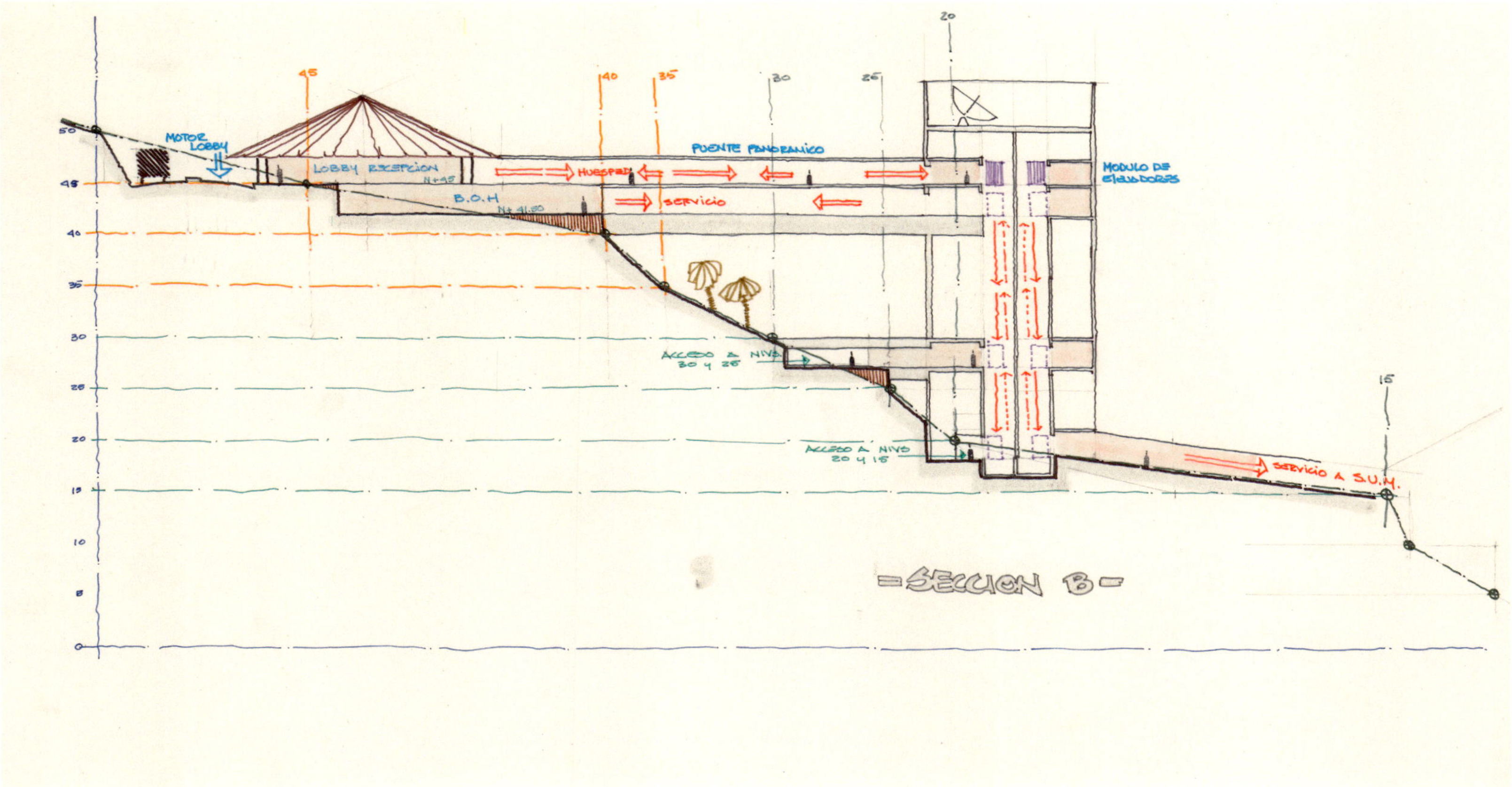

Sketch of condominiums in longitudinal section.

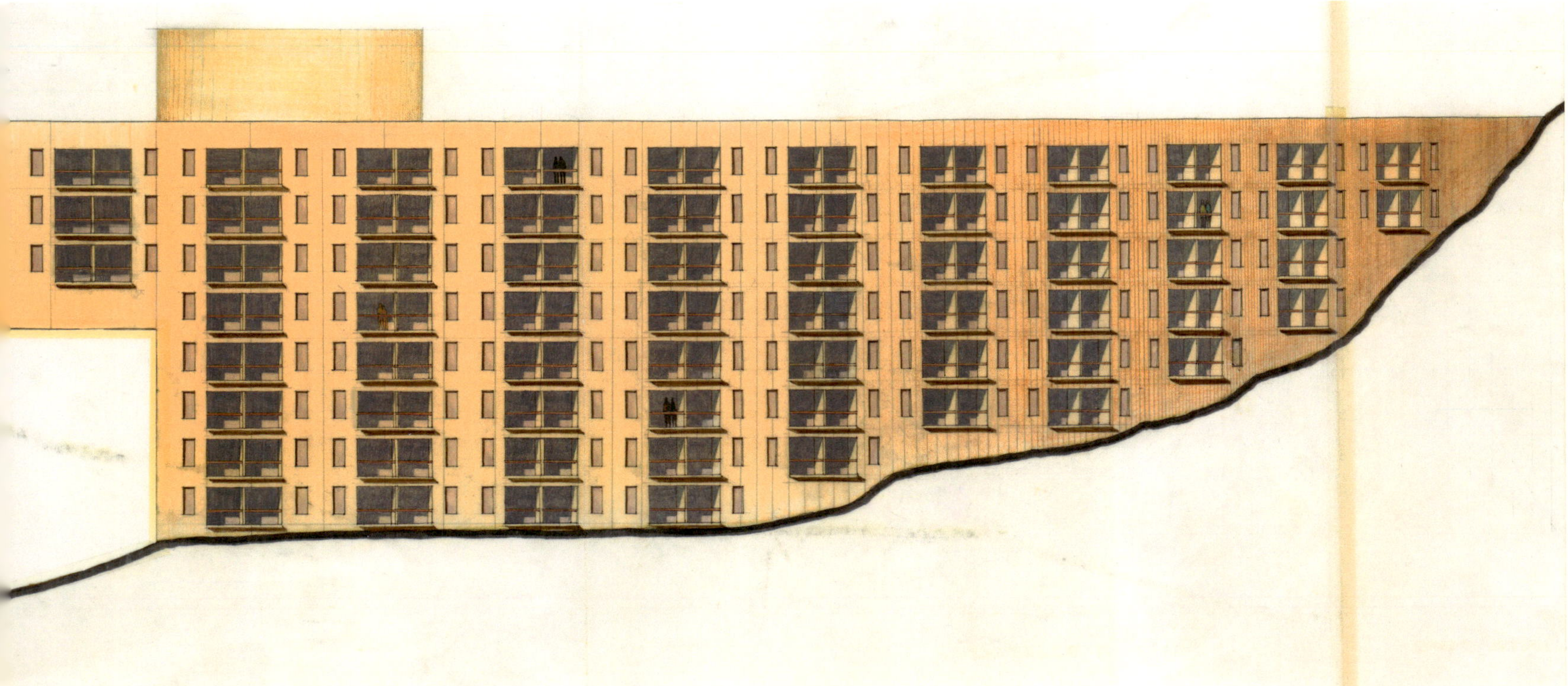

2015
GRAND HYATT
PLAYA DEL CARMEN

Above: motor lobby, cascading fountain. Below: access corridor to hotel reception; *Kukulcán*, by César López Negrete and Claudia Turrent.

Above: lap pool. Below: shopping kiosk in El Paseo.

Longitudinal section in perspective. El Paseo is a descending corridor that connects the hotel elements from the reception to the beach.

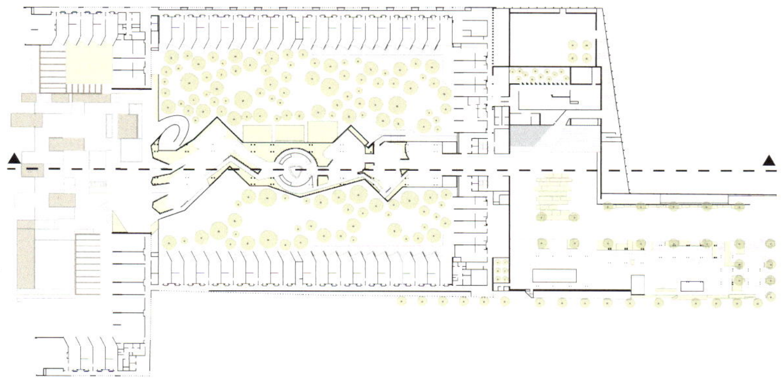

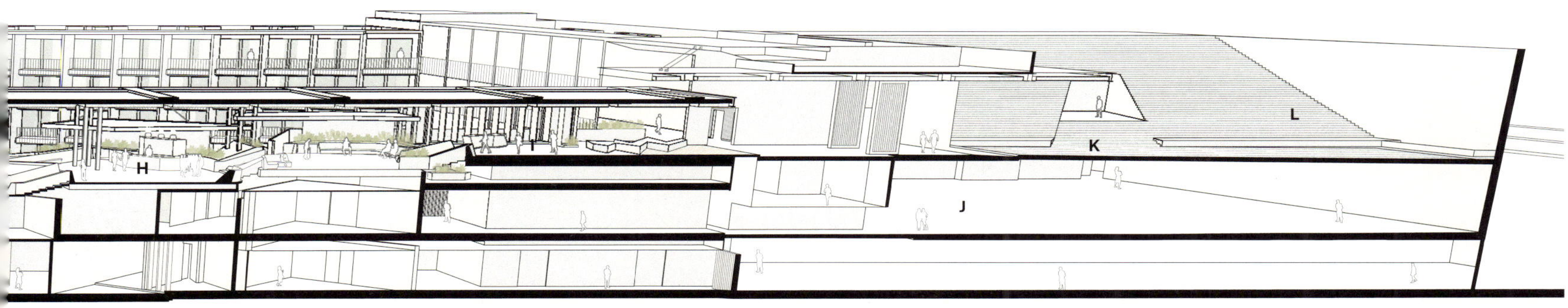

A. Beach
B. Swimming Pool
C. Restaurant
D. Gym
E. Inner Garden (mangrove)
F. Spa
G. Cenote
H. Kiosks
I. Lobby
J. Salon for Events
K. Motor Lobby
L. Fountain

0 20 m

Left hand page, above: El Paseo. View of the sea, vertex of the conic volume of the cenote-spa. Below: waiting room and exterior view of the cenote-spa.

Right hand page: interior view of the cenote-spa.

2018
SOLAZ LOS CABOS

Above: aerial view of the platforms of rooms and ravines.

Below: aerial view with details of hallways, swimming pool, terraces and private access patio to the rooms.

Above: villa-type room terrace.

Below, left: exterior passageway to the rooms.
Right: private access patio to each room.

Above: hotel reception with Baja Gold, wooden seats and benches by César López Negrete. Below: space between volumes in the main building.

Above: access to Mako Restaurant.

Below: exterior passageways, rear facade facing the highway.

3.

INHABITING THE CITY: URBAN HOUSES

LOURDES CRUZ GONZÁLEZ FRANCO

A Juan Sordo Madaleno, ground floor of the house complex at 2388 Reforma, 1952.
B Juan Sordo Madaleno, inner patio of the house at 2388 Reforma, 1952.
C Juan Sordo Madaleno, interior swimming pool and living room of the house at 2388 Reforma, with furniture design by Clara Porset, 1952.

B

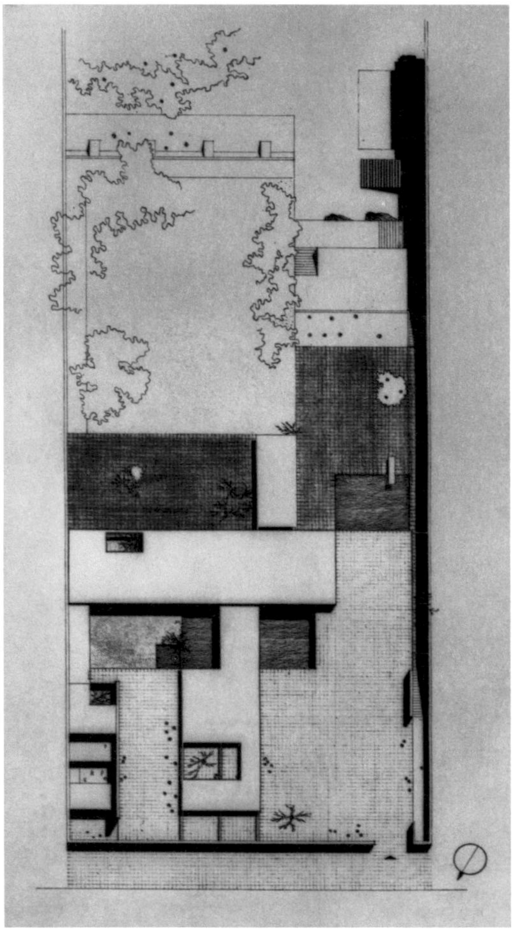

A

C

The first house by Juan Sordo Madaleno to appear in a publi-
252 cation was his own, located at Calle de Sierra Fría, number 725 (1946). It was chosen for the book *18 Residencias de Arquitectos Mexicanos* (18 Residences of Mexican Architects), which featured some of the houses built by the most highly regarded architects between 1930 and 1950.[1] In 1946, Juan Sordo
260 Madaleno was a young man of thirty. In partnership for some
256 years with Augusto H. Álvarez, he had built several apartment buildings in well-to-do districts of Mexico City. His architecture was associated with the Modern movement because he had successfully assimilated its characteristics. Although his prestige was based above all on his public buildings—financial headquarters, office blocks, and hotels—his houses appeared in publications as notable examples of the residences of the post-revolutionary social class with the highest economic resources, the fruit of the so-called "Mexican miracle."

The selected residences share characteristics, including that they are built on extensive grounds where the architect could design his project in total freedom practically without restrictions. In each case, there was hardly any direct engagement with the city because the houses were set back behind esplanades, like the ones at his house, 725 Sierra Fría—notable for its river stone texture—and at 940 Corregidores (1956), or gardens like the grove in front of the house at 100 Conscripto (1953). Because of this setback, a viewer had some perspective from which to appreciate their intersecting volumes in composition with terraces and bridges, as seen in the house at 2388 Reforma (1952) (A). Like his contemporaries,

1. Enrique Yáñez, *18 Residencias de Arquitectos Mexicanos* (Mexico City: Ediciones Mexicanas, S.A. 1951), 39–44, and *Arquitectura México*, Mexico City, September, no. 35 (1951).

Juan Sordo Madaleno designed compact and asymmetrical volumes that were occasionally perforated by gardens of varying proportions. These volumes were laid out around courtyards as a way of organizing the plan into functional zones and finding the best orientation for services, social areas, and private areas. Another feature of the exterior was the generous area allotted to parking—cars being a symbol of high purchasing power and social status—designed with protective roofing that could be integrated with an access walkway flanked by vegetation and reflecting pools, as in the house at 940 Corregidores. At the back of the plot, besides a large garden, there might also be a ball court as an additional leisure component.

Moreover, the open or partially covered terraces and the swimming pool functioned as elements articulating the social spaces and open spaces—resources that were not employed by this architect alone. The terraces provided means of enjoying views of the garden from both the ground floor and the upper story, which housed the bedrooms. Green areas were an integral and substantial part of the project. A pool sometimes formed part of the family quarters, partially intersecting a social area that could be double-storied, as in the houses at 940 Corregidores, 100 Conscripto, and the architect's own house at 2388 Reforma (C).[2] The interior and exterior blended together through the large windows on the ground floor, whose transparency opened views right to the end of the property. These were honest, generous, and functional homes with no nooks or crannies. It should be mentioned that the use of glass diminished in time, as the architect himself pointed out in an interview: "I started to build with glass, with glass windows so big that they were really glass walls. But then I realized that for my part, I had never lived or wanted to live in a glass cage, exposed to everyone's gaze. And it is even less pleasant to hide behind curtains. And so, I built in accordance with my own desire, which is to seek isolation."[3] Instead of large expanses of glass, lattices were often used both the exterior and the interior, a feature probably owing something to the influence of his architect friend Luis Barragán.

On the exterior, horizontality prevails thanks to the proportions of the volumes—specifically, the window rows along the upper floor that provide greater privacy and the emphatically continuous cantilever slabs. He generally used a mixed structure for his houses with horizontals of reinforced concrete and verticals of reinforced concrete or steel. If the pillars remained exposed, he would often paint them in a dark color to reduce their impact and emphasize horizontality. He also employed supporting walls which could be of volcanic stone. The social area of the house was kept free of structural supports by incorporating them into the walls or setting them immediately adjacent to the facade. By doing so, he created a flowing space of modernity linking the living room with its fireplace, the dining room, the breakfast area, the study, the bar, the partially uncovered terraces, and the pool. This continuous space could be double-height or partially divided with doorless walls. Services like the kitchen, the pantry, laundry room, and the servants' quarters were grouped together without letting these functions encroach on the rest of the house. The bedrooms were on the upper floor each with its own bathroom and large closet and always with views over the garden. The bathrooms were generally located on the interior—away from the facades—and were therefore lit by overhead glazing or skylights.

D

To this space of modernity, Juan Sordo Madaleno incorporated warm materials like wood and added artworks, including such major pieces as Mathias Goeritz's *Christ* on the side wall of the entrance plaza of his house at 2388 Reforma and later at the house located at 2076 Reforma (1981) (D), where the influence of Barragán was very evident in the use of vibrant color, rustic wooden furnishings, and beams also of wood (E). All the houses were unique and made to measure, and represented the social customs and private lives of their inhabitants.

---

2. *Espacios*, May, no. 15 (1953), and *Arquitectura México*, June, no. 42 (1953).
3. *Arquitectura México*, April-July, no. 100 (1968): 79.

D *Auschwitz Savior* by Mathias Goeritz, iron sculpture, 1951–1952, in the entrance court to the house on 2388 Reforma.

E Juan Sordo Madaleno and Javier Sordo Madaleno Bringas, entrance court to the house on 2076 Reforma, 1981.

E

From the 1970s, the Sordo Madaleno studio distanced itself from the orthodox postulates of the Modern movement,
270 as did many of their contemporaries. Moreover, the presence
274 from the early 1980s of the architect Javier Sordo Madaleno Bringas breathed energy into a new highly productive phase characterized by great compositional freedom. Sordo Madaleno Arquitectos has upheld its prestige as a firm since it was founded and has also produced some luxury residences in recent decades that have received high praise for their quality. All had the good fortune to be set back in grounds privileged in terms of both their size and their surroundings. This has allowed the studio great expressive freedom, not only because of the dimensions involved but also because the needs and habits of society have changed which bring a demand for new spaces that architects have generally met by appealing to their imagination in the absence of pre-established rules. Plans and elevations have remained predominantly orthogonal, although
264 in the case of the Bosques de las Lomas house (2007) volumes are rotated at a different angle.

There remain some continuities of compositional features used previously, like the solution of surrounding the house with green areas, with the large garden at the back so that the view of it could be enjoyed from the social areas and the bedrooms.
266 This is the case of the Vistahermosa house (2009), where the entrance plaza allows a full view of the three white rectangular parallelepipeds of the upper floor, which rest on a perpendicular volume that supports and embraces them.

Whether in the city, in the forest, or on the coast, Sordo Madaleno Arquitectos always seeks an integration of exterior and interior spaces. This integration can be achieved by means of terraces or by fully-open folding or sliding windows, as in the award-winning house on the island of Cozumel (2017) or in the internationally-renowned clubhouse in the Valle San Nicolás residential complex in the State of Mexico (2021), which although not exactly a private house is part of the lifestyle and living space of those who reside in this exclusive country club. Other persistent traits are the use of reflecting pools as a compositional element, double or triple height vestibules, and extreme care in the choice of artworks. However, this new phase with Javier Sordo Madaleno Bringas also has made its own mark through outstanding, distinctive characteristics, such as the overhead light filtered through beams, single-ramp staircases protected by glass banisters, and a careful choice and combination of woods with white walls and paving on both the exterior and the interior. There is a special interest in concealing the parking and service areas from the view of guests. One striking aspect, as in many residences of the class with high purchasing power, is the number of square meters devoted to bathrooms and closets, all as a reflection of lifestyle.[4] These are unique houses whose predominant feature is light; light that filters through, inundates, and reveals the domestic space.

4. David Leatherborrow, "The Architecture of Javier Sordo Madaleno", in *Javier Sordo Madaleno* (Mexico City: Arquine, 2011).

1946
725 SIERRA FRÍA

Left hand page, above: entrance court and parking area. Below, exterior patio.

Right hand page: pool house.

1953
100 CONSCRIPTO

Above: interior view of the swimming pool with furniture designed by Clara Porset. Below: interior view of the swimming pool.

Above: rear patio. Below: exterior view from the swimming pool with diving platform.

1956
940 CORREGIDORES

Left hand page, above: interior view of the living room and swimming pool. Below: exterior view from the rear patio.

Right hand page, above: interior patio with vegetation. Below: interior view of the stairway to the ground floor.

2007
BOSQUES DE LAS LOMAS

2009
VISTAHERMOSA

Above: exterior view from entrance courtyard.

Below, left: main entrance. Right: interior circulation.

Interior view of the corridors.

2017
COZUMEL HOUSE

A. Lobby
B. Room 1
C. Bathroom
D. Room 2
E. Room 3
F. Room 4
G. Main Room
H. TV Room, Storm Room
I. Bar

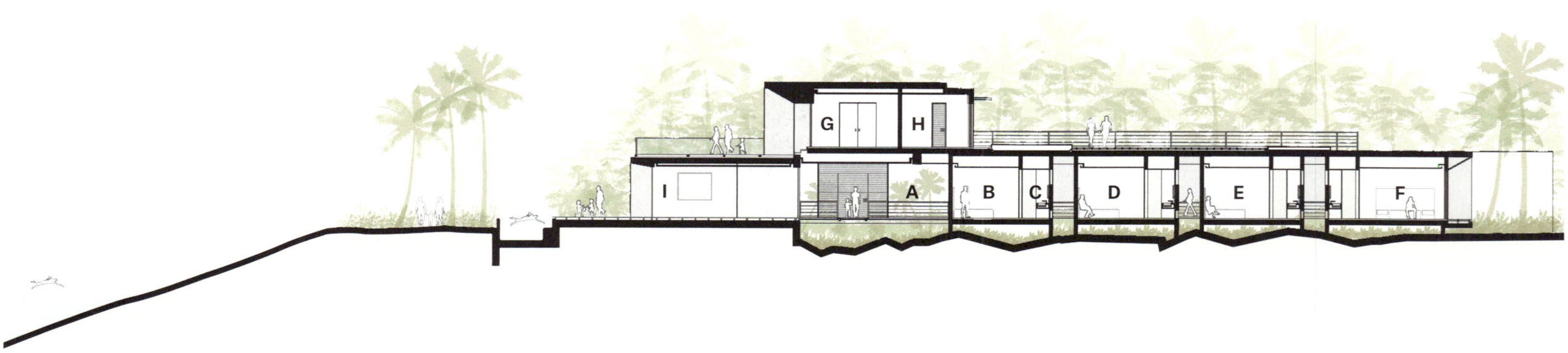

Longitudinal section.

0 6m

Left hand page, above: west facade.

Right hand page, above: exterior view of the swimming pool. Below: exterior view of the swimming pool.

2021
VALLE SAN NICOLÁS

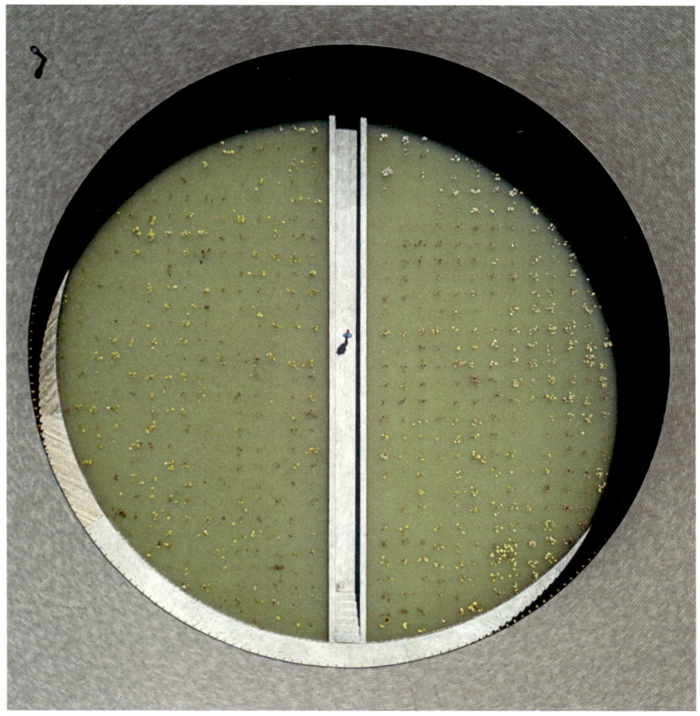

Left hand page, above: exterior view from the dock at sunrise. Below: aerial view of the clubhouse in its context.

Right hand page, above: exterior view of the dock and pool to the southeast. Below: interior view from the central corridor.

4.

INHABITING THE CITY: APARTMENT BUILDINGS

SARA TOPELSON

In collaboration with Jimena Orvañanos

A

A Plaza Melchor Ocampo. From left to right: Luis Barragán and José Creixell, apartment building; Luis Barragán and Max Cetto, painter's studio; Juan Sordo Madaleno and Augusto H. Álvarez, apartment building; Enrique del Moral, apartment building, Mexico City, 1936–1947.

B

B Aerial view of Colonias Cuauhtémoc and Anzures in 1949, Mexico City.

In the decades from 1920 to 1950, Mexico City underwent a rapid process of urbanization that saw the beginning of a new model of dwelling. Apartment buildings of this era are the reflection of the demographic changes in the city and the search for a suitable model for multistoried accommodation. In those three decades, Mexico City went from a small city of 400,000 inhabitants to a metropolis of four million.[1]

The most frequent collective model for dwellings in the nineteenth and early twentieth centuries was the *vecindad*, characterized by community life around a central courtyard with shared washing facilities and passageways connecting the rooms and dwellings.[2] Until then, there had been no traditional habitation or residential type for the petty bourgeoisie, and it was this that prompted the development of the first apartments, originally in four-story buildings without elevators known as *casas de departamentos*, and afterwards in higher buildings of eight to ten floors with elevators, the type still known today as *edificios de departamentos* or apartment buildings (A, B).[3]

These new models modified the way neighbors lived together, a response to the needs and aspirations of a Mexican bourgeoisie with a contemporary spirit inspired by European models, especially from Madrid and Paris. Apartment buildings proposed a solution to the housing problem by increasing densification in new residential districts, an economically viable model thanks to "stacking," which "increases the real estate value of a property by expanding the square footage and usable capacity of a building without increasing its footprint."[4]

The challenge was to foster a relationship between the inhabitants of these buildings and their environment, between the individual and the city. Reserving the ground floor for commercial use succeeded in creating a sensation of neighborhood community, not only inside the building but also in its context through echoes of neighboring buildings of the same type. Juan Sordo Madaleno's first incursion into the apartment building genre was his first project in 1936. This is a five-story building in the Historic Center of Mexico City, on Isabel la Católica and Regina, with the ground floor destined for commerce and three levels of apartments with balconies, except on the corner, where horizontal windows are integrated in the volume to emphasize the building's presence. The fifth

1. Alejandro Pérez-Duarte Fernández, "Nacimiento del modelo de apartamento en la Ciudad de México 1925–1954: lectura del archivo de un arquitecto," *Scripta Nova: revista electrónica de geografía y ciencias sociales* 7 (2003), https://www.raco.cat/index.php/ScriptaNova/article/view/60235.
2. José Luis Noriega, "El origen de las vecindades en la Ciudad de México," *Milenio* (September 6, 2019), https://www.milenio.com/cultura/el-origen-de-las-vecindades-en-la-ciudad-de-mexico.
3. Vladimir Kaspé, "La habitación colectiva," *Arquitectura México* no. 17 (1943): 67, https://fa.unam.mx/editorial/wordpress/wp-content/Files/raices/RD06/REVISTAS/17.pdf.
4. Paul Lewis, Marc Tsurumaki, and David J. Lewis, *Manual of Section* (New York: Princeton Architectural Press, 2016).

C

level is set back and has small horizontal windows, forming a clear conclusion to the building.

In 1940, the architect assumed the full challenge of designing a large building on the outer edge of a city block. Located at the crossing of Avenida Insurgentes and Avenida Álvaro Obregón and Monterrey in Colonia Roma, its ground floor is also given over to shops, which occupy the longer front along Álvaro Obregón. The entrance to the building is on Insurgentes, the main avenue, with a longitudinal vestibule leading to the elevators and the stairs. The facades have different treatments. The horizontal windows and balconies facing Álvaro Obregón evoke the two-story apartments of Le Corbusier's Immeubles-Villas in their alternation of windows and terraces, but the front-facing Insurgentes looks like another building altogether. Israel Katzman is of the opinion that the set-back structure on the first floors emphasizes "the horizontal lengthening of openings and closures." (C)[5]

Four years later, in collaboration with the architect Augusto H. Álvarez, Juan Sordo Madaleno carried out another intervention on the edge of a residential block, this time located between the streets of Río Lerma, Melchor Ocampo, and Río Ródano. He implemented the project in phases, starting with the trapezoidal building on the corner, its form accentuated by the terraces that allow views over the two streets. The surface of the wall facing Melchor Ocampo provides an attractive contrast, with horizontal windows newly evoking the rationalist language he adopted in the whole set of four buildings. Louise Noelle comments on these buildings: "The works designed by Juan Sordo Madaleno have always been in the avant-garde of the Modern movement, faithfully reflecting the designs of more developed countries. They always have the stamp of an architecture based on functionalist ideas and on the constructions of the Bauhaus and Le Corbusier."[6] In her analysis of this complex, Lourdes Cruz notes: "These constructions were an early display of modulation both in the plan and in the stone-faced facades with large windows from floor to ceiling."[7]

In 1947, he constructed one of his best and most visible apartment buildings at the intersection of Avenida Mariano Escobedo, Paseo de la Reforma, and Melchor Ocampo. Known as the Edificio Larín after the name of a chocolate shop on the 286
ground floor, its main facade had a curved morphology owing to its position on the former Glorieta de Simón Bolívar, a round plaza with a splendid view of the castle in the Bosque de Chapultepec (Chapultepec Forest). These were the views enjoyed from the living and dining rooms of the sixteen apartments with balconies and large windows that defined the character of the building. All vertical circulation was in the center of the building while the bedrooms faced the side streets with small windows. The ground floor was intended for shops and the main entrance hall. The building was one of the city's landmarks until its demolition.

From the 1950s, because of the city's constant growth
and the American post-war economic boom, resources were 282
allocated to the development of urban infrastructure in areas outside the center, and new perspectives emerged in the preferences of the population, who started to transfer their choice of apartments to new locations. Juan Sordo Madaleno continued to design apartment buildings, especially in areas like Polanco, Lomas de Chapultepec, and Bosques de las Lomas. In 2006, Javier Sordo Madaleno took over the baton from his father and designed an apartment building in Lomas de Chapultepec, a project informed by the steep incline of the site and
its magnificent views over Mexico City. Cumbres Residential 290
is formed of nine stepped apartments attached onto a large, inclined wall, which acts as the container and distributor of vertical circulation and services while at the same time defining the overall geometry. Communication with the apartments is by bridges that allow lighting and ventilation into the service areas. The amenities and communal zones are located on a large terrace on the lowest part of the terrain.

Also in Lomas de Chapultepec, this time on the complicated road intersection formed by Paseo de la Reforma and Avenida Constituyentes, Sordo Madaleno built an apartment complex called Arbolada Lomas (2006) (D), made up of four blocks connected by a circular ring providing access to the four towers, with views of the greenspace and the pool. The main facade on Paseo de la Reforma has four levels of offices in an interesting design of white triangular volumes with upward-facing windows to reduce the impact of the large avenue, which is really the main exit from the city on the road to Toluca. At the

5. Israel Katzman, *La arquitectura contemporánea en México* (Mexico City: Instituto Nacional de Antropología e Historia, 1964).
6. Louise Noelle, *Arquitectos Contemporáneos de México* (Mexico City: Trillas, 1989), 144.
7. Lourdes Cruz González-Franco, *Augusto H. Álvarez: Arquitecto de la modernidad* (Mexico City: Facultad de Arquitectura UNAM, Departamento de Arquitectura, UIA, 2008), 37.

C Le Corbusier, Immeubles-Villas, 1922.

D Interior view of Arbolada Lomas, 2006.

130 

D

back of the site is a fifteen-story apartment block, far from the noise of the avenue. The complex is complemented by two eleven-story lateral towers with a total of seventy-eight apartments between them.

298 The apartment building in Alcázar de Toledo, completed in
2018, is located in a privileged spot. The design is based on
300 respect for the complex topography on which the five apartments with large terraces are installed, framed horizontally by a zigzag line that defines the attractive volume of the stacked apartments; vehicular and pedestrian access is located on the highest part and a ramp descends to the reception. The five apartments enjoy magnificent views of the Mexico City valley and the surrounding mountains.

294 Artesia (2014), an apartment project on Avenida Campos Elíseos in Polanco, marks a return to the consolidated urban fabric of the city, alongside hotels, restaurants, shops, Polanco Park, and the Bosque de Chapultepec. Two sober twenty-three-story towers, contrasting and complementary, contain single- and double-story apartments of different types, sizes, and concepts. The two towers rise over a shared base that houses the entrance, reception, and communal areas. Like yin and yang, black and white, they engage in a volumetric dialogue—one in black granite and the other with a glass facade—standing out thanks to these contrasts amidst the context of other existing tower blocks. At the base, a set of magnificent works by Jan Hendrix brings continuity to the dialogue.

To conclude this tour of the apartment buildings of Sordo Madaleno Arquitectos in Mexico City, we mention the res-
304 idential complex at 225 Rubén Darío (2020). Located on a major city thoroughfare opposite the Bosque de Chapultepec, it stands on a site of 100 acres on the edge of a residential block in Polanco. Two thirty-story towers define the silhouette of the complex and mold the skyline of the area, rising on a three-story base that leaves a vast area of terrain free. These three levels contain the amenities, the pool, and the communal areas. Several terraces enjoy views toward the Bosque de Chapultepec and the urban district of Polanco. The large double-story apartments create the sensation of living amongst the trees of the forest.

In Guadalajara, the country's second most populous city, Sordo Madaleno Arquitectos has been involved over the last decade with several urban reconversion projects that have included apartment buildings. The design of the Andares mixed-use complex in Zapopan, Jalisco, responds to the concepts of integrality and mixed land use with a building of 168 apartments (2009), a shopping center (2009), an office building (2017), and a hotel (2017) all articulated on the design based of various volumes, such as the ascending diagonal that defines the entrance to the complex. Rising above two stories of shops is a triangular block containing apartments with large balconies facing the diagonal facade. The inclusion of shops in the base of the building links the inhabitants of Andares with their surroundings and makes the avenue leading into the complex—the axis around which the master plan is articulated—a crowded and busy place.

The mixed-use complex The Landmark (2019)—the immediate neighbor of Andares—is defined by a central plaza that generates the fluid and organic forms which integrate the project, like a space that distributes the different blocks of offices and apartments which form it. The apartment building continues the elliptical curve around the central space, and like Andares, it rises above a base dedicated to commercial use. The large apartments have balconies with views over the city and the interior of the complex. The block is segmented with a diagonal rift forming spaces for amenities and open areas for the use of residents.

Apartment buildings that started to be adopted as solutions in the last century have led to a new option for habitability and have continually transformed both the morphology and the outline of the city. These buildings are now regarded as milestones that define, distinguish, and mark the complex fabric of their urban settings.

1940
MONTERREY AND ÁLVARO OBREGÓN

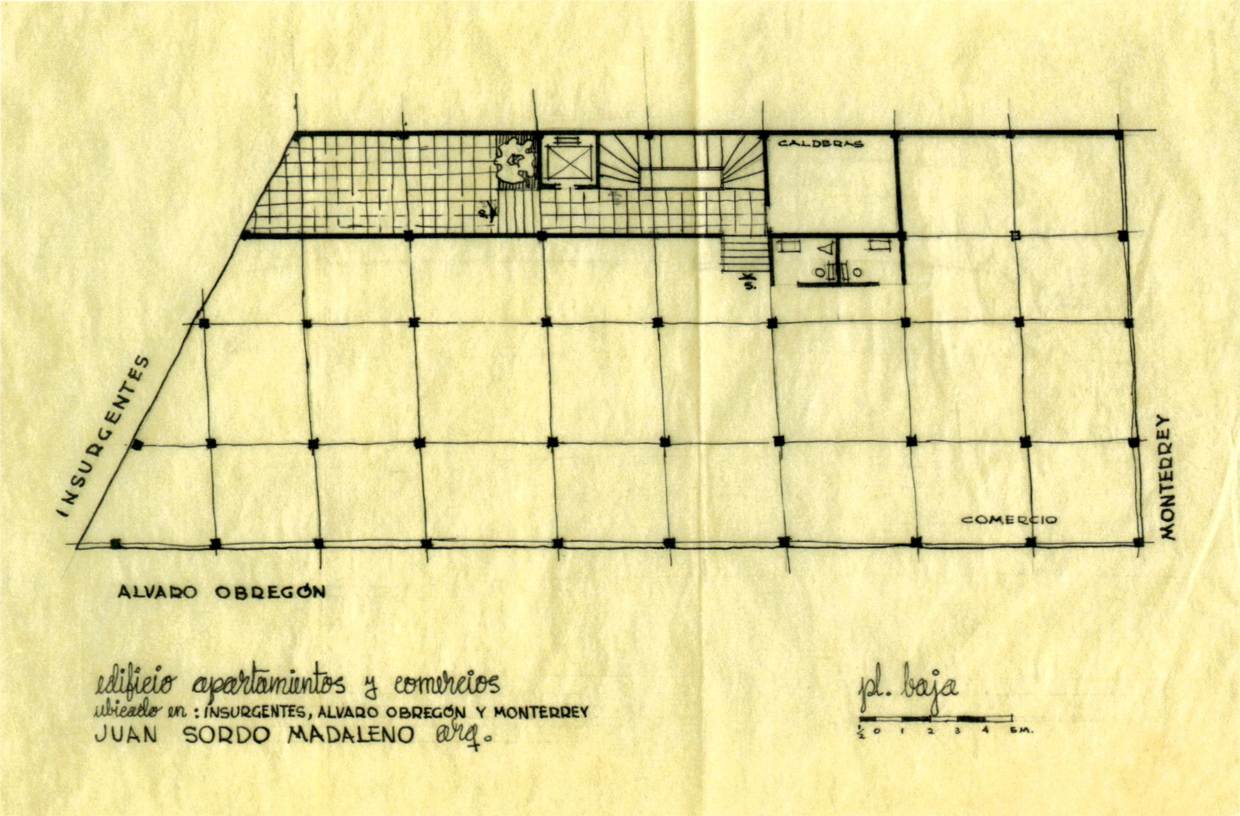

Schematic layout plan.

FREY
S.A.

1945
333–335 RÍO LERMA

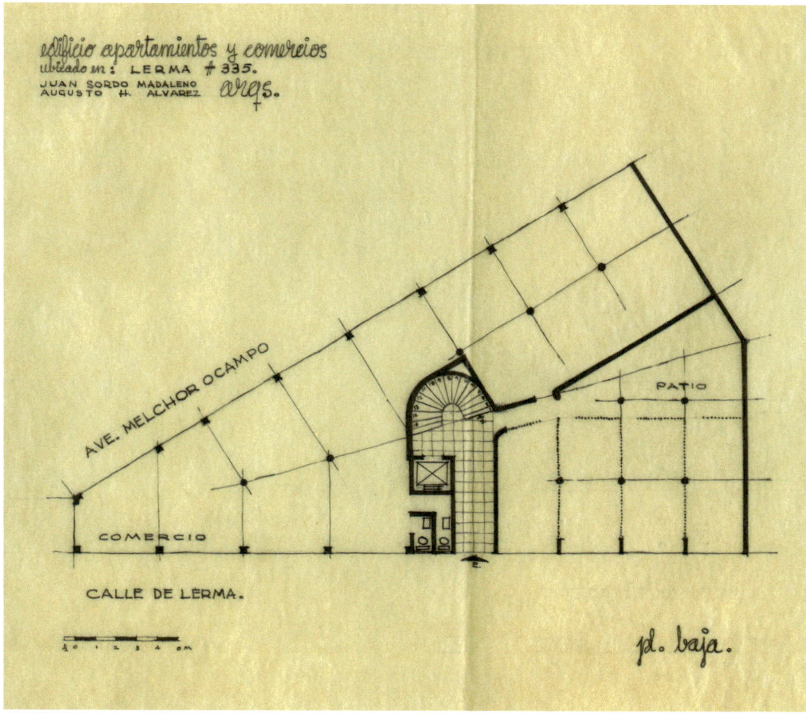

General distribution plan.

1947
EDIFICIO LARÍN

SALONES DE BELLEZA
Dr. Rodolfo del Rosal
ENFERMEDADES DEL CORAZON
BOMBONES
DULCES
REGALOS

Side facade from Circuito Interior.

Above: entrance lobby.

Below: interior view. Interior-exterior connection by means of a large terrace designed for views of the Chapultepec Castle.

2006
CUMBRES RESIDENTIAL

2014
ARTESIA

200
CAMPOS
ELISEOS
200

Above: entrance lobby with art work by Jan Hendrix on the columns. Below: inner hallways with access to apartments.

Above: motor lobby. Below: inner hallways that connect the amenities areas.

2018
ALCÁZAR DE TOLEDO

Left hand page, above: exterior night view of Paseo de los Ahuehuetes. Below: aerial view.

Right hand page: exterior view of the terraces.

2019
THE LANDMARK

Left hand page, left: facade of the residential corporate tower. Right: detail of the facades of both towers.

Right hand page, left: ground floor of the commercial area. Right: outer stairway that connects different commercial levels with the terrace on the fourth floor.

2020
225 RUBÉN DARÍO

Exterior view from Ruben Darío Street.

Skyline of Rubén Darío Street from the Chapultepec Lake.

Rear facade of the second tower from the plaza and the lower level of the apartment building.

Detail of facade between the two towers of the complex.

5.

CHURCHES AND CHAPELS

IVAN SAN MARTÍN

A Juan Sordo Madaleno, ground floor plan of the San Ignacio de Loyola Church, Mexico City, 1961.

Architects seldom have an opportunity to design and build temples—constructions that are likely to survive for several generations—since religious communities tend to preserve the spaces of sacred significance to them, maintaining them as places of gathering for a communal understanding of the destiny of human existence. Temples express the theological, liturgical, religious, and moral concepts of a people, beliefs inspired by sacred books, and norms that govern worshippers materially and spiritually. Religious architecture constructed in Mexico during the twentieth century and up to the present day displays some noteworthy examples of churches designed for the practice of the Roman rite. Throughout the world, there are various Catholicisms and accompanying rites; in Mexico, it is the Catholic Apostolic church that is the most common.

During the 1930s and 1940s, after the end of the "Cristero War" between the Mexican state and the Catholic Apostolic Church (other churches did not actively take part in these religious conflicts, though they were also affected by the strict application of the Constitution) the engineers and architects who designed churches began to experiment with new solutions. Innovative silhouettes and interior spaces thus started to appear with the incorporation of hyperbolic arches, unconcealed construction systems including reinforced concrete and ceramic brick began to be employed, and there was a general abandonment of the traditional Latin cross and basilica plans that had been used for at least four centuries. Nevertheless, it was during the 1950s that architectural innovation became most evident, above all because of the use of thin-shell reinforced concrete roofs and spatial experimentation with circular, triangular, rhomboid, and fan-shaped plans; still, the Latin cross was not necessarily abandoned altogether (A). By mid-century, church architecture displayed a broad range of morphological expressions, such as those which displayed and emphasized the structure employed, which favored flat roofs on supporting walls, or those which continued to explore the possibilities of vaults and domes with new developments and sections.

In this context, the places of worship designed by Juan Sordo Madaleno from the 1950s onwards opted for a path of synthesis between the traditional and the modern, introducing innovative spatial explorations without abandoning traditional plans and materials. Qualitatively, what was sought was an effective handling of natural light, powerful chromatic effects using stained glass, and an extreme iconic simplicity recommended by the Vatican II Council (1959–1965) both in hospital or domestic chapels and in parish churches located within the metropolitan area, which now informed the identity of their flock.

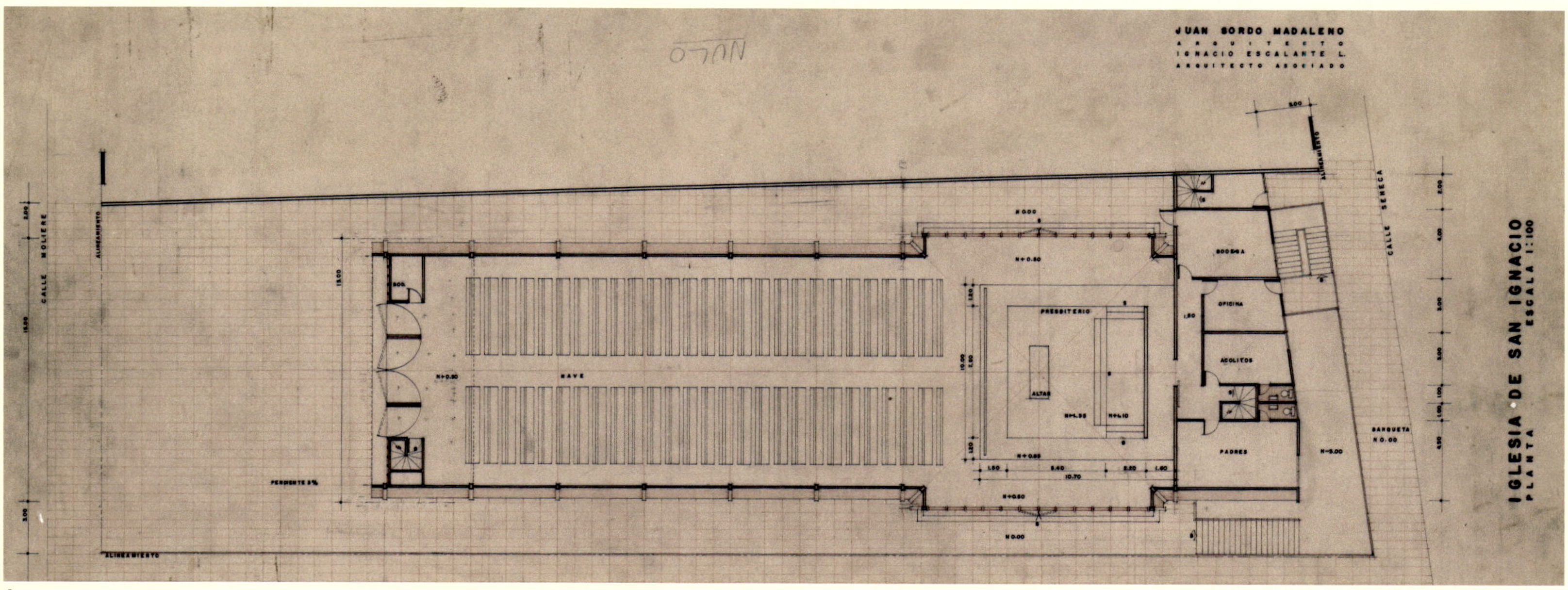

A

B Luis Barragán, interior and ground floor
C plan of the chapel of the Capuchinas Sacramentarias del Purísimo Corazón de María, Tlalpan, 1952–1955.

B

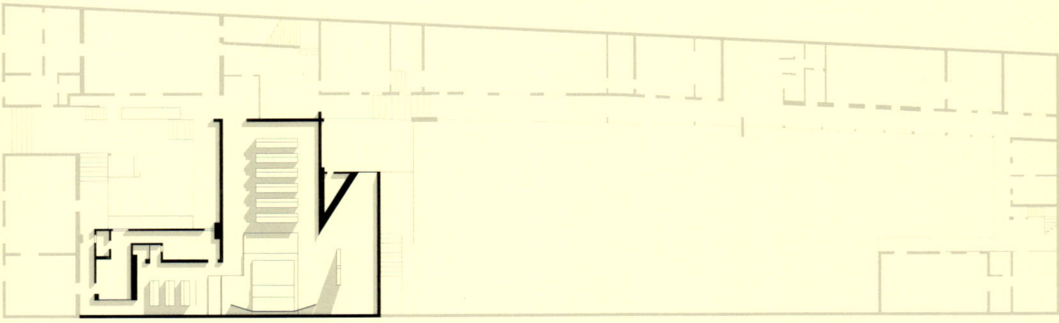

C

Sanatorio of the Sociedad de Beneficencia Española Chapel, 1955

Mexico City

This hospital chapel forms part of a larger architectural complex, today's Hospital Español. Founded in 1942, this institution's facilities grew gradually as needs required and as available resources allowed additions like the tuberculosis and infectious disease wards (1953–1956) and the hospital chapel (1955), for which Juan Sordo Madaleno was commissioned. The tradition of including chapels in hospitals dates back several centuries—the intimation of death and the hope of recovering health are recurrent circumstances of human life, in this case under the care of the Catholic Apostolic faith predominant in Mexico.

Immersed amidst the gardens and wards, the small, simple space of the hospital oratory was built thanks to various donations, as indicated on a plaque by the entrance: "Private oratory chapel, constructed entirely with funds raised by the Ladies' Committee and the donations of other benefactors, opened in an inaugural ceremony chaired by Don Pablo Diez on 8 December 1955. Project by architect Juan Sordo Madaleno."

Opposite the chapel, an atrium is suggested by a small plaza overlooked by the striking facade—two solid walls of exposed brick, a material used for several of the surrounding wards, flank a monumental cross, an element used both in Catholic Apostolic churches and by many Protestant denominations. Slightly recessed, it announces the building's Christian affiliation. This facade was modified in 2000, when the beautiful wooden lattice screen immediately behind the cross was removed and replaced with a figurative stained-glass window for the choir loft. Compositionally speaking, the original solution created an attractive contrast it now lacks between the textures and colors of the materials, but the new windows add a beautiful chromatic effect, a tradition in church architecture. 314

The plan used was a very traditional one of a single rectangular nave without intermediate supports with the altar at the east end. There was another lattice on the side that was also removed to insert an additional figurative stained-glass window. In the meantime, a small underchoir separated by a wooden screen served as a vestibule for the church's two entrances—the main one from the small plaza, opened only for the daily religious services, and the subsidiary entrance, always open to offer hope and consolation to the faithful day and night, as the thin line between human life and death can be broken at any moment.

This is a great work on a small scale that requires no technological wizardry or innovative ground plans, since a simple facade and a cubic volume of bare brick are enough to integrate it completely within the hospital complex. In fact, this fondness for traditional cubic forms is also found in the work of other great mid-century architects, like Luis Barragán in the chapel of the Capuchin Sacramentarian convent of El Purísimo Corazón de María (1952–1955) (B, C), or Ludwig Mies van der Rohe in the university chapel of St. Savior (1956), built on the campus of the Illinois Institute of Technology (IIT) in Chicago (D, E).

Chapel Mausoleum in La Herradura Ranch, 1956 318

State of Mexico

This private chapel is located at the end of a property in the woodlands to the west of the Mexican capital. The land had formed part of a large ranch given in 1931 by General Pascual Ortiz Rubio to General Manuel Ávila Camacho. The main house, the work of the architect Manuel Giraud Esteva, was built in 1946 for Don Manuel and his wife, Soledad Orozco

D Mies van der Rohe, St. Savoir University
E Chapel, IIT Chicago, 1956.

D

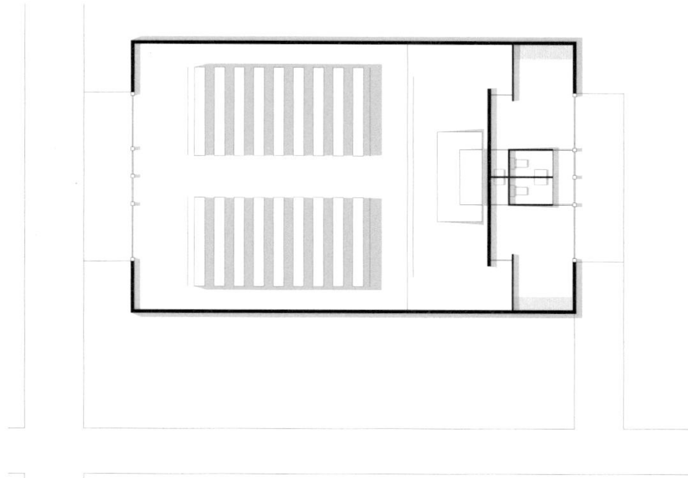

E

García, who planned to make it their residence after the end of the general's administration as President of the Republic (1940–1946), a period when the political regime in Mexico was still based on the predominant strength of an official party.

Juan Sordo Madaleno designed the chapel in collaboration with the architects Raúl Henríquez and Agustín Caso Bercht in 1956, three years after the death of the former president. It was to be a mausoleum holding his remains and a chapel for saying private masses, as his widow, a very religious woman, was always drawn to a discreet and spiritual life. The small
322 chapel has two entrances, one in the side for those walking from the nearby house, and another main entrance in the front with a vestibule to receive outside guests, who have separate access from the street. It thus functions as a chapel for both private and semi-public use.

The volumetric scheme is a parallelepiped intersecting transversally with a second to form the traditional Latin cross, whose crossing receives indirect light that illuminates the presbytery. In front of the vestibule, the facade incorporates an exact replica of the Plateresque facade of the church of the convent of San Agustín (1539) in Acolman, a small town near Teotihuacán, while a gilt Baroque altarpiece was set up against the end wall on the interior, thereby allowing the measured white forms of the chapel to set off the viceregal art forms of the private mausoleum (F). The remains of the former president were kept there until 1989, when the estate was donated to the federal government at the decision of the widow—the couple had no children. After her death in 1996, the remains of both were transferred to the Panteón Francés in Mexico City, while the large estate was used to accommodate distinguished foreign visitors.

The project for this small private work was a considerable challenge for the architect, since this was to be a family chapel aligned with the conservative forms of the residence, yet with its own formal autonomy owing to its integration in the landscape as a rural hermitage. It was a synthesis between the simplicity of the evangelizing monasteries and the luxury of Baroque altarpieces. Here, the architect had to renounce sophisticated technological solutions and innovative forms in the interests of harmony with the pre-existing surroundings. This meant an authorial restraint and discretion to which few architects would be willing to submit.

San Ignacio de Loyola Church, 1961

Mexico City

This church was designed by Juan Sordo Madaleno for the Jesuit order in collaboration with the architects José A. Wiechers and Ignacio Escalante. It was to be consecrated to the advocation of the saint who founded the Society of Jesus, a congregation with a long educational tradition in the country. The plot where it was built was on the outer edge of a block bounded by three avenues in Colonia Polanco, a site that enhanced its urban dominance when the neighboring buildings were not as high as they are today. A single rectangular nave was laid out longitudinally on the narrow plot with a small vestibule at the end, a transitional space between the secular and the sacred, which was originally open to the public space of the street, but later closed on one side to protect the parishioners from the traffic (many churches have had to transform their vestibules owing to the increase of motor traffic in recent decades). At the opposite end, a small volume with a separate entrance houses the sacristy, the office, and other facilities, while the parochial residence, located between the church and the southern boundary, is reached from the street behind it.

Unlike in his previous commissions for religious buildings, the architect was able on this occasion to release his creativity with a powerful volumetric design since the goal was precisely to contribute an attractive and innovative morphology that would serve as an urban referent. The prismatic volumetrics were the result of using a pitched metal roof rising from ground level, a solution that eliminated the perimeter supporting walls traditionally used in churches. This omission of vertical walls constituted an emphatically modern feature. Although it had already been used in other churches with hyperbolic vaults, it was achieved here with a metal structure that imparts a sensation of spatial ascent in the interior, very much like the Gothic churches of the Middle Ages. Girders and frames were mounted under the roof for fitting with prefabricated concrete panels coated on the exterior with hand-crafted ceramics, a stroke of popular nationalism that anticipated the typical regionalist attempts of the 1960s to achieve a harmonious synthesis between the regional and the modern.

The prismatic roof was raised on the plan of a single rectangular nave, but because its volumetrics resulted from the intersection of two gables, the resulting interior space was perceived as a Latin cross plan, with the presbytery occupying the virtual crossing. The points of entry of natural light played a strategic role in the spatial quality, since brightness entered only through two zones: the reddish stained-glass window beneath the tympanum, with its energetic abstract design, and the pair of triangular stained-glass windows flanking the presbytery. The result is a dramatic contrast with the semi-darkness of the nave, a strategy that once more recalls the interplay of luminosity in medieval churches. During the day, the natural light thrusts its way into the interior, while by night, artificial light radiates towards the exterior like a great beacon of faith for the surrounding urban environment.

This church was designed before the conclusion of the Vatican II Council—when liturgical ceremonies were held with the priest facing the altar and with his back to the congregation. Hence, against the end wall, a small cross was placed over a slightly raised altar. For the same reason, the ritual act took place at the far end of the nave with no attempt to bring it closer to the assembly. As the years went by, the altar was slightly modified to adapt it to post-Council practices. A second piece of furnishing was added in front so that the officiant could face the congregation while saying mass flanked by a lectern and an image of the Virgin of Guadalupe. The original cross was also replaced by a large bronze sculpture of

F

F Juan Sordo Madaleno, Chapel Mausoleum in La Herradura Ranch, Huixquilucan, 1956.

Christ on the cross, a piece with expressionist forms by Claudio Favier Orendáin—an architect and artist from Guadalajara with a solid career in the design of religious imagery. The result was a modern church tied to liturgical tradition, with simple geometrical forms and powerful strategies of luminosity, as part of the search common in the 1960s for an effective synthesis of the regional and the international.

Santa Elena Chapel, 1974 328

Texas, United States

This private chapel was built on a ranch in Texas then owned by Robert and Helen Kleberg, close friends of Juan Sordo Madaleno, whose descendants retain the family property today. The project was commissioned in 1963 in memory of Helen Campbell Kleberg, who died that year; although its construction was delayed for some years. A small building, it exhibits architectural solutions unusual in church design in those years. Asymmetry, so infrequent in religious architecture, appeared here in the massive walls—originally painted bright orange—that form large planes enclosing the exterior and interior spaces. The asymmetrical design is carried throughout, as well as in the position of the sacristy at the foot of the chapel, and in the arrangement of benches at one end of the nave to allow a processional route to the monumental cross.

An extraordinary solution was also proposed for the interior. Instead of an end wall closing off the building behind the altar, there is a large window framing the surrounding landscape that bathes the interior in light and exhibits the splendor of nature as a metaphor of divine creation. A similar expedient is found in other contemporary works like the parish church of Santa María Reina (1970) by the architects Jaime Herrasti Donde and Eduardo Jiménez Galindo in the Unidad Habitacional San Jerónimo to the south of the Mexican capital. This innovative building explored new planning strategies in Catholic religious architecture, while the robust traditional walls evoke the old missions and forts of northern New Spain.

332 **San Josemaría Escrivá de Balaguer Parish, 2009**
Mexico City
The church was built in the west of the city where it forms part of a dispersed urban context in constant transformation. It is consecrated to the advocation of Josemaría Escrivá de Balaguer, the Spanish priest who founded the Opus Dei congregation, who was beatified in 1992 and canonized in 2002, a few years before the construction of this parish church. This great religious building in the thriving commercial and residential area of Santa Fe was designed by the architect Javier Sordo Madaleno and was planned and constructed thirty years after the religious works designed by his father. Its concepts, spaces, technologies, and morphologies therefore respond to very different historical and urban contexts.

The parish church presents a sculptural volume built on several levels containing the chapel, the crypts, and the other complementary services; although these are camouflaged by slopes of stone and vegetation so that the facade seems to emerge out of the terrain. It stands on an inclined triangular plot previously used as a rubbish tip, almost like a moral allegory of spiritual renewal after a previous state of degradation. In front is an entrance plaza with parking spaces—parishioners habitually arrive by car—while the religious character is accentuated by a slender free-standing bell tower, reminiscent of a Renaissance *campanile*, and a monumental cross located at the opposite end. These features reinforce the urban dominance of this innovative work which made the most of the isolation of the terrain since there was nothing pre-existing on neighboring plots to inform the formal proposal.

For the volumetric scheme, a very simple configuration was adopted. Two large curved and inclined walls—made with a steel structure lined on the exterior with zinc sheets and on the interior with wood—approach each other to frame the ritual space. This marked directionality evokes the longitudinal solution of his father's design for the church of San Ignacio de Loyola in Polanco; although here it is in consonance with the architectural contemporaneity of the start of a new millennium. Overhead, a continuous skylight illuminates the interior dramatically, forming a zenithal cleft that shapes the main entrance in its descent. At the far end, the presbytery and altar are oriented towards the northeast. Crowning the altar is a graceful and monumental image of Christ on the cross, the upright of which constitutes the only vertical element serving as a stabilizing spatial referent, and on either side are images of the Spanish saint and of the Virgin of Guadalupe. All this is inside a longitudinal space in the form of a fish, a figure with Christological connotations that contrasts with the traditional floor plans of Catholic Apostolic churches. The success of this work has led to an increase in the number of visitors on days of observance making it necessary to enlarge the lateral areas and so expand the capacity of the longitudinal nave.

Final considerations
Over several decades, Juan and Javier Sordo Madaleno developed a solid architectural practice as designers of religious buildings for the Catholic Apostolic faith professed by both. This was begun by the father with two chapels in the 1950s, when he was forced to adhere to a previously established architectural context—a hospital complex and a large residence—to achieve a simple and austere result with few elements. He then moved on in the 1960s to a Jesuit parish church in Polanco, where he explored a synthesis between regionalism and modern technology, creating a landmark within its residential environment. In the 1970s, finally, he designed a private chapel on a ranch in Texas, where he experimented with asymmetry in both plan and elevation as well as a new relationship with the natural surroundings.

At the start of the new century, church design was resumed by his son, Javier, with the parish church of San Josemaría Escrivá, where he succeeded in freeing himself from the orthogonal tradition of ecclesiastical architecture, opting for new spatialities and a dramatic use of natural light, all without ceasing to comply with the liturgical norms of the Roman Catholic Apostolic rite. Its powerful morphology and strategic siting managed to attract and strengthen the faith of contemporary Catholic worshippers in an increasingly multireligious social context, where religious institutions must find a renewed spirituality that offers answers to old questions in the same way as the architect achieved monumental creativity at the start of a new millennium.

1955 SANATORIO DE LA SOCIEDAD DE LA BENEFICENCIA ESPAÑOLA CHAPEL

Interior view of the nave looking towards the entrance with view of the upper cloistered choir, with wooder latticework.

Interior view of the altar. Detail of illumination of wooden window.

1956
CHAPEL MAUSOLEUM IN LA HERRADURA RANCH

View of the side facade.

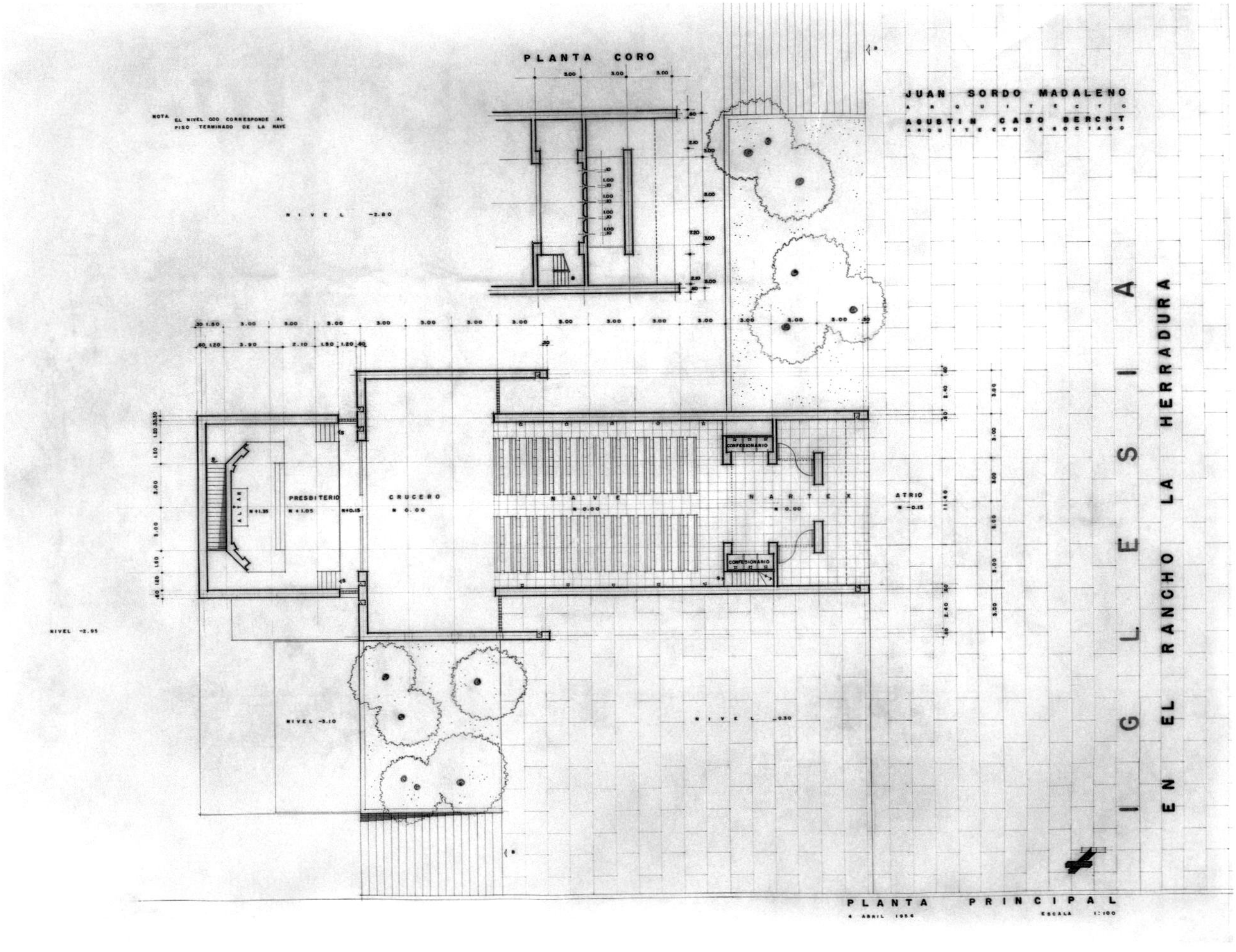

Above: interior view towards altar. Below: floor plan.

1961
SAN IGNACIO DE LOYOLA CHURCH

OREX
11-16-75

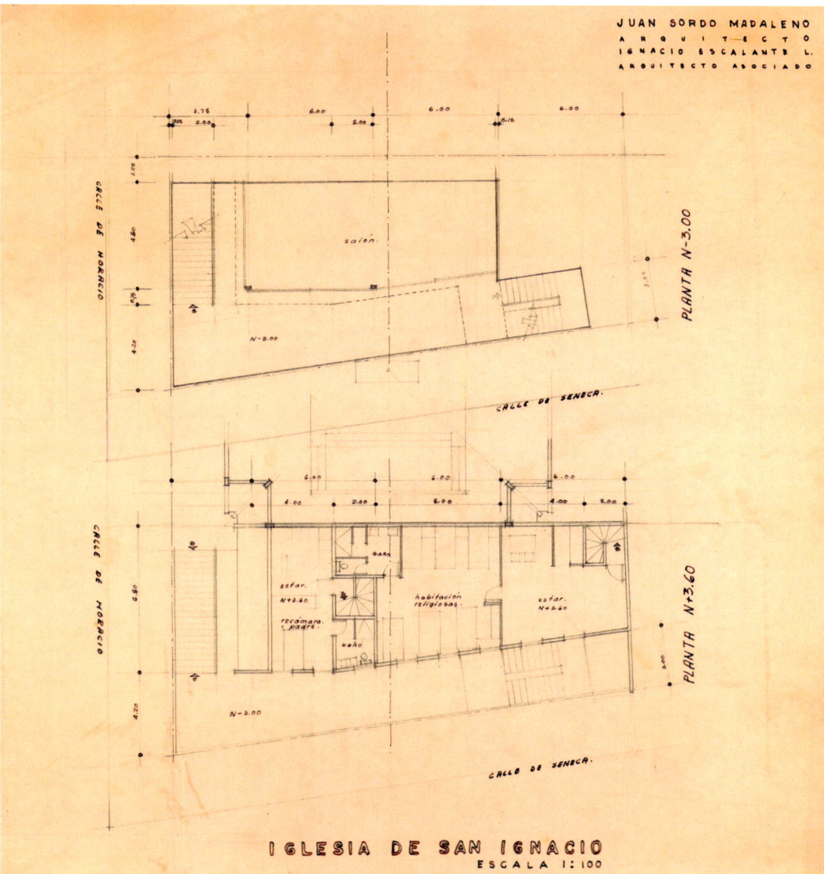

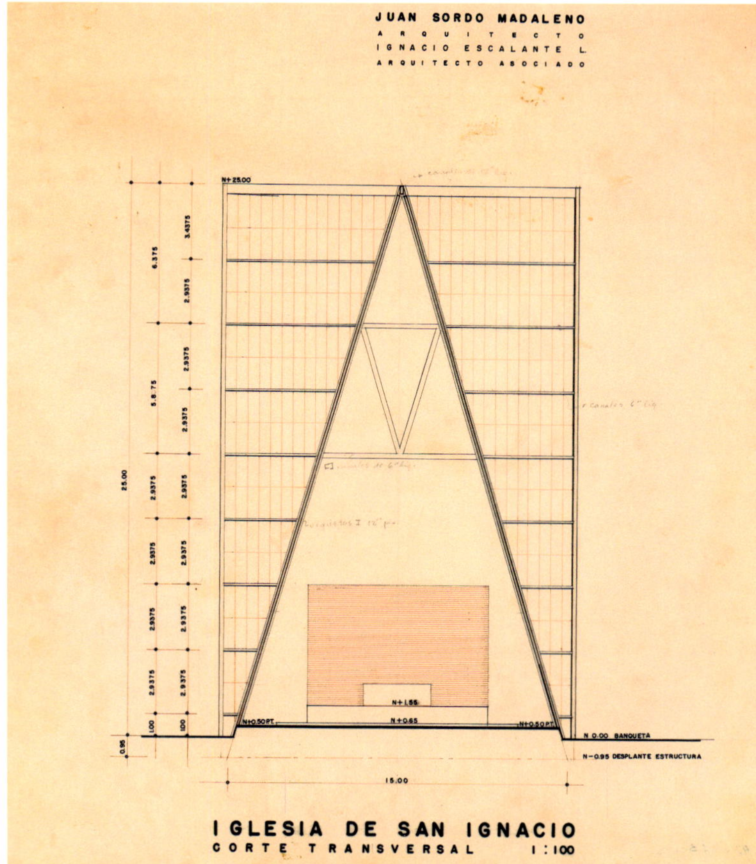

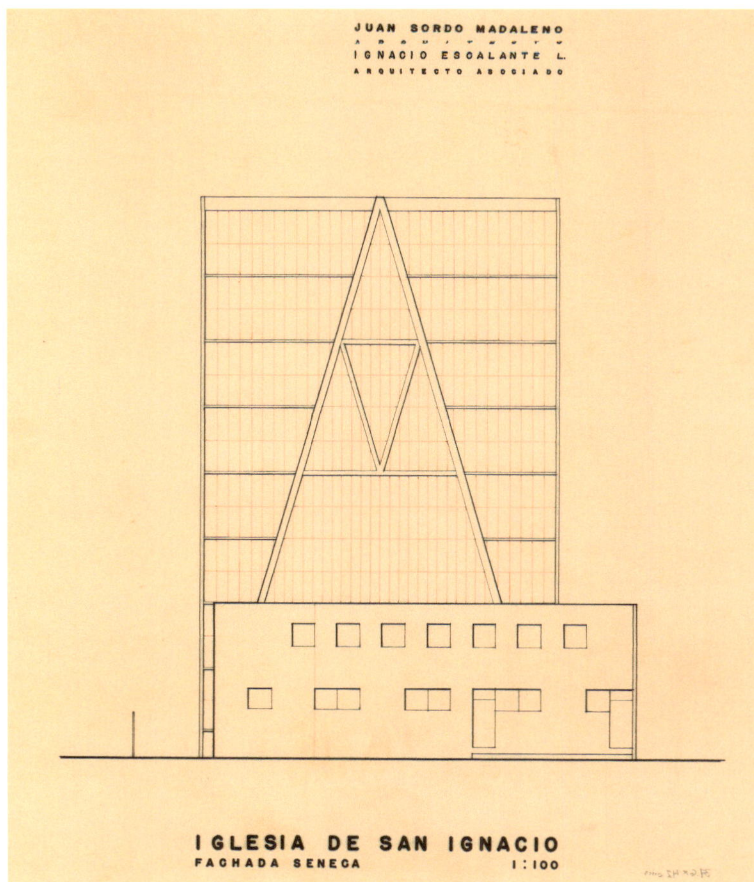

Left hand page: construction photograph, detail of the metallic structure and prefabricated panels.

Right hand page: ground plan of the rectory, facade and cross-section of the church.

Left hand page: view of the roof structure over the altar area.

Above: view of the nave.

Below: interior view with detail of stained glass window.

1974
SANTA ELENA CHAPEL

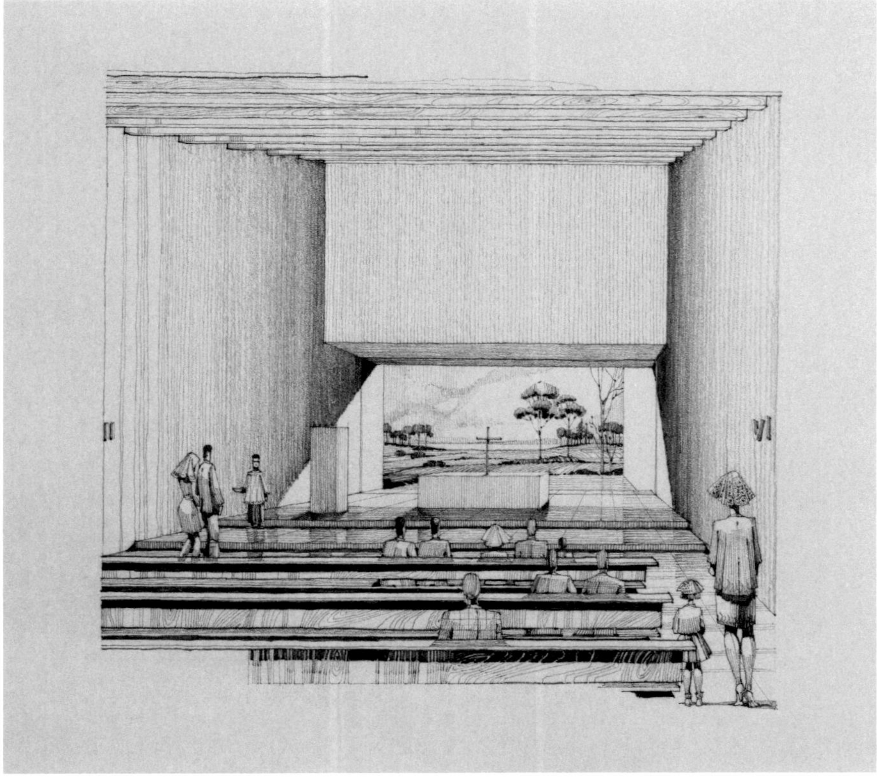

Perspective renderings of the interior (left) and exterior (right).

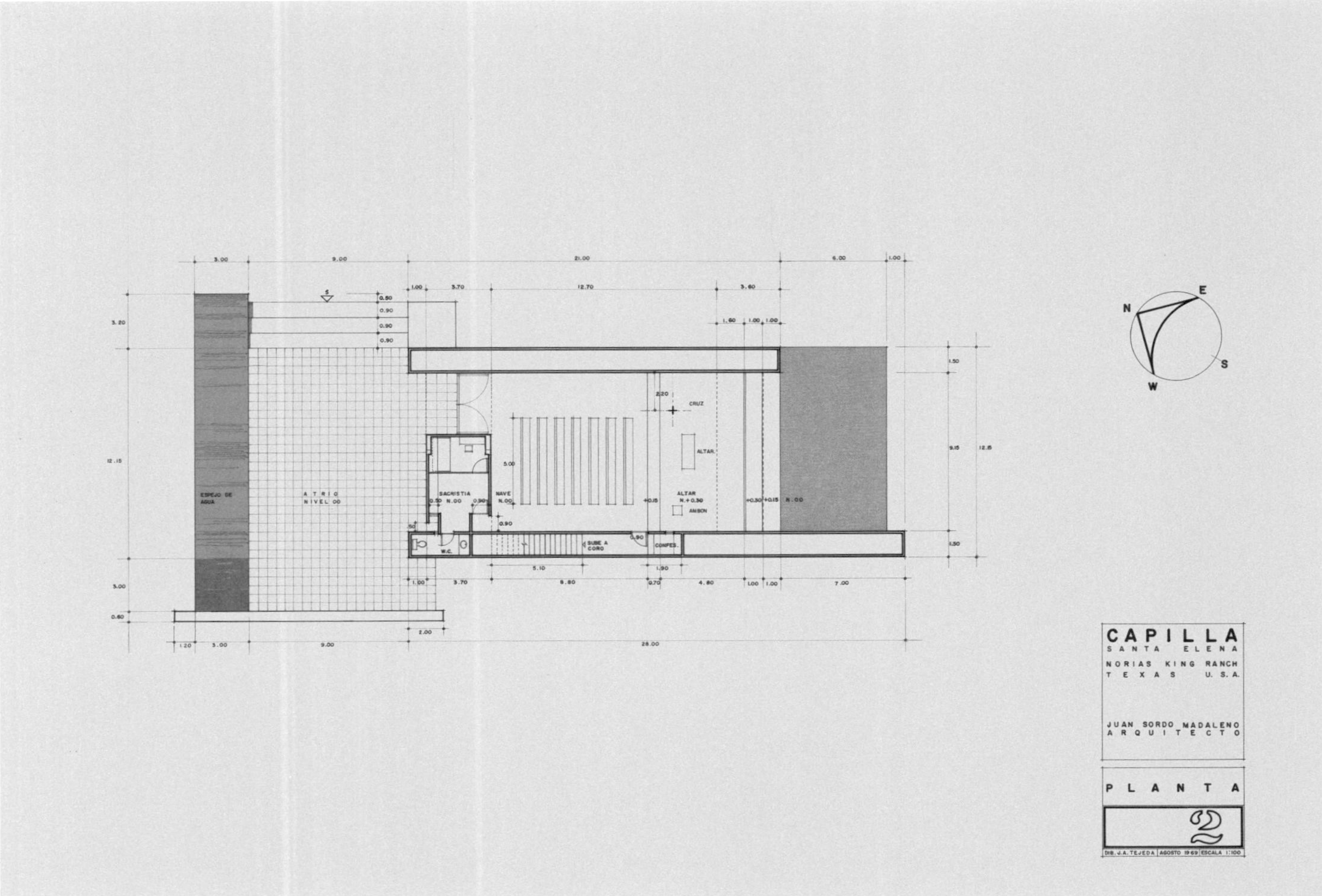
CAPILLA
SANTA ELENA
NORIAS KING RANCH
TEXAS U.S.A.
JUAN SORDO MADALENO
ARQUITECTO
PLANTA
2
DIB. J.A. TEJEDA | AGOSTO 1969 | ESCALA 1:100

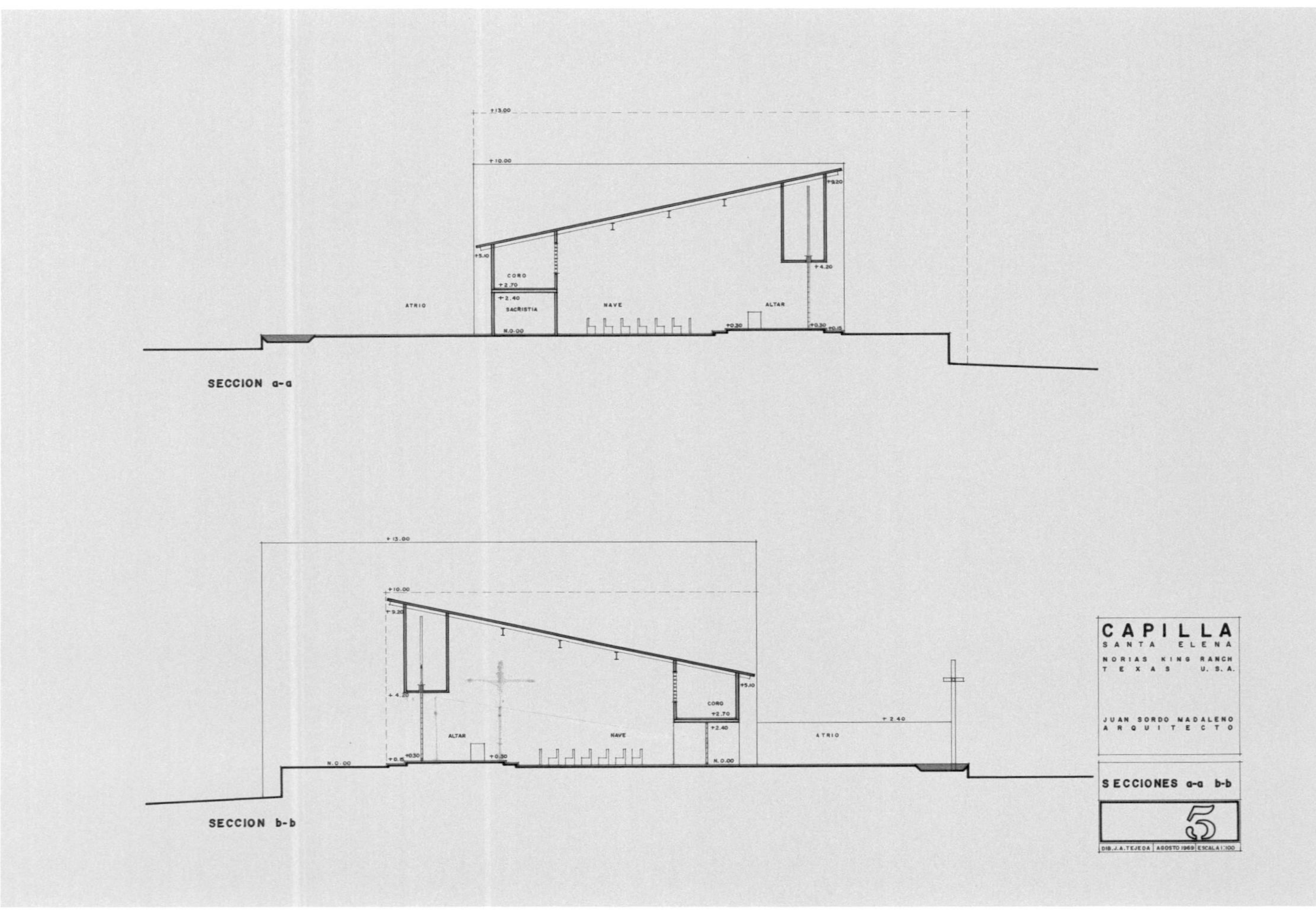
SECCION a-a
SECCION b-b
CAPILLA
SANTA ELENA
NORIAS KING RANCH
TEXAS U.S.A.
JUAN SORDO MADALENO
ARQUITECTO
SECCIONES a-a b-b
5
DIB. J.A. TEJEDA | AGOSTO 1969 | ESCALA 1:100

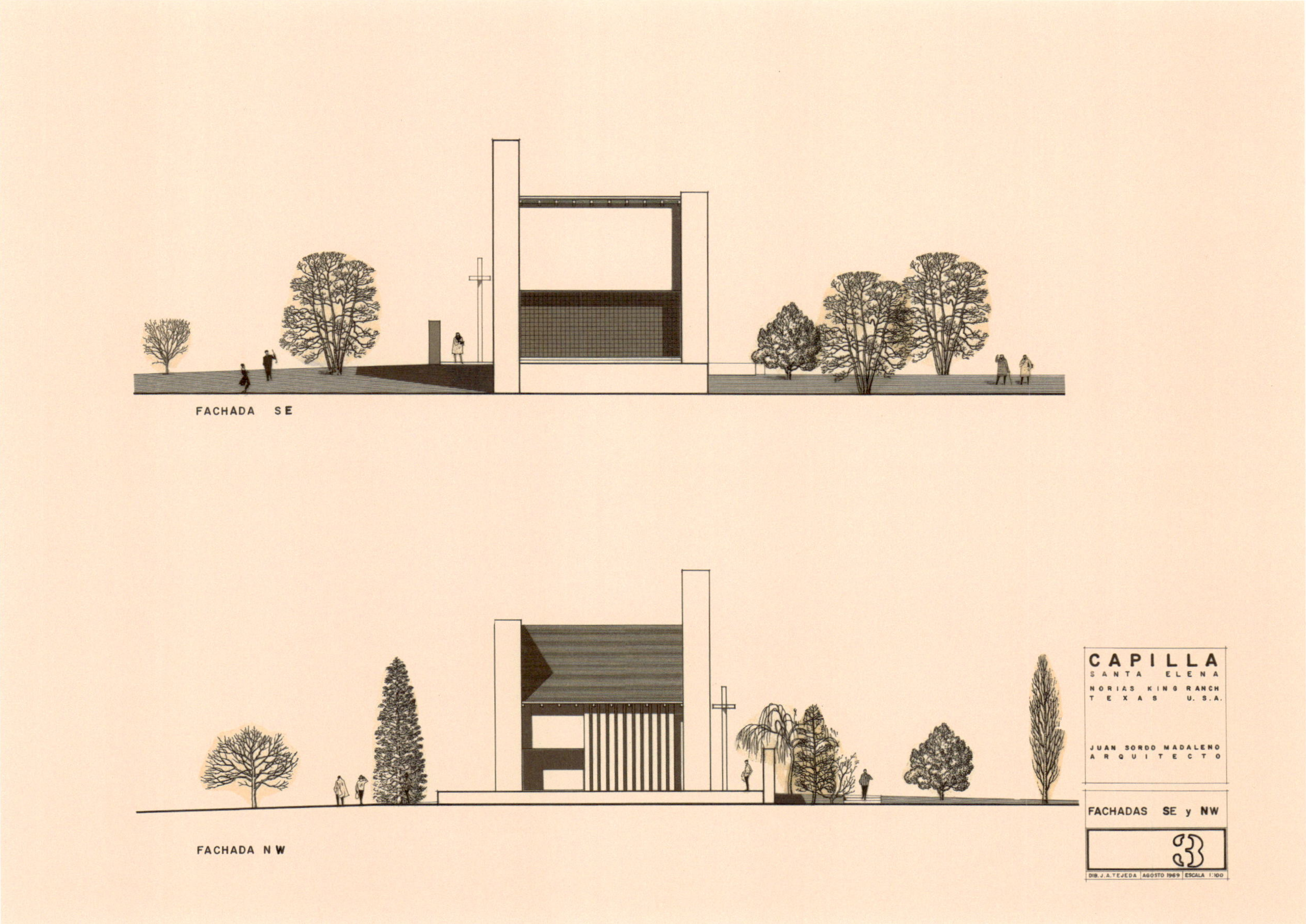

Left hand page, above: plan.
Below: sections.

Right hand page: facades.

2009
SAN JOSEMARÍA ESCRIVÁ DE BALAGUER PARISH

Left hand page: night view of main entrance.

Above: side facade.

Below: detail of the facade surface, covered with zinc panels.

Interior view towards the altar.

Above: view of the entrance.

Below: interior view of the crypt.

6.

SPACES FOR OFFICES AND THOUGHTS

JOSE CASTILLO

A *Mexican Modernisms* exhibition, Brussels, Belgium, 2010.

The personal and the architectural

My connection to the architecture of the Sordo Madaleno prac-
tice is at once personal and long-standing: my parents were
married, and I was baptized, in Juan Sordo Madaleno's iconic
322 San Ignacio de Loyola Church in Polanco. In turn we baptized
my daughters in the church and held memorial services there
for my grandmother and my father. I have memories of shop-
190 ping with my mother at Plaza Satélite, and of a vacation at
230 Javier Sordo Madaleno's Westin Regina Los Cabos Hotel. Years
later, Javier Sordo Madaleno de Haro was my student at the
Iberoamericana University. But probably the architectural work
that has been the most engaging for me both personally and
348 professionally is 555 Palmas (B), an office building that in
my youth seemed as bizarre in its architecture as it was rele-
vant to the "*pre-temblado*" times of my student years housing
Tofanetti, a popular pizza place, and Vips, a hangout offering
no-frills breakfasts that was beloved by high school and col-
lege students.

Sometimes the personal connects with the professional and the intellectual. In 2010 I co-curated the exhibition *Mexican Modernisms* (A) in Brussels. There, alongside works by Ricardo Legorreta, Agustín Hernández, and others, we showcased 555 Palmas, probably the first international exhibition to do so. A few months later we choose that remarkable building for our architectural office since we had outgrown a tiny apartment space in Colonia del Valle. As our office has grown, we have expanded three times, now occupying two floors; the building has become something of an active partner, a laboratory for our own investigations on the nature of our work. It has further nourished for me a renewed interest in the oeuvre of Juan Sordo Madaleno, his role in the evolution of modern architecture in Mexico, and the ways that work has shaped the recent architectural production at Sordo Madaleno Arquitectos (SMA). Subsequently, 555 Palmas appeared in other international exhibitions. In 2015, the Museum of Modern Art in New York (MoMA, NYC) included it in the exhibition *Latin America in Construction: Architecture 1955–1980* curated by Barry Bergdoll, Carlos Eduardo Comas, Jorge Francisco Liernur and Patricio del Real. Featured amongst the original material exhibited were original and historical photographs by Guillermo Zamora, donated by SMA to the museum.

A

The architect vs. the architecture

Juan Sordo Madaleno is one of the most elusive architects of twentieth-century Mexico, even though he is also one of the most prolific, recognized, and published. Writers on his work have often had resort to adjectives such as "precise, discreet, elegant, harmonious, well-proportioned, detailed."[1] However these descriptors fail to explain why his production is so relevant to the history of Mexican modern architecture; the aim of this essay is to offer a personal interpretation of the work.

Sordo Madaleno has always been considered a pragmatist and the little evidence we have of his ideas, methodology and theories give only limited clues about what really interested him.[2] Perhaps the aphorism of the acerbic Viennese critic Karl Kraus, "If anyone has something to say, let him come forward and be silent!" captures it. Sordo Madaleno preferred to let his buildings speak for themselves. Silence should not be mistaken for lack of depth or ideas. Rather, his work on office

1. It has been Juan Manuel Heredia who has written the most comprehensive account of Sordo Madaleno's work and gone beyond the adjectives to analyze how proportions and an understanding of spatial relationships was at the core of his work.
2. In the short interview he gave to *Arquitectura México* in 1968 among many other renowned architects, he avoids answering two of the questions and rather develops a short essay on the role of technique in Mexican architecture.

buildings represents a radical departure in form and in the evolution of this key building type in the modern city. His architecture is not about compositional elegance alone, but about the subversion of architectural elements to produce new typologies in the urban landscape somewhere between the language of canonical modern architecture and a local tradition of monumentality. This innovative and unconventional transformation of an existing architectural language is what constitutes the radicality in Sordo Madaleno's oeuvre.

It is no less interesting to note that Juan Sordo Madaleno's work established the basis for the professionalization of the architectural office that is now SMA. The ongoing work in that office continues to develop key issues already at play in the work of the firm's founder.

The lobby, the stair, and the facade

For Juan Sordo Madaleno the office interior was never simply a matter of systems, efficiencies, and standardization; it was also a place of material speculation and of defining new forms of work and leisure as well as for crafting new relationships between the office building, its users, and the city.[3] The lobbies of his office buildings and the integrated cinemas were exercises in material complexity. In these spaces he developed a rich and seemingly contradictory materiality: concrete, tropical woods, volcanic rocks, stucco, and glass as well as custom modern furniture. A dialogue is set up between the public nature of the street and the private interior space. The motor lobby at the Mariano Escobedo building, the double-height spaces at DM Nacional in Paseo de la Reforma, and the Reforma and Morelos project all attest to an interest in engaging building and city—both the building's occupants and the passersby—in an interactive fashion. There is a lusciousness to these spaces, almost as if they want paradoxically to extend out toward the city and offer a respite from it.

Similarly, stairs play a role in creating surprising effects of scale, of spatial fluidity and rigor. In the Dirección de Policía y Tránsito of 1956, five almost imperceptible steps provide both access and a sense of scale to the vestibule with its luminous ceiling. In the Palacio de Justicia two diagonal volumes with solid parapets distort the apparent classic patio scheme. Three bridges connect the towers at different points transforming the scale of the space in-between. In the María Isabel Hotel of 1961, designed with José Villagrán and José A. Wiechers, and the Ford Corporate building of 1963, with José Villagrán, Ricardo Legorreta and José A. Wiechers, there is already an initial version of the gently sloped stairs that Legorreta would later develop brilliantly in the Camino Real Hotel.

In his handling of the curtain wall and the facade—somehow imprecise terms, since they fall short of describing the design operation—Sordo Madaleno's work evolves most profoundly and reveals a major transformation in his architectural language. Although often categorized as an "International Style" architect, Sordo Madaleno seems to have been less concerned with the fetishistic qualities of glass—thinness, transparency, or reflectivity—and more with material and formal complexities and the construction of depth. Volumetric abstraction was always more of a result than an initial premise in his work.

In the building at Reforma and Morelos of 1946, the north-facing facade acknowledges the slab of each floor. The sophistication here comes in the tripartite arrangement of glazing including the middle section that provides natural ventilation. In 543 Mariano Escobedo, alternating balconies produce a perception of "overweight" elements that are in tension with the thin glazing. The facades of Reforma and Versalles (1954), 98
Reforma and Lieja (1956), and Anáhuac Tower (1958), now 346, 100
called Torre Contigo, are likewise exercises on the articulation and scale of mid-rise buildings through careful proportions in the parapet and the horizontal ribbon window.

In the 1960s more complex material relationships begin to appear. In Ford Corporate and in the María Isabel Hotel (1961), marble and glass work together, alternating as horizontal and vertical elements. This material combination is 344
used again in the Palacio de Justicia (1964) where dark glass 106
volumes are "caged" in institutional white marble.[4] Also inno- 90
vative is the way that the glass—designed as smaller horizontal pieces—is placed in a slanted fashion achieving a quality closer to shingles.

It seems that for Sordo Madaleno the notion of "free design of the facade" and the "horizontal window"—two of the tenets of Le Corbusier's five points of architecture—are trans- 48
formed into a new language where the wall ceases to be a
wall and the facade as a concept is neither "composed" in the 64

3. It is no surprise that some of his tenants included the designer Clara
Porset, the artist Abel Quezada, and later on architect and furniture 58
designer Oscar Hagerman with LOGADO at Palmas 555.
4. This particular aesthetic is somehow related to Oscar Niemeyer's work in Brasília but anticipates Francisco Artigas's CAPFCE building of 1965-1970, which has a similar architectural scheme.

B 555 Palmas, exterior view of the entrance plaza and the terraced commercial volume.

B

classical sense nor treated only as elegant glazing in a Miesian tradition. Rather elements, such as the slab, the parapet, the beam, the lintel, and the window, are transformed to produce a new architectural language. A similar attitude that appears in the later work is the idea of "weight" in the building, the strategy of placing the thick and heavy elements on top of lighter ones—a theme that would appear in many buildings
52 such as the Merck, Sharp & Dohme laboratories and offices
226 and the Presidente Cozumel Hotel. I believe these buildings are the genesis of the office projects from the 1970s and would also inform a new direction in Mexican architecture in the 1970s and '80s that is concerned with weight, scale, volumetric presence, and monumentality.

The radical, the monumental, and the iconic

Two projects of the 1970s are emblematic of the morphological transformations of the office building type in both plan and section. They also serve as a hinge between the early works of Juan Sordo Madaleno and the work of Sordo Madaleno Arquitectos of the 1980s.

352 In the Centro Operativo Bancomer, an office building for nine thousand employees, developed in partnership with Augusto H. Álvarez and José Adolfo Wiechers, the plan achieves one of the most complex and radical forms of office space—a singular building comprised of interlocked open courtyards and built floor plates. After decades in which both worked to evolve the office tower type, Sordo Madaleno and Álvarez made a profound change in direction; rather than design a single tall skyscraper, they divided the program into nearly fifty small buildings of five floors each connected at the corners and alternating in a checkerboard of courtyards.[5] The complex, yet systemic approach to the building is indebted to the idea of mat-building,[6] where a low-rise but high-density structure organized as a modulated grid with little interest in the facade, resolves programmatic connections, natural light, monumental tectonics, and the corporate organization of this large financial institution. It is not an exaggeration to state that this building is a utopian attempt at organizing modern work.[7]

The most interesting office building by Sordo Madaleno is without doubt 555 Palmas; it is probably also his most iconic. Designed in collaboration with José Adolfo Wiechers and José Ignacio de Abiega and finished in 1975, it is a sophisticated urban building that acknowledges site and type in unexpected ways. Occupying the full front of a block along a major avenue, the building negotiates the slope of the street with

5. Probably due to organizational challenges, decades later BBVA would decide to consolidate again in a skyscraper in Reforma, designed by Legorreta Arquitectos and Richard Rogers. It comes as an irony that the corporation moved from a Sordo Madaleno building to the site where a former building by Sordo Madaleno (now demolished) used to exist, at Reforma and Lieja.
6. See for example Alison Smithson, "How to Recognise and Read Mat-Building: Mainstream Architecture as it has Developed Towards the Mat-Building," *Architectural Design*, September (1974): 573–590.
7. In a strange way, one could also connect Centro Bancomer's radical checkerboard scheme to BBVA's headquarters in Madrid by Herzog & DeMeuron, where a low-rise mat building is combined with an iconic, round-shaped tower. This combination seems to address a decades-long question of the organization of workspaces in relationship to horizontal and vertical connectivity.

c Sordo Madaleno Arquitectos, Herdez Corporation, Mexico City, 1995.

c

a combination of plaza and staircase in front of a solid horizontal volume that creates a plinth. A nine-story office tower rises from this plinth and is perceived as a stack of "dislocated slabs" and overhangs in different sizes and alternating directions. These parapets both contain and hide the slab within the building's section. By using a 1.6-meter-high window, the 1:1 ratio between built parapet and the ribbon window, together with the shifts in plan, creates a combination of spatial revelations and eccentricities. The horizontal window between the extended parapets and lintels frame views of the Lomas de Chapultepec neighborhood, of the skyline, and even of the distant volcanoes of the Valley of Mexico.

What appears to be a complicated structural operation is, in fact, straightforward—a nine-meter structural grid of columns with only variations on the side towards which it cantilevers and whose shifts repeat every four floors. This operation creates a building that is perceived completely differently as one moves around it, depending upon location in the city or position within the interior. From the immediate sidewalk the windows can disappear from view—the building becomes a "jenga-like" stack of solids. From the higher ground of Lomas de Chapultepec, the ribbon windows can give a sense of lightness that reinforces horizontality. This tension between the elements and the changing modes of perceiving the building has no comparison in architecture in Mexico City; it is truly an uncanny urban building.

I speculate that these three projects from the 1970s place Sordo Madaleno's architecture as a "hinge" between the early decades of modern architecture with its imported architectural languages and the more volume-driven and monumental architectures of the '70s and '80s concerned with local ideas and aesthetics. Probably no less important is the fact that the prolific work and speculations by Sordo Madaleno expanded into more diverse building types and consolidated an architectural practice that extends into today.

SMA projects from the 1980s, such as the Centro Internacional de Prensa 356—built in record time for the 1986 Soccer World Cup and the first solo project by Javier Sordo Madaleno Bringas after Juan's death—have architectural qualities that became motifs in later projects. This building is an exercise in sections—a central atrium configured by receding floor plates, massive parapets, and a set of escalators give scale to the space. Probably as interesting is its capacity to evolve and be adapted after the World Cup into the Televisa Foundation for

D 1500 Américas, Guadalajara, Jalisco, 2016.

D

Contemporary Art—a private art collection that was fundamental to cultural life in '80s and '90s Mexico City.

SMA's work since the 1990s has expanded to include headquarters for some of the leading Mexican corporations such as Herdez (C), Cuervo, Grupo BAL, and many others, mirroring the achievements of Juan Sordo Madaleno's work of producing the workspaces of global modernity. In the 1997 project for Grupo BAL Headquarters in Polanco, a massive triangular tower makes a wink to the San Ignacio Church, just across the street, designed in 1961 by Juan Sordo Madaleno. Molière
198 Dos22 is a case of adaptation and growth, since the building grew in height in a transformation of 2015 that included the new Palacio de Palacios retail hub.

Over the past two decades SMA has increasingly focused on other types such as mixed-use developments and hotel design— all explored at length in other essays in this book. My impression is that some of these projects have reclaimed some of the design topics that arose during the 1970s, in par-
130 ticular the notions of stacking and vertical articulation. The language that began with 555 Palmas remains one of the re-
84 current themes of the office's recent work. If the early question of the heavy and the light were explored with solid volumes, these recent buildings achieve with glass volumes a playfulness with the sense of proportions and a carefulness with the design of the facade elements.

360 In the tower of Andares Corporate in Zapopan, Jalisco, there is an articulation of volumes through small horizontal gaps that appear intermittently. This slight separation gives a sense of levity because of the shadow created and also of weight due to the nature of the stacked "boxes" of differentiated heights. These concerns with stacking of program and volumes appear in other projects such as Solaz Los Ca-
242 bos hotel and the mixed-use building Américas 1500 (D), in Guadalajara.

173 In Artz Pedregal—a mixed-use complex organized around
116 an open-air shopping mall that follows the success of Antara—the horseshoe-shaped plan follows a traditional scheme of placing the office towers at the perimeter, taller on the southern and northern edges and midrise on the eastern edge. Most remarkable is the way that the towers are slanted in a subtle and elegant way and also complemented with the mullions and the facade design that reinforce the theme with thin "fin-like" extruded elements. No minor achievement is the way the corners of the towers are resolved as well as the horizontal gap that appears midway in the vertical development of the building, making this building closer to the notion of stacking than to the simple oblique geometric extrusion.

This possibility of multiple ways of perception of the built form is becoming more relevant in the recent work since the ensemble of individual buildings that are shaping Antara, Andares, and other projects are somehow connected to the early urban sensibilities that Juan Sordo Madaleno initiated around the Reforma and Colón roundabout almost seventy-five years ago—the idea that buildings in themselves are not only independent speculations on form and space, but that when placed in proximity, they produce urban affects.

The challenge of remaining relevant for an architectural office that endures over many decades requires a double task: to understand what has changed in the profession, in the city, in society and what has changed in the way we practice. Probably more important is to ask what connects us to our legacy—the "big questions" that became our ethos and the source of our prolific oeuvre.

SMA's recent work is engaging in this double dialogue—the act of becoming a third-generation studio and one of the largest, most robust, and successful offices in the country. They have managed to keep alive the spirit of both radicality and pragmatism initiated by Juan Sordo Madaleno. This is no small achievement.

1947
543 MARIANO ESCOBEDO

1956
REFORMA AND LIEJA

Perspective view and urban surroundings.

1975
555 PALMAS

phidias
LIBROS DISCOS
EXPOSICION DE DISEÑO PARA
DISTRIBUIDORES AUTORIZADOS

Left hand page: detail of the gaps between tiles and aluminum materials on the facade.

Right hand page: longitudinal section in perspective of 555 Palmas, Mexico City, 1975.

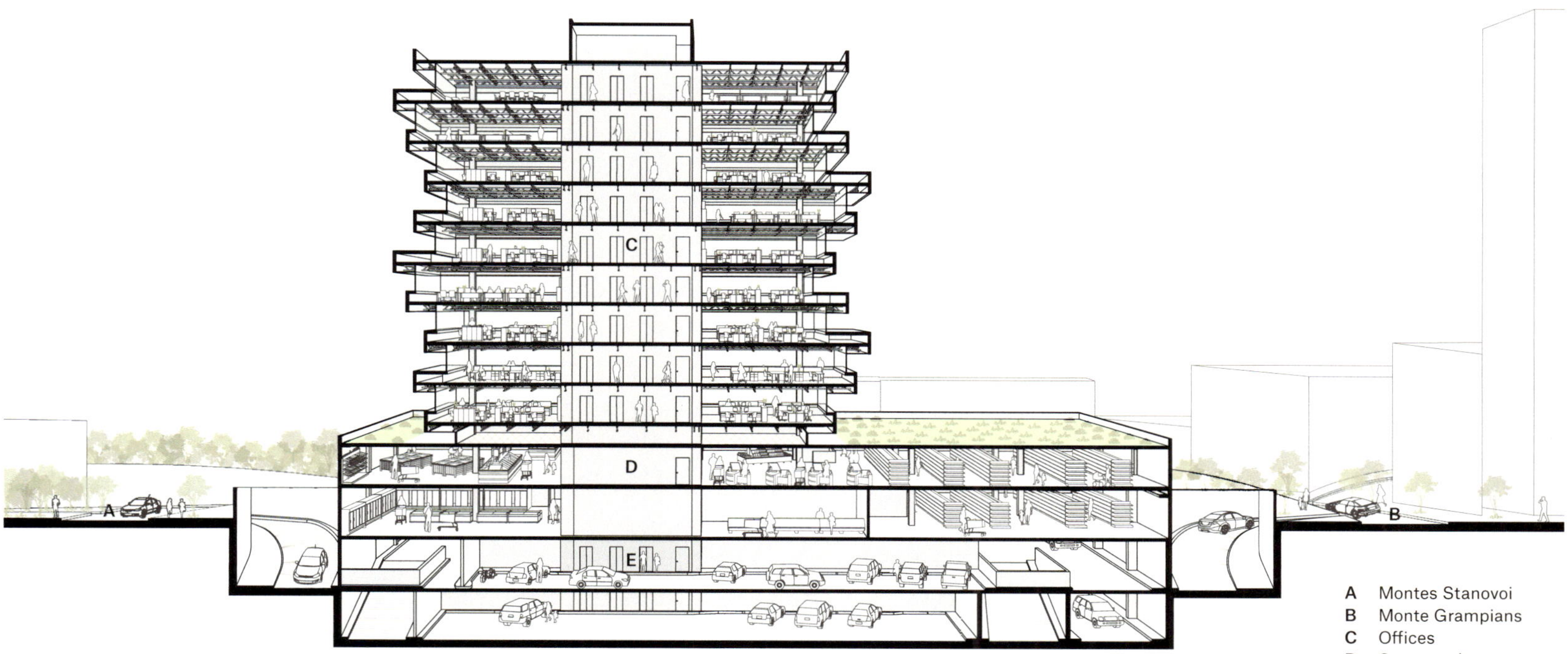

A Montes Stanovoi
B Monte Grampians
C Offices
D Supermarket
E Parking Lot

1976
CENTRO OPERATIVO BANCOMER

Aerial photograph of Coyoacán in 1980. Centro Operativo Bancomer in frame.

Left hand page: interior views of main patio with domes to capture natural lighting.

Right hand page: interior view of the module open to the facade.

1986
CENTRO INTERNACIONAL DE PRENSA

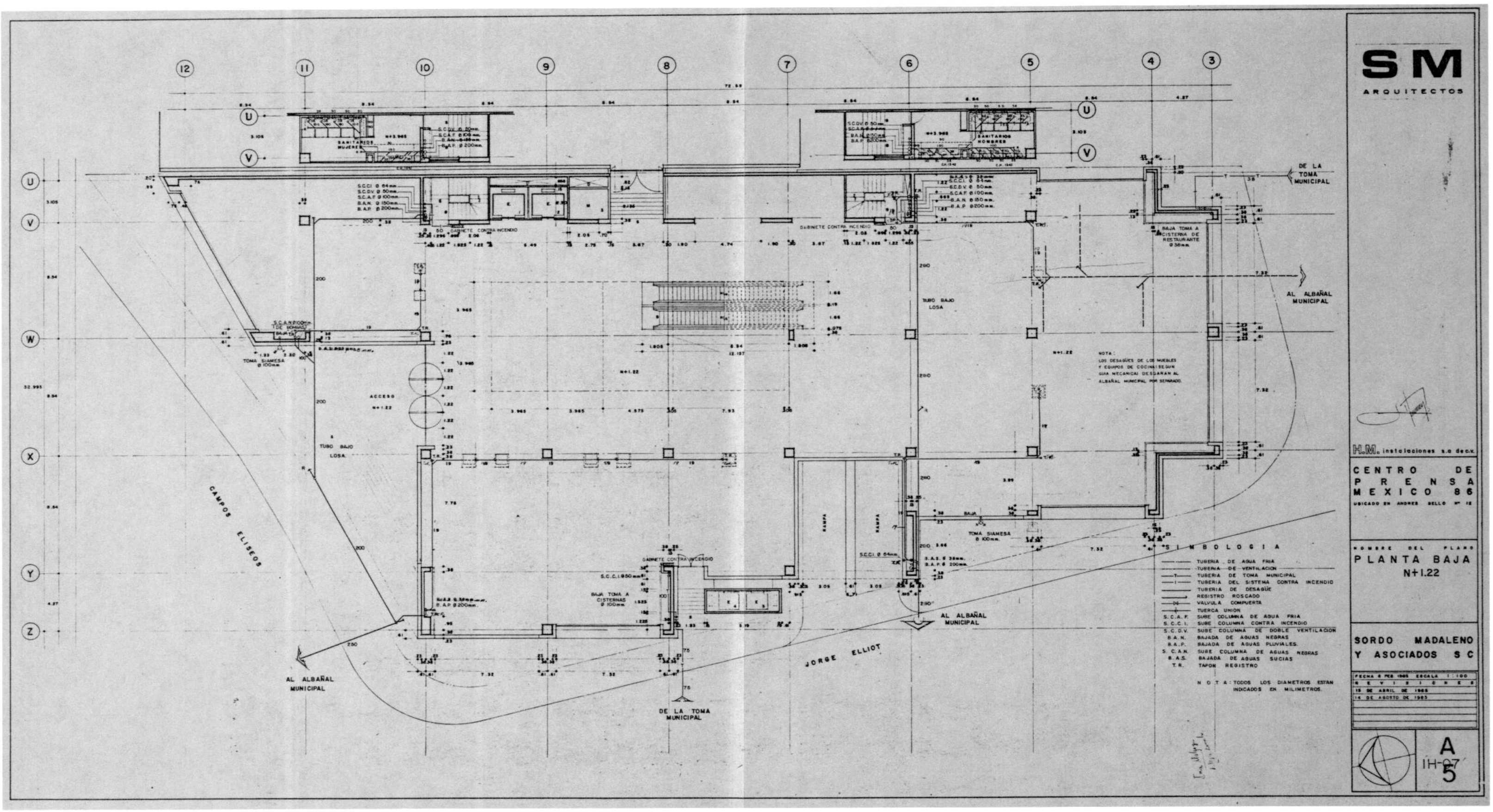

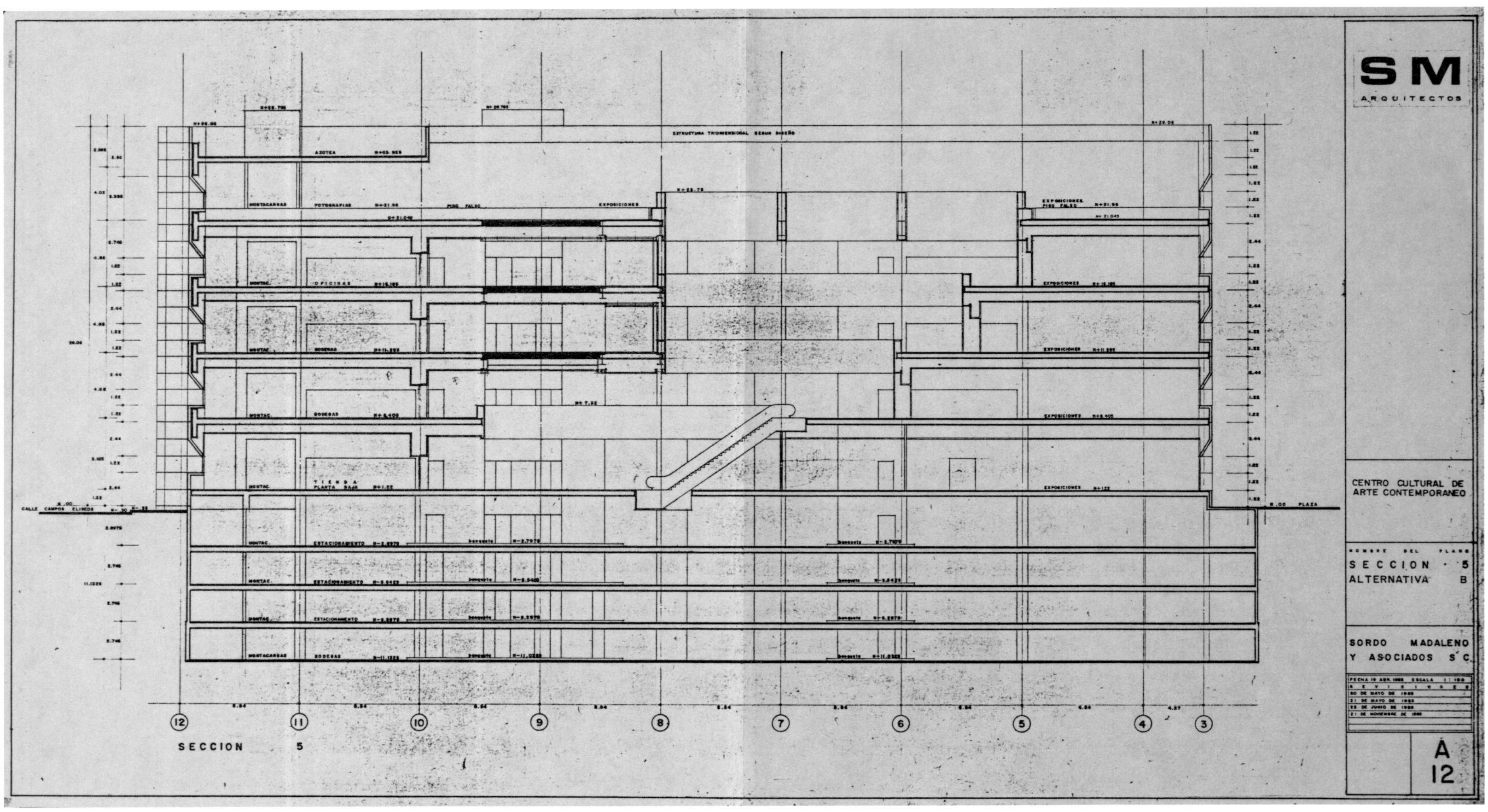

Ground floor and longitudinal section.

Above: entrance stairway. In detail, perforated stone platform.

Below: interior view, main patio. Three upper levels with stairs can be observed.

2017
ANDARES CORPORATE

NO ES
CUALQUIER
TEQUILA.

P.F. CHANG'S

Left hand page: exterior view from Andares Masterplan.

Right hand page, above: exterior view of the common-use corporate terrace on the third floor.

Below: interior view of the offices lobby.

7.

SOCIAL ARCHITECTURE

SARA TOPELSON

A Main corridor, Tlalnepantla CRIT, State of Mexico, 1999.

A

When approaching any of the twenty-three Teletón Children's Rehabilitation Centers (CRITs) located in different Mexican cities, we immediately recognize its presence. A common language with its own identity defines this network of architectural complexes, creating a referent in the collective imagination with colorful, attractive, and playful forms related to traditional Mexican architecture, as reflected in the surfaces and colors of villages all over the Republic.

The concept of the CRIT was born in 1997. Beforehand, there was little information or experience in Mexico on this model of children's rehabilitation, and the premises used for such purposes were adapted houses or some other adapted pre-existing space. Fernando Landeros, the director of the CRIT system, tells us that "we started from scratch, so we visited rehabilitation centers in other countries like Brazil, Chile, the United States, and some European countries with interesting experiences."[1] The great challenge was to create a model of rehabilitation that would apply the lessons learned to an environment that would foremost consider the location, climate, and culture of Mexico.

The basis of the concept is the recognition that rehabilitation is a long process in which the child remains for an average of three years. The objective was therefore to create a center and an environment where the child would feel at home and want to return. It was decided to avoid the appearance of a hospital which could seem intimidating and unfriendly. A magical moment—and a happy coincidence—came when the architect Javier Sordo Madaleno was consulted. He immediately proposed distinguishing such centers in Mexico with generous colors, textures, and materials in active forms that would positively stimulate the children and their senses.

Since the first CRIT, Javier has been directly involved, *pro bono*, intensely working on the creation, design, and development of all the projects confirming the commitment of Sordo Madaleno Arquitectos to social responsibility and spreading the benefits of their work inclusively to the whole community, particularly the under-resourced. In the rehabilitation centers, patients are offered treatment with personalized care, cutting-edge technology, current global standards of care, training in self-management of care, and assistance with reintegration into community. The therapeutic concept, reflected in all areas that comprise the rehabilitation system—from assessment and laboratories to treatment and adaptation to the surroundings—was developed simultaneously with architectural concepts and intended as a gift to the children of Mexico. With skill and talent, Sordo Madaleno adapted the CRIT's aspirations to the architectural project, integrating ludic features in the facades, forms, and spaces as well as the interior design, which even considers such details as the position of children undergoing treatment. For example, rooms where they have to lie down have ceilings covered with geometrical forms and colors that invite children to play with their imagination.

The CRIT model is strictly speaking a center that provides only outpatient care with the objective of serving children and their families with excellent medical care and human warmth. Javier Sordo Madaleno mentions that "the general concept of the project presupposed the design of a building with a colorful, comfortable, and pleasant ambience, so that children would not feel as though they were in a hospital but in a place where they could play and have fun. The interiors and exteriors had to be inspiring and motivate them to come back and continue their treatments until they were fully rehabilitated."[2]

The first CRIT, built in 1999, is in Tlalnepantla (State of Mexico). With this building, Javier can be said to have created the model that revolutionized the predominant criteria for hospital architecture in Mexico. Of course, the concept has evolved and been continually perfected, incorporating various features of both a functional and a formal nature. The CRIT Tlalnepantla is a building whose color and form stand out from its monochrome context. The entrance is via a motor lobby plaza with

1. Fernando Landeros (CRIT System Director) in discussion with the author, September 19, 2019.
2. Javier Sordo Madaleno Bringas (architect) in discussion with the author, August 16, 2019.

Tlalnepantla CRIT, State of Mexico, 1999.

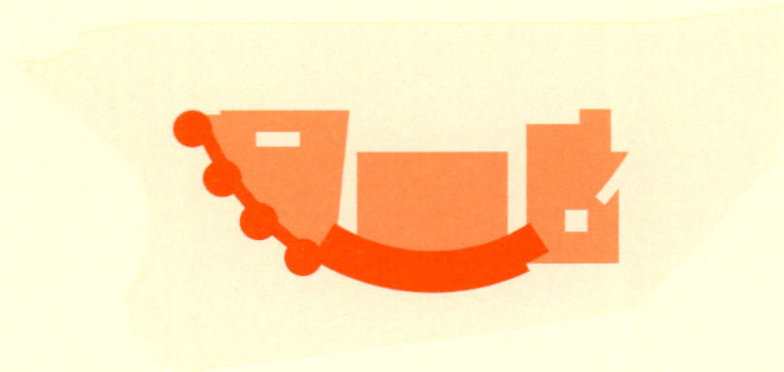

Jalisco CRIT, 2000.

Oaxaca CRIT, 2001.

Hidalgo CRIT, 2004.

Chiapas CRIT, 2006.

Chihuahua CRIT, 2006.

Teletón Autism Center (CAT), Ecatepec, State of Mexico, 2007.

Yucatán CRIT, 2008.

Tamaulipas CRIT, 2008.

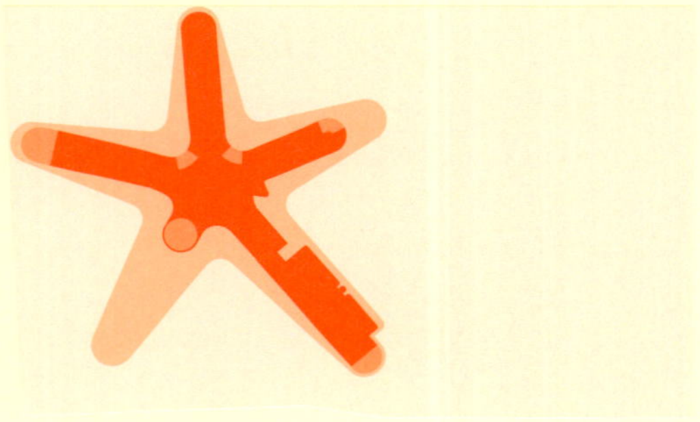

Baja California Sur CRIT, 2010.

Guerrero CRIT, 2012.

Teletón Infant Oncology Clinic (HITO), Querétaro, 2013.

Aguascalientes CRIT, 2002.

Guanajuato CRIT, 2004.

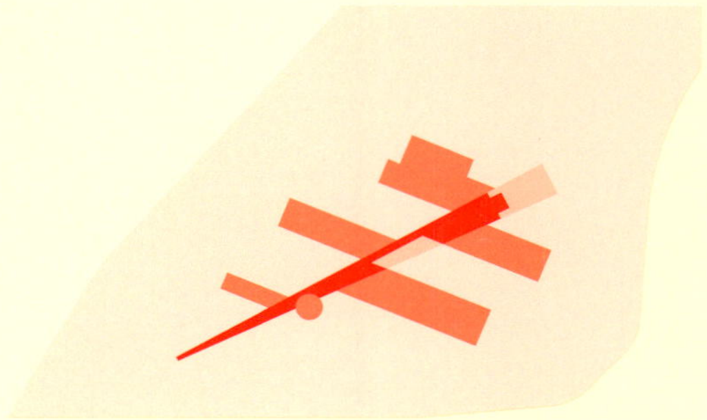

Coahuila CRIT, 2004.

Puebla CRIT, 2007.

Quintana Roo CRIT, 2007.

Nezahualcóyotl CRIT, State of Mexico, 2007.

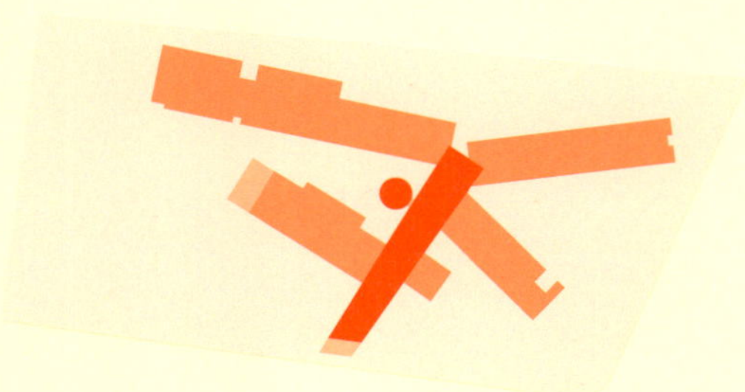

Veracruz CRIT, 2009.

Durango CRIT, 2009.

Sonora CRIT, 2010.

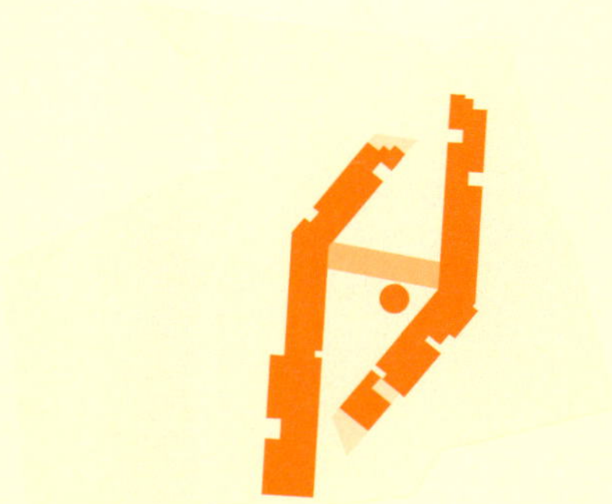

Michoacán CRIT, 2013.

San Antonio CRIT, Texas, USA, 2014.

Baja California CRIT, 2015.

B Interior view of rehabilitation hall, Guanajuato CRIT, 2004.

B

no physical barriers to impede access for anyone. Next to the motor lobby plaza is an attractive cylindrical volume of Mexican pink. The vestibule and reception hall are a welcoming space decorated with the distinctive colors of the CRIT—yellow, orange, Mexican pink, blue, and purple. We immediately find indications on the floor leading to the main axis of distribution and all the services. The area is a generous curve that visually reduces the perception of its length while articulating the various functions of the rehabilitation center.

The project is structured in two differentiated areas. One is the public zone which includes classrooms, a library, an auditorium, and a cafeteria. The other is the zone for medical and psychosocial care, made up of assessment facilities, laboratories, surgeries, areas for mechanical and aquatic therapy, and a social integration zone. Plastically and morphologically, the predominant features are identifiably Mexican, with design elements based on geometrical patterns in bright colors, openings for lighting overhead and in the facades, and ceilings at heights that emphasize the light, the shadows, and the changing perspectives with ludic elements predominating in the finishes. The volumetrics and spatial diversity are based on octagonal blocks that intersect with cylindrical volumes. The spaces are defined with attractive colors and figures on ceilings, walls, and floors in accordance with the function and use of each. In every case, openings onto plazas and gardens encourage expansion and dialogue with the exterior. In the gardens, recreational facilities include ramps and games adapted to the capacities of patients. On the upper level are the administrative offices with views over the curved axis, the main passage for circulation and the articulator of all the spaces. The complex is completed with a chapel, a cylindrical space bathed in carefully measured light suitable for meditation and reflection.

What we might call the CRIT model of pediatric rehabilitation has proved very successful in the twenty-three centers distributed all over Mexico and which are studied all over the world. As a result, other facilities have been built, among them the Teletón Infant Oncology Clinic (HITO) of Querétaro. Here the children are hospitalized for surgical operations or receive chemotherapy or radiation treatment over extended periods while housed with a relative in another structure purpose-built as a patients' residence. The facilities at HITO retain the cheerful colors and multitude of forms that define the model. It has 91 beds and full hospital services, operating theaters, laboratories, chemotherapy units, and lead-lined rooms for isolation during radiation treatment. The intensive therapy rooms are complemented by an adjacent room for parents and relatives, as children recover better if they keep up a close and continuous relationship with their loved ones.

This hospital encourages a close relationship with the parents or relatives who form an integral part of the care team. The result of this combination of attractive and cheerful architectural spaces with humanized medical attention is that this hospital now has the third-highest survival rate in the world after the Children's Cancer Hospitals of Boston and Egypt, with results 30% higher than the national average.

All CRITs serve children with a variety of issues, like musculoskeletal disorders, cancer, and autism. Yet another feature that

C Main entrance, San Antonio CRIT, Texas, USA, 2014.
D Main entrance, Michoacán CRIT, 2013.

C

D

distinguishes one CRIT from another is integration of the local culture of the place where they are located; they retrieve local symbols and derive their morphology from them. The Aguascalientes CRIT acknowledges the tree-lined avenue where it stands, the plan of the Acapulco CRIT is in the form of a fish, the Puebla CRIT an angel, the La Paz CRIT a starfish, and the Cancún CRIT a snail. The Tamaulipas CRIT in Altamira was named the best building in the health category at the 2009 World Architectural Festival in Barcelona, a distinction for which the building was selected from among more than 300 projects from 67 countries. Mentioning this fact, Javier Sordo Madaleno adds that "the design concept of the Teletón Children's Rehabilitation Centers comes from the use of color and geometrical shapes so that they look like toys." Indeed, the ceilings, walls, and floors display a wide range of designs bathed in light and color to entertain and distract the youth, constantly stimulating their senses and inviting them to have fun.

Finally, a few words about the Baja California CRIT in Tijuana, built on elevated terrain. It feeds off the culture of Baja California with forms that recall bunches of grapes, while the plan resembles wine glasses. A central axis structures the complex and provides access to three curved segments that house the different areas of the center. The first is for reception, offices, and assessment, the second is made up of surgeries and treatment rooms, and the third contains the aquatic therapy and social integration zones, all rendered in the architectural language that today characterizes the CRITs.

I should like to finish by stressing the full dimension of the social work performed by the architect Javier Sordo Madaleno with 23 CRITs, a cancer hospital, an autism center in Tabasco, and the Teletón University—all projects carried out *pro bono* and with a large social impact, inspired by a spirit of cooperation and solidarity with the families as a service to the communities of his country. Javier sees the children as the object of his commitment. "They're marvelous," he says, explaining how they have infused him spiritually, along with everyone else involved with the concept with conviction and enthusiasm in helping to promote health, equity, diversity, and social inclusion.

The CRITs make up the world's largest system of children's rehabilitation, and their approach to space and architecture has proved very positive. The flow of ample spaces within each complex and the color that characterizes them constantly refer users to other buildings by Sordo Madaleno, like hotels, houses, and shopping centers, with the same care here put into the color and form for low-income families and their children. It is an architectural focus worth celebrating.

Left hand page: cactus garden, Coahuila CRIT, 2004.

Right hand page: corridor and exterior garden, Oaxaca CRIT, 2001.

Above: esplanade entrance, Aguascalientes CRIT, 2002. Below: corridor and main garden, Guanajuato CRIT, 2004.

Above: esplanade entrance, Puebla CRIT, 2006. Below: interior view of waiting room, Baja California CRIT, 2015.

Above: intersection of volumes and play of colors, Tamaulipas CRIT, 2008.

Below: detail of exterior corridor, Mexico City CRIT, 2010.

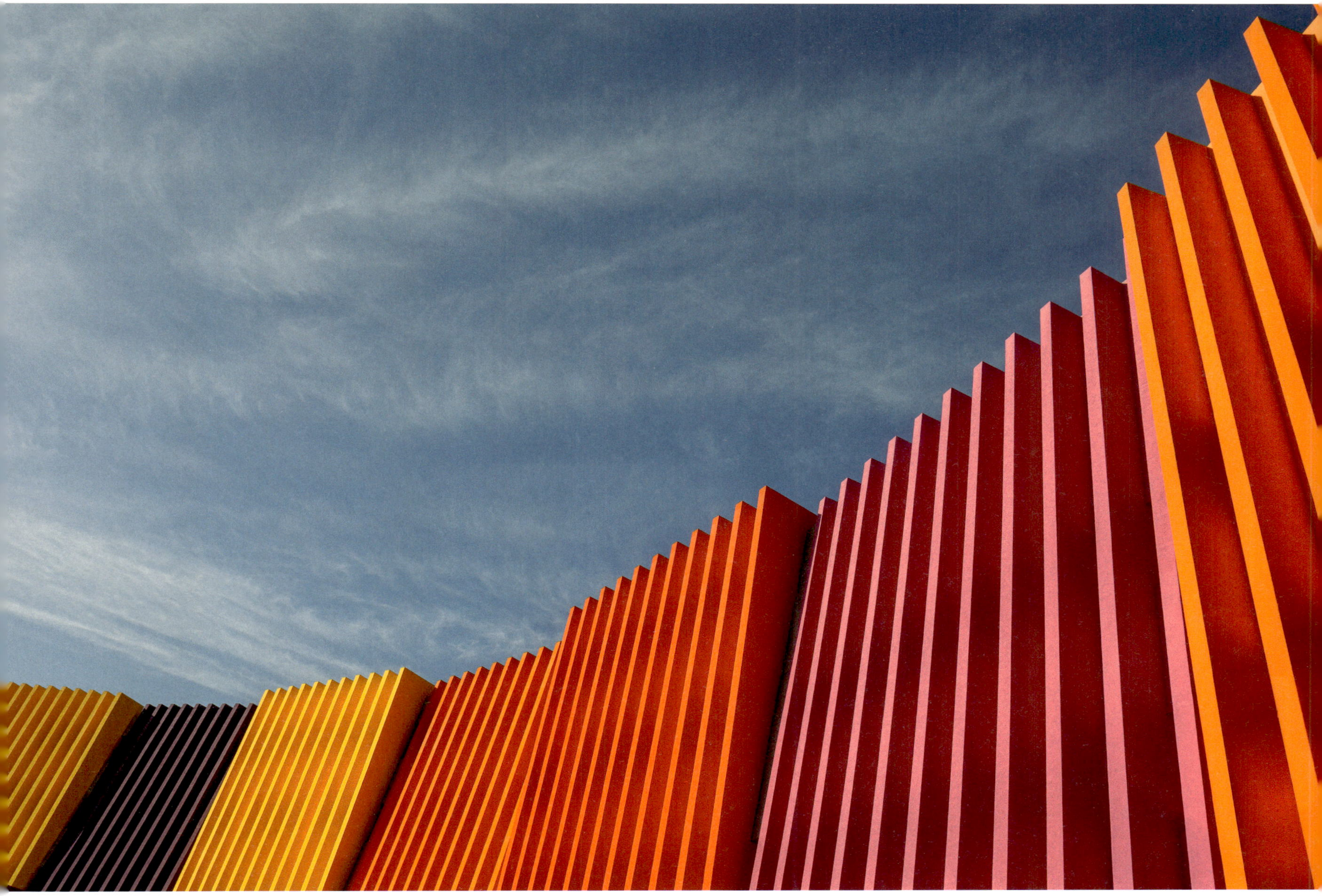

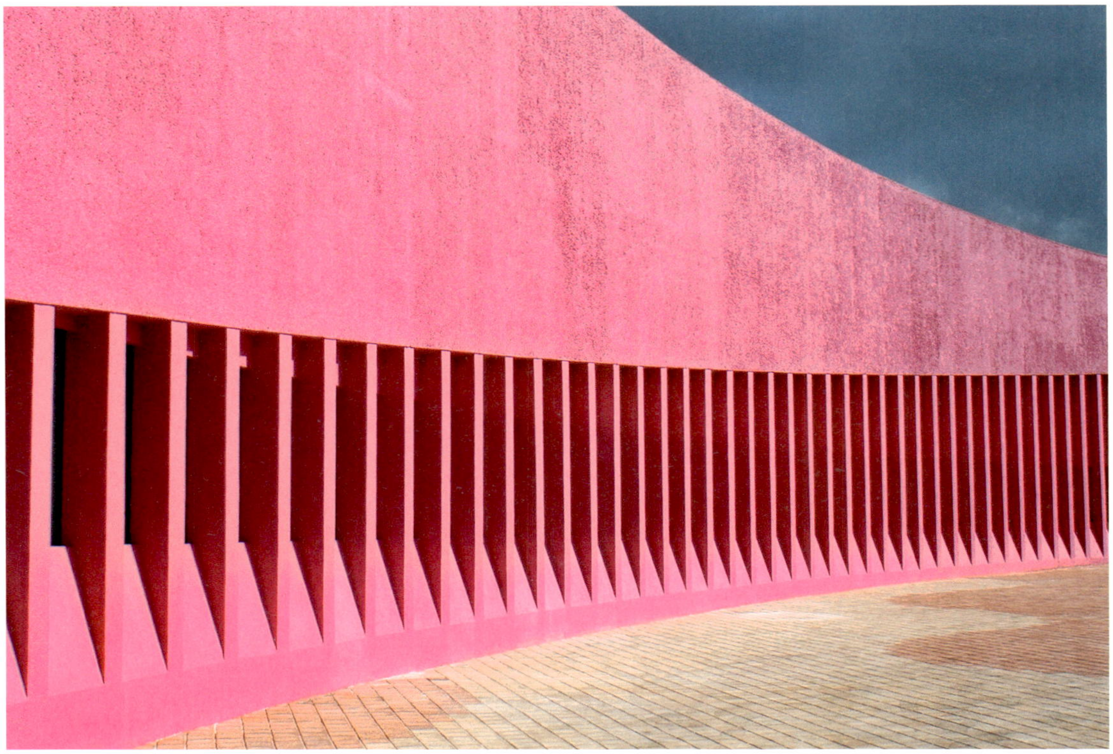

Above: detail of the main facade, Querétaro HITO, 2013.

Below: detail of the access wall, Quintana Roo CRIT, 2007.

ANNEXES

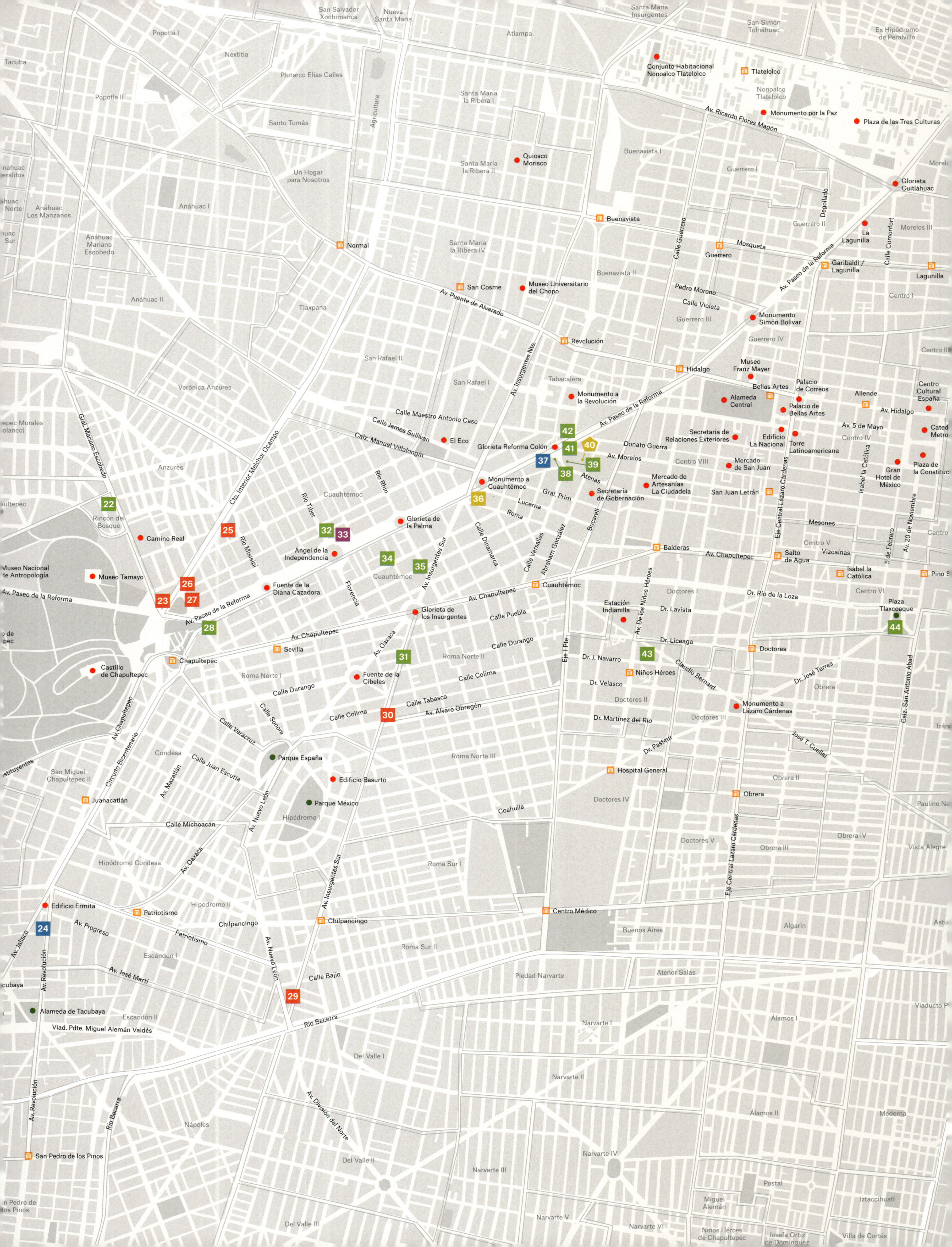

San Salvador Xochimanca
Nueva Santa María
Santa María Insurgentes
San Simón Tolnáhuac
Ex Hipódromo de Peralvillo
Popotla I
Atlampa
Tacuba
Nextitla
Conjunto Habitacional Nonoalco Tlatelolco
Tlatelolco
Plutarco Elías Calles
Popotla II
Santa María la Ribera I
Agricultura
Nonoalco Tlatelolco
Monumento por la Paz
Plaza de las Tres Culturas
Av. Ricardo Flores Magón
Santo Tomás
Quiosco Morisco
Buenavista I
Santa María la Ribera II
Guerrero I
Un Hogar para Nosotros
Glorieta Cuitláhuac
Anáhuac I
Degollado
Anáhuac Los Manzanos
Buenavista
Guerrero II
Morelos III
Anáhuac Mariano Escobedo
Normal
Santa María la Ribera IV
Calle Guerrero
Mosqueta
La Lagunilla
Calle Comonfort
Guerrero
Garibaldi / Lagunilla
Lagunilla
Av. Paseo de la Reforma
Buenavista II
Anáhuac II
San Cosme
Museo Universitario del Chopo
Pedro Moreno
Centro I
Av. Puente de Alvarado
Calle Violeta
Tlaxpana
Guerrero III
Monumento Simón Bolívar
Revolución
Guerrero IV
San Rafael II
Hidalgo
Museo Franz Mayer
Centro II
Av. Insurgentes Nte.
Tabacalera
San Rafael I
Bellas Artes
Palacio de Correos
Verónica Anzures
Centro Cultural España
Alameda Central
Allende
Monumento a la Revolución
Palacio de Bellas Artes
Av. Hidalgo
Calle Maestro Antonio Caso
Av. Paseo de la Reforma
Catedral Metropolitana
Av. 5 de Mayo
Calle James Sullivan
Secretaría de Relaciones Exteriores
Torre Latinoamericana
Gral. Mariano Escobedo
El Eco
Edificio La Nacional
Centro IV
Donato Guerra
Calz. Manuel Villalongín
Glorieta Reforma Colón
Av. Morelos
Centro VIII
Cto. Interior Melchor Ocampo
Anzures
Río Rhin
Atenas
Mercado de San Juan
Gran Hotel de México
Plaza de la Constitución
Isabel la Católica
Monumento a Cuauhtémoc
Mercado de Artesanías La Ciudadela
Cuauhtémoc
Gral. Prim
Secretaría de Gobernación
San Juan Letrán
Eje Central Lázaro Cárdenas
Río Tiber
Lucerna
Rincón del Bosque
Roma
Mesones
Glorieta de la Palma
Calle Dinamarca
Camino Real
Río Misisipi
Ángel de la Independencia
Calle Versalles
Abraham González
Bucareli
Centro V
Balderas
Av. Chapultepec
Salto de Agua
Vizcaínas
5 de Febrero
Av. 20 de Noviembre
Museo Nacional de Antropología
Museo Tamayo
Av. Insurgentes Sur
Cuauhtémoc
Isabel la Católica
Pino Suárez
Fuente de la Diana Cazadora
Florencia
Doctores I
Dr. Río de la Loza
Centro VI
Av. Paseo de la Reforma
Av. Chapultepec
Glorieta de los Insurgentes
Estación Indianilla
Av. De los Niños Héroes
Dr. Lavista
Plaza Tlaxcoaque
Calle Puebla
Av. Paseo de la Reforma
Av. Chapultepec
Sevilla
Av. Oaxaca
Calle Durango
Dr. Liceaga
Doctores
Chapultepec
Roma Norte II
Eje 1 Pte
Dr. J. Navarro
Castillo de Chapultepec
Roma Norte I
Fuente de la Cibeles
Calle Colima
Niños Héroes
Claudio Bernard
Dr. José Terres
Calle Durango
Dr. Velasco
Obrera I
Calle Sonora
Calle Tabasco
Doctores II
Monumento a Lázaro Cárdenas
Calle Colima
Av. Álvaro Obregón
Dr. Martínez del Río
Doctores III
Calz. San Antonio Abad
Calle Veracruz
Av. Chapultepec
Condesa
José T. Cuellar
Dr. Pasteur
Parque España
Circuito Bicentenario
Calle Juan Escutia
Roma Norte III
Constituyentes
San Miguel Chapultepec II
Hospital General
Edificio Basurto
Obrera II
Av. Mazatlán
Obrera
Juanacatlán
Parque México
Doctores IV
Paulino Navarro
Av. Nuevo León
Calle Michoacán
Hipódromo I
Coahuila
Doctores V
Obrera IV
Obrera III
Vista Alegre
Hipódromo Condesa
Av. Oaxaca
Roma Sur I
Eje Central Lázaro Cárdenas
Edificio Ermita
Av. Insurgentes Sur
Hipódromo II
Centro Médico
Patriotismo
Algarín
Chilpancingo
Chilpancingo
Av. Progreso
Buenos Aires
Patriotismo
Av. Jalisco
Av. Nuevo León
Roma Sur II
Escandón I
Av. Revolución
Av. José Martí
Atenor Salas
Calle Bajío
Piedad Narvarte
Tacubaya
Viaducto Piedad
Alameda de Tacubaya
Escandón II
Río Becerra
Álamos I
Viad. Pdte. Miguel Alemán Valdés
Narvarte I
Del Valle I
Narvarte II
Av. Revolución
Río Becerra
Av. División del Norte
Álamos II
Nápoles
Moderna
San Pedro de los Pinos
Del Valle II
Narvarte IV
Narvarte III
Postal
Miguel Alemán
Iztaccíhuatl
San Pedro de los Pinos
Narvarte V
Del Valle III
Narvarte VI
Niños Héroes de Chapultepec
Josefa Ortiz de Domínguez
Villa de Cortés
22
23
24
25
26
27
28
29
30
31
32
33
34
35
36
37
38
39
40
41
42
43
44

1

Torres Toreo
Nueva Argentina (Argentina Poniente)
Torre Blanca
Argentina Antigua
Legaría
San Joaquín
Torre Blanca
Ventura Pérez de Alba
México Nuevo
Pensil San Juanico
Deportiva Pensil
Panteón Francés
Pensil Norte
Lomas de Sotelo
Ahuehuetes Anáhuac
Reforma Pensil
5 de Mayo
Francisco I. Madero
Modelo Pensil
Loma Hermosa
Av. Río San Joaquín
Popo
Cuauhtémoc Pensil
San Joaquín
Anáhuac Dos Lagos
Irrigación
Granada (Ampl.)
Museo Soumaya
Museo Jumex
Blvd. Miguel de Cervantes Saavedra
Granada
Militar 1k Lomas de Sotelo (U. Hab.)
Av. Ejército Nacional
Los Morales (Polanco)
Ferrocarril de Cuernavaca
Av. Molière
Morales Sección Palmas (Polanco)
Av. Homero
Del Bosque (Polanco)
Anillo Periférico
Polanco Reforma (Polanco)
Morales Sección Alameda (Polanco)
Av. Cicerón
Av. Horacio
Polanco
Conservatorio Nacional de Música
Av. Pdte. Masaryk
Palmitas (Polanco)
Reforma Social
Chapultepec Polanco (Polanco)
Parque Lincoln
Paseo de las Palmas
Calle 3 Picos
Fuente de Petróleos
Campos Elíseos
Rubén Darío
Prado Norte
Anillo Periférico
Auditorio
Auditorio Nacional
Av. Paseo de la Reforma
Lomas de Barrilaco (Lomas de Chapultepec)
Lomas de Chapultepec
Calz. Chivatito
Lomas Virreyes (Lomas de Chapultepec)
Prado Sur
Blvd. de los Virreyes
BOSQUE DE CHAPULTEPEC
San Miguel Chapultepec I
Av. Explanada
Los Pinos
BOSQUE DE CHAPULTEPEC II SECC.
Av. Corregidores
Bosque de Chapultepec I, II y III Sección (Polanco)
Montañas Rocallosas
Paseo de las Palmas
Constituyentes
Bosques de la Reforma
Museo de Historia Natural
Papalote Museo del Niño
Casa Barragán
Lomas de Reforma (Lomas de Chapultepec)
Bosque de las Lomas
Daniel Garza (Ampl.)
Av. Parque Lira
Av. Constituyentes
Anillo Periférico
BOSQUE DE CHAPULTEPEC III SECC.
Parque Lira
Paseo de los Ahuehuetes Sur
Cumbres de Acultzingo
Daniel Garza
Observatorio
América
Av. Paseo de la Reforma
16 de Septiembre
Av. Observatorio
Lomas de Reforma
Lomas Altas
Cove
Tacubaya
Paseo Lomas Altas
Estado de Hidalgo
Las Palmas
Av. Constituyentes
Acueducto
Observatorio
El Capulín
Anillo Periférico
El Capulín
Belén de las Flores
Reacomodo Pino Suárez
Real del Monte
Bella Vista
Av. Constituyentes
Lomas de Santo Domingo
Molino de Santo Domingo
Molino de Santo Domingo
Ocho de Agosto
Liberales de 1857
Torres de San Pedro
Santa Fe
Industrias Militares de Sedena
La Conchita
Pólvora
Tolteca
El Paraíso
El Cuernito
Zenón Delgado
Santa Fe (U. Hab.)
Cristo Rey
María G. de García Ruiz

LOCATION OF PRINCIPAL BUILT PROJECTS

A

Mexico and the United States

■ **JSM** JUAN SORDO MADALENO (1937–1985)
● **JSMB** JAVIER SORDO MADALENO (FROM 1985)
⬟ **SMA** SORDO MADALENO ARQUITECTOS (FROM 2010)

MEXICO AND THE UNITED STATES:

RESIDENTIAL
24. Valle San Nicolás (2021) **SMA**
38. Cozumel House (2017) **SMA**
43. Vistahermosa (2009) **JSMB B→**
44. Bosques de las Lomas (2007) **JSMB B→**

COMMERCIAL
20. Antea (2013) **SMA**
27. Luxury Hall (2010) **SMA**
28. Angelópolis (1998, expansion) **JSMB**
41. Plaza Satélite (1971, modified/ expansion) **JSM B→**

MIXED USE
14. Andares Masterplan (2009–2017) **JSMB**
15. The Landmark (2019) **SMA**
16. Midtown (2019) **SMA**
40. Lomas Verdes (1966, project) **JSM B→**

PUBLIC: CHURCHES, MOVIE THEATERS AND EDUCATION
9. Santa Elena Chapel (1974) **JSM**
45. San Josemaría Escrivá de Balaguer Parish (2009) **JSMB B→**

HOTELS
5. Solaz Los Cabos (2018) **SMA**
6. Westin Regina Los Cabos (1994) **JSMB**
13. Westin Regina Puerto Vallarta (1993) **JSMB**
29. Presidente Acapulco (1958, expansion) **JSM**

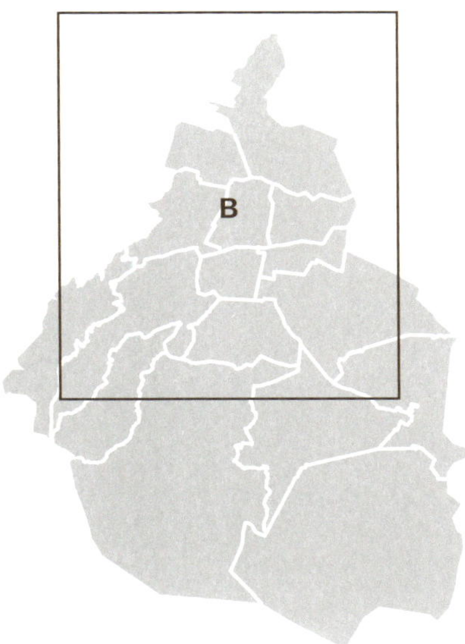

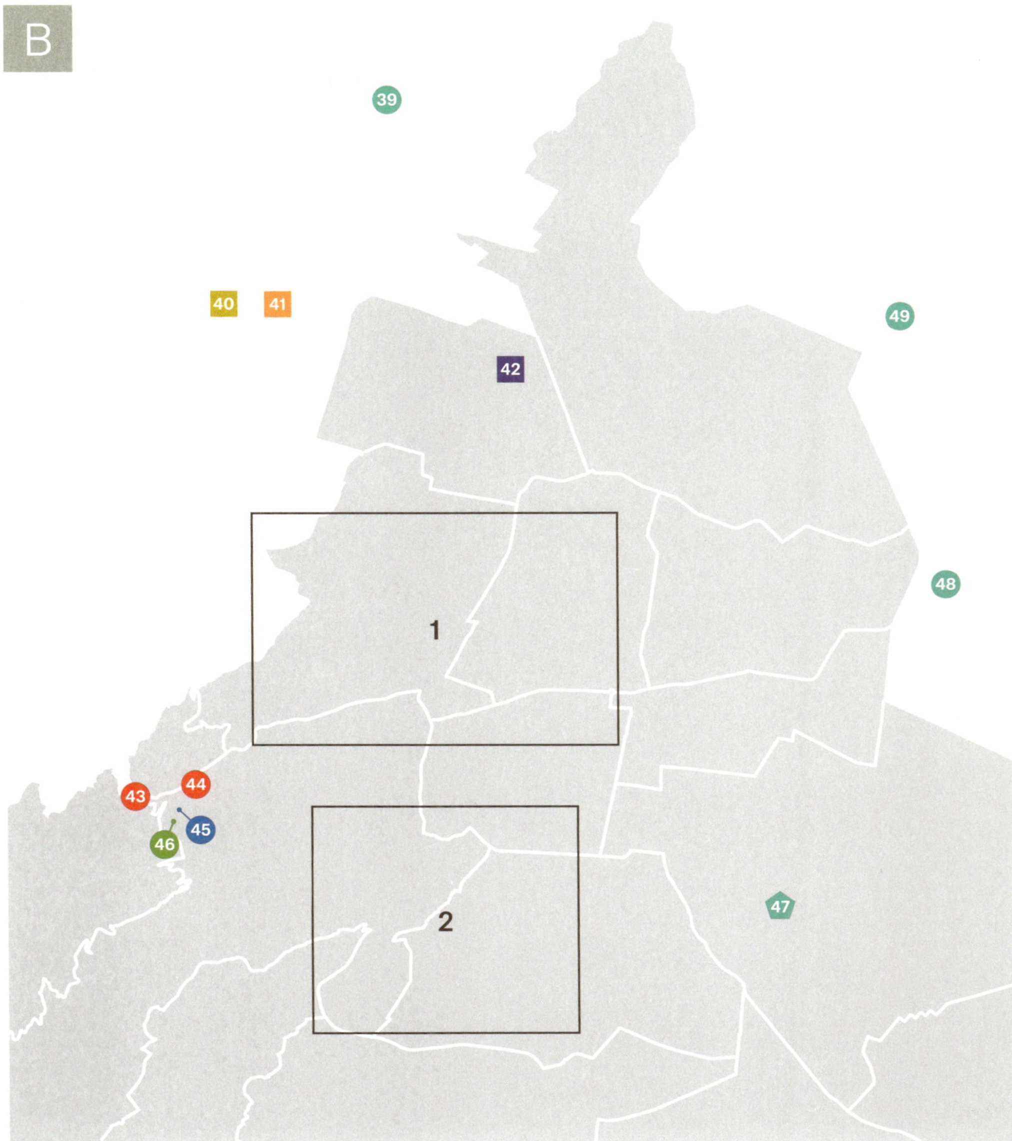

Mexico City and Metropolitan Area

34. Grand Hyatt Playa del Carmen (2015) **SMA ←A**
36. Presidente Cancún (1974) **JSM ←A**
37. Presidente Cozumel (1969) **JSM ←A**

OFFICE BUILDINGS

46. Cuervo Corporate (1996) **JSMB**

HEALTH

1. Baja California CRIT (2015) **SMA ←A**
2. Sonora CRIT (2010) **SMA ←A**
3. Chihuahua CRIT (2006) **JSMB ←A**
4. Baja California Sur CRIT (2010) **SMA ←A**
7. Durango CRIT (2009) **JSMB ←A**
8. Texas CRIT (2014) **SMA ←A**
10. Coahuila CRIT (2004) **JSMB ←A**
11. Tamaulipas CRIT (2008) **JSMB ←A**
12. Aguascalientes CRIT (2002) **JSMB ←A**
17. Jalisco CRIT (2000) **JSMB ←A**
18. Guanajuato CRIT (2004) **JSMB ←A**
19. Michoacán CRIT (2013) **SMA ←A**
21. Teletón Infant Oncology Clinic (2013) **SMA ←A**
22. Hidalgo CRIT (2004) **JSMB ←A**
23. Veracruz CRIT (2009) **JSMB ←A**
26. Puebla CRIT (2007) **SMA ←A**
30. Guerrero CRIT (2012) **SMA ←A**
31. Oaxaca CRIT (2001) **JSMB ←A**
32. Chiapas CRIT (2006) **JSMB ←A**
33. Yucatán CRIT (2008) **JSMB ←A**
35. Quintana Roo CRIT (2007) **JSMB ←A**
39. Tlalnepantla CRIT (1999) **JSMB**
47. Mexico City CRIT (2010) **SMA**
48. Nezahualcóyotl CRIT (2007) **JSMB**
49. Teletón Autism Center (2007) **JSMB**

INDUSTRIAL

25. Cartuchos Deportivos (1962) **JSM ←A**
42. Wyeth-Vales (1950, demolished) **JSM**

OTHER COUNTRIES:

HOTELS

- Villamagna (Spain, 1963) **JSM**
- Torremolinos Hotel Complex (Spain, 1963) **JSM**
- Meliá Castilla (Spain, 1968) **JSM**
- Saudi Arabia Hotel (Saudi Arabia, project) **SMA**

* The mapped projects refer only to those mentioned throughout the book, not to the completed work built by SMA.

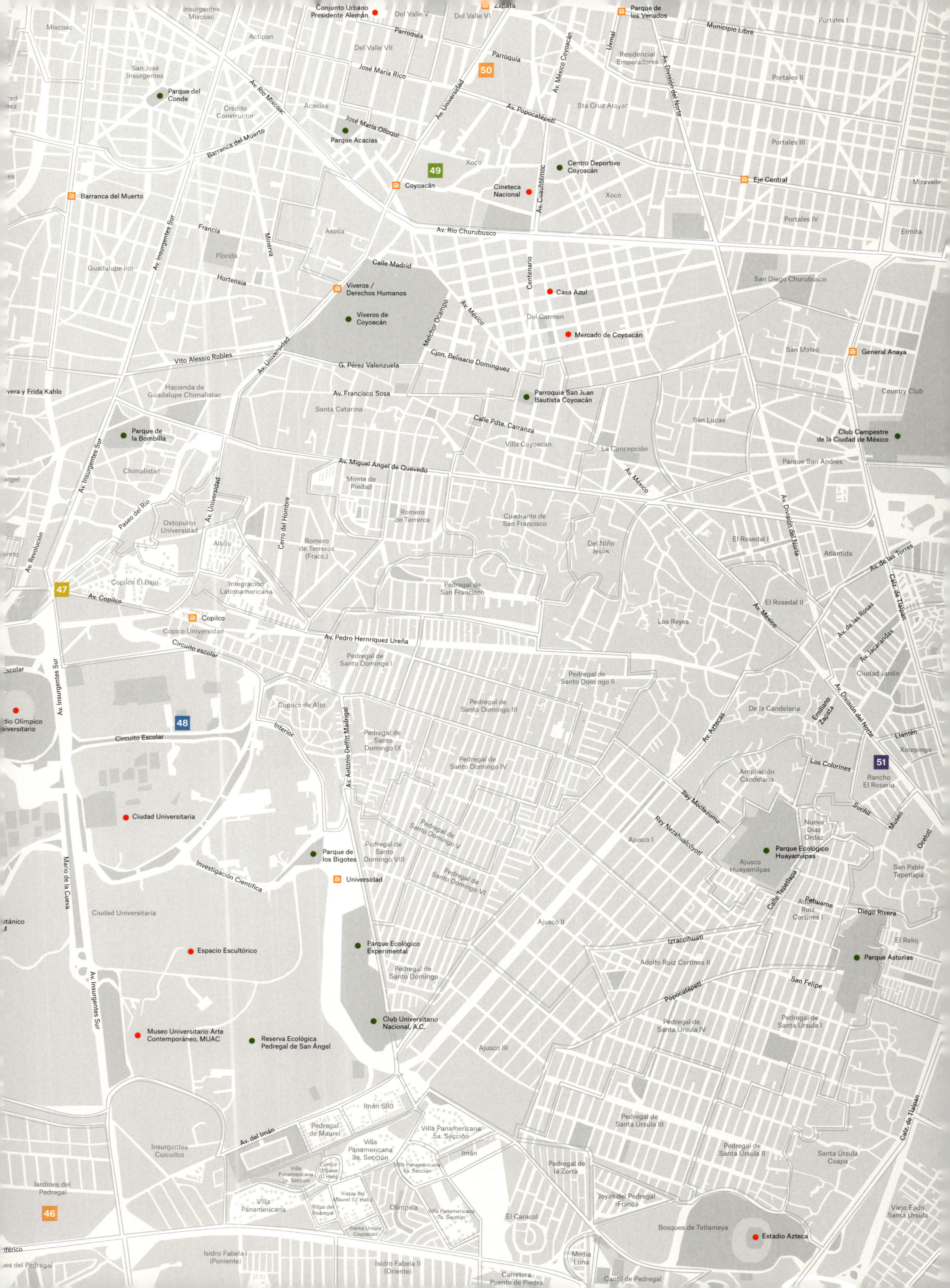

Mixcoac
Insurgentes Mixcoac
Conjunto Urbano Presidente Alemán
Del Valle V
Zapata
Del Valle VI
Parque de los Venados
Portales I
Municipio Libre
Actipan
Parroquia
Del Valle VII
Uxmal
Residencial Emperadores
Av. División del Norte
San José Insurgentes
José María Rico
50
Parroquia
Av. México Coyoacán
Portales II
Parque del Conde
Av. Río Mixcoac
Crédito Constructor
Acacias
Av. Universidad
Av. Popocatépetl
Sta Cruz Atoyac
José María Olloquí
Parque Acacias
Barranca del Muerto
Portales III
Xoco
49
Centro Deportivo Coyoacán
Av. Cuauhtémoc
Coyoacán
Cineteca Nacional
Eje Central
Miravalle
Xoco
Barranca del Muerto
Av. Insurgentes Sur
Francia
Minerva
Axotla
Av. Río Churubusco
Portales IV
Ermita
Florida
Guadalupe Inn
Calle Madrid
Centenario
Hortensia
Viveros / Derechos Humanos
Casa Azul
San Diego Churubusco
Av. México
Viveros de Coyoacán
Melchor Ocampo
Del Carmen
Mercado de Coyoacán
Av. Universidad
Cjon. Belisario Domínguez
San Mateo
General Anaya
Vito Alessio Robles
G. Pérez Valenzuela
Hacienda de Guadalupe Chimalistac
Av. Francisco Sosa
Parroquia San Juan Bautista Coyoacán
Country Club
Santa Catarina
Calle Pdte. Carranza
San Lucas
Parque de la Bombilla
Club Campestre de la Ciudad de México
Villa Coyoacán
La Concepción
Av. Insurgentes Sur
Av. Miguel Ángel de Quevedo
Parque San Andrés
Chimalistac
Av. México
Av. Universidad
Monte de Piedad
Paseo del Río
Av. División del Norte
Oxtopulco Universidad
Romero de Terreros
Cuadrante de San Francisco
Cerro del Hombre
El Rosedal I
Av. Revolución
Altillo
Romero de Terreros (Fracc.)
Del Niño Jesús
Atlántida
Av. de las Torres
Copilco El Bajo
Integración Latinoamericana
Pedregal de San Francisco
Calz. de Tlalpan
47
Av. Copilco
El Rosedal II
Av. México
Copilco
Los Reyes
Av. de las Rosas
Copilco Universidad
Av. Pedro Henríquez Ureña
Av. Jacarandas
Circuito escolar
Pedregal de Santo Domingo I
Pedregal de Santo Domingo II
Ciudad Jardín
Av. Insurgentes Sur
Av. División del Norte
Copilco de Alto
Pedregal de Santo Domingo III
De la Candelaria
Emiliano Zapata
48
Av. Antonio Delfín Madrigal
Interior
Pedregal de Santo Domingo IX
Av. Aztecas
Llantén
Circuito Escolar
Xotepingo
Pedregal de Santo Domingo IV
Los Colorines
51
Rancho El Rosario
Ampliación Candelaria
Rey Moctezuma
Ciudad Universitaria
Suchil
Pedregal de Santo Domingo V
Ajusco I
Rey Nezahualcóyotl
Nueva Díaz Ordaz
Museo
Ocelotl
Mario de la Cueva
Parque de los Bigotes
Pedregal de Santo Domingo VIII
Parque Ecológico Huayamilpas
Ajusco Huayamilpas
San Pablo Tepetlapa
Investigación Científica
Universidad
Pedregal de Santo Domingo VI
Calle Tepetlapa
Pefuame
Adolfo Ruiz Cortines I
Diego Rivera
Ciudad Universitaria
Ajusco II
El Reloj
Espacio Escultórico
Parque Ecológico Experimental
Iztaccíhuatl
Adolfo Ruiz Cortines II
Parque Asturias
Av. Insurgentes Sur
Pedregal de Santo Domingo
San Felipe
Popocatépetl
Museo Universitario Arte Contemporáneo, MUAC
Reserva Ecológica Pedregal de San Ángel
Club Universitario Nacional, A.C.
Pedregal de Santa Úrsula IV
Pedregal de Santa Úrsula I
Ajusco III
Calz. de Tlalpan
Imán 580
Pedregal de Maurel
Villa Panamericana 5a. Sección
Pedregal de Santa Úrsula III
Av. del Imán
Villa Panamericana 3a. Sección
Insurgentes Cuicuilco
Imán
Pedregal de la Zorra
Pedregal de Santa Úrsula II
Santa Úrsula Coapa
Villa Panamericana 2a. Sección
Centro Urbano (U Hab)
Villa Panamericana 4a. Sección
Jardines del Pedregal
Vistas del Maurel (U. Hab)
Joyas del Pedregal (Fracc.)
Villa Panamericana
Villas del Pedregal
Olímpica
Villa Panamericana 7a. Sección
El Caracol
Viejo Ejido Santa Úrsula
46
Santa Úrsula Coyoacán
Bosques de Tetlameya
Estadio Azteca
Isidro Fabela I (Poniente)
Isidro Fabela II (Oriente)
Media Luna
Carretera Puente de Piedra
Cantil de Pedregal

■ JSM JUAN SORDO MADALENO (1937–1985)
● JSMB JAVIER SORDO MADALENO (FROM 1985)
⬟ SMA SORDO MADALENO ARQUITECTOS (FROM 2010)

MEXICO CITY:

RESIDENTIAL

2. 100 Conscripto (1953) **JSM**
5. 2388 Reforma (1952, modified/demolished) **JSM**
6. Arbolada Lomas (2006) **JSMB**
7. 725 Sierra Fría (1946) **JSM**
8. 2076 Reforma (1981) **JSM**
9. Cumbres Residential (2006) **JSMB**
10. 940 Corregidores (1956) **JSM**
20. Artesia (2014) **SMA**
21. 225 Rubén Darío (2020) **SMA**
23. Edificio Larín (1947, demolished) **JSM**
25. Melchor Ocampo (1943) **JSM**
26. 333–335 Río Lerma (1945) **JSM**
27. Ródano and Atoyac (1947, demolished) **JSM**
29. 533 Insurgentes (1950) **JSM**
30. Monterrey and Álvaro Obregón (1940, demolished) **JSM**

COMMERCIAL

46. Perisur (1980) **JSM 2→**
50. Plaza Universidad (1969, expansion) **JSM 2→**

MIXED USE

1. Toreo Parque Central (2014) **SMA**
4. Bosques de las Lomas Complex (1974) **JSM**
12. Reforma Complex (1969, project) **JSM**
13. Antara Masterplan (2006–2024, under construction) **JSMB**
14. Molière Dos22 (1997, expansion) **JSMB**
18. Centro Internacional de Prensa (1986, demolished) | Cultural Center for Contemporary Art (1987, demolished) **JSMB**
36. Reforma and Insurgentes (1954, project) **JSM**
40. Reforma Colón (2025, first phase under construction) **SMA**
45. Artz Pedregal (2018) **SMA 2→**
47. Universidad Complex (project/study) **JSM 2→**

PUBLIC: CHURCHES, MOVIE THEATERS AND EDUCATION

3. Chapel Mausoleum in La Herradura Ranch (1956) **JSM**
15. San Ignacio de Loyola Church (1961, restaured) **JSM**
17. Sanatorio de la Sociedad de la Beneficencia Española Chapel (1955) **JSM**
24. Cine Ermita (1951, demolished) **JSM**
37. Cine París (1954, demolished) **JSM**
48. Geology Institute (1953) **JSM 2→**

HOTELS

19. Presidente Chapultepec (1977) **JSM**
33. María Isabel (1961, modified) **JSM**

OFFICE BUILDINGS

11. 555 Palmas (1975) **JSM**
16. Herdez Corporate (1995) **JSMB**
22. 543 Mariano Escobedo (1947, modified) **JSM**
28. Reforma and Lieja (1956, demolished) **JSM**
31. 15 Tonalá (1945, partially demolished) **JSM**
32. Ford Corporate (1963, modified) **JSM**
34. Génova and Hamburgo (1956, modified) **JSM**
35. Londres and Niza (1953, demolished) **JSM**
38. DM Nacional (1963, demolished) **JSM**
39. Reforma and Versalles (1954, demolished) **JSM**
41. Reforma and Morelos (1946, demolished) **JSM**
42. Anáhuac Tower (1958) **JSM**
43. Palacio de Justicia (1964) **JSM**
44. Dirección de Policía y Tránsito (1956, demolished) **JSM**
49. Centro Operativo Bancomer (1976) **JSM 2→**

INDUSTRIAL

51. Merck, Sharp & Dohme (1960, modified) **JSM 2→**

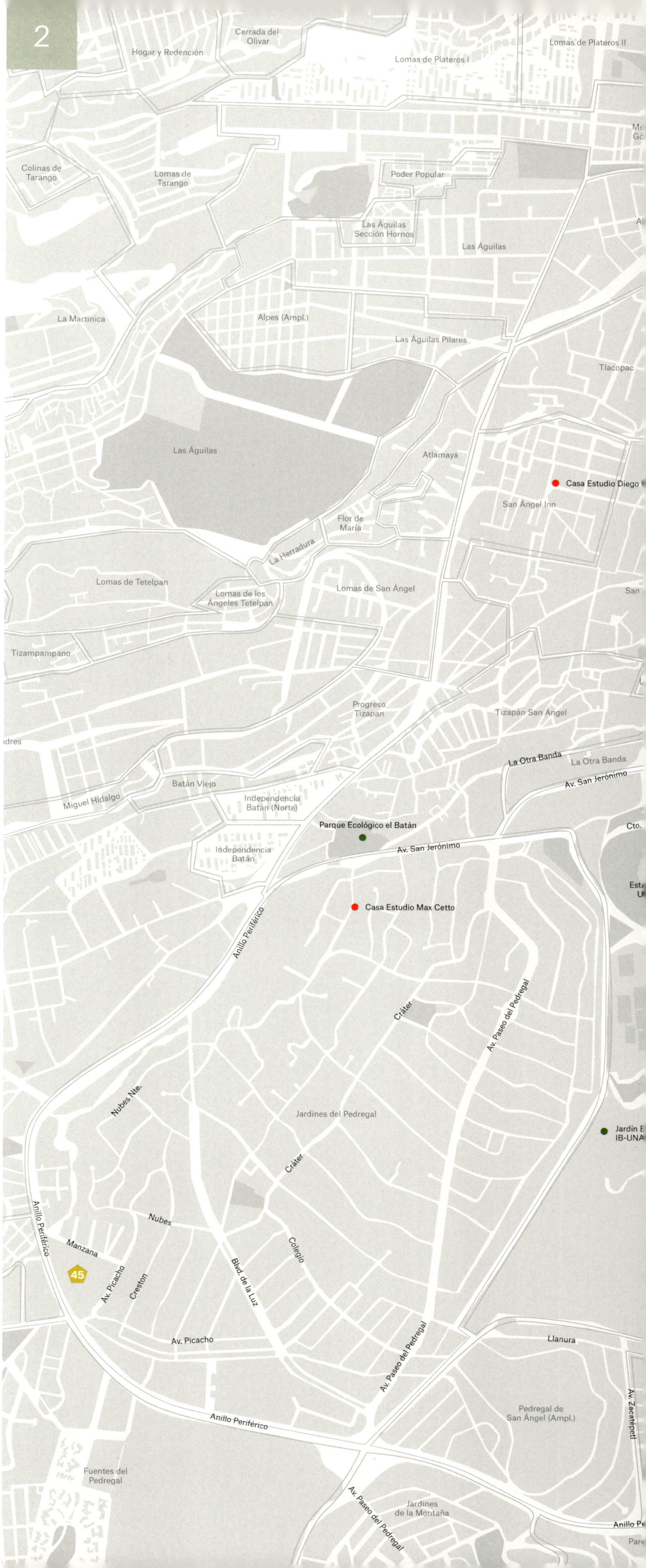

CATALOG OF INCLUDED PROJECTS

EDUCATIONAL

1953
UNAM Geology Institute
Mexico City
Luis Martínez Negrete and José Luis Certucha, Associate architects
pp. 9, 20, 43, 381

INDUSTRIAL

1950
Wyeth-Vales
Mexico City (demolished)
pp. 43, 379

1960
Merck Sharp & Dohme
Mexico City (modified)
José Adolfo Wiechers and Imanol Ordorika, Associate architects
pp. 9, 21, 23, 44, 52–57, 112, 341, 381

1962
Cartuchos Deportivos
Cuernavaca, Morelos
José Adolfo Wiechers, Imanol Ordorika and Félix Candela, Associate architects
pp. 9, 10, 21, 379

MOVIE THEATERS

1951
Cine Ermita
Mexico City (demolished)
pp. 13, 20, 21, 43, 112, 381

1954
Cine París
Mexico City (demolished)
Jaime Ortiz Monasterio, Associate architect
pp. 13, 20, 22, 43, 88, 89, 94–97, 140, 381

URBAN

1954
Reforma and Insurgentes Complex
Mexico City (unbuilt)
pp. 42, 111, 112, 381

***ca.* 1960**
Universidad Complex
Mexico City (unbuilt)
pp. 112, 381

1966
Lomas Verdes
Naucalpan, State of Mexico (unbuilt)
José Adolfo Wiechers and Luis Barragán, Associate architects
pp. 44, 45, 187, 378

1969
Reforma Complex
Mexico City (unbuilt)
José Adolfo Wiechers and José Ignacio de Abiega, Associate architects, Steve Pappas, Architect consultant
pp. 112, 381

MIXED USE

1997, 2015
Molière Dos22
Mexico City (expanded)
Jorge Isaías, Project leader
pp. 29, 46, 198–201, 343, 381

2006, 2013, 2017, +2024
Antara Masterplan
Mexico City (under construction)
Jorge Isaías and José María Zarazúa, Project leaders; expansion, Andrés Cajiga, Project leader
pp. 116–129, 167–171, 381

2009, 2017
Andares Masterplan
Zapopan, Jalisco
Humberto Mendoza and Andrés Cajiga, Project leaders
pp. 11, 15, 30, 115, 130–135, 189, 281, 343, 363, 378

2014
Toreo Parque Central
Mexico City
Jorge Isaías, Project leader
pp. 115, 189, 202–209, 381

2016
1500 Américas
Guadalajara, Jalisco
Boris Pena, Project leader
p. 343

2018
Artz Pedregal
Mexico City
Andrés Cajiga, Project leader
pp. 11, 13, 14, 30, 34, 115, 174, 175, 177, 178, 180, 189, 343, 381

2019
Midtown
Guadalajara, Jalisco
Andrés Cajiga, Project leader
pp. 10, 189, 210–213, 378

2019
The Landmark
Zapopan, Jalisco
Alejandro Quiros and Andrés Muñoz, Project leaders
pp. 10, 11, 133, 281, 300–303, 378

Reforma Colón
Mexico City (under construction)
Andrés Cajiga and Luis Hernández (architecture), Jorge Gerini (urban design), Project leaders
pp. 13, 32, 115, 137–159, 177, 185, 381

COMMERCIAL

1963
DM Nacional
Mexico City (demolished)
Jesús García Collantes and Alfredo Terrazas de la Peña, Associate architects
pp. 89, 106–109, 140, 340, 381

1969, 2002
Plaza Universidad
Mexico City (expansion)
José Adolfo Wiechers and José Ignacio de Abiega, Associate architects; expansion, Humberto Mendoza, Project leader
pp. 19, 36, 44, 112, 187, 381

1971, 1993, 2018, 2020
Plaza Satélite
Naucalpan, State of Mexico (expansion)
José Adolfo Wiechers and José Ignacio de Abiega, Associate architects; expansion, Humberto Mendoza, Project leader
pp. 10, 11, 32, 36, 44, 112, 188, 190–197, 339, 378

1980
Perisur
Mexico City (modified)
José Adolfo Wiechers, Associate architect
pp. 44, 112, 381

1998
Angelópolis
Puebla, Puebla (expanded)
Humberto Mendoza, Project leader
pp. 115, 378

2010
Luxury Hall
Puebla, Puebla
pp. 115, 189, 378

2013
Antea
Querétaro, Querétaro
Humberto Mendoza, Project leader
pp. 115, 378

2014
Andamar
Boca del Río, Veracruz
Humberto Mendoza, Project leader
p. 189

HOTELS

1958
Presidente Acapulco Hotel
Acapulco, Guerrero (modified)
José Adolfo Wiechers and Félix Candela, Associate architects
pp. 9, 14, 15, 23, 44, 216, 217, 220–225, 378

1961
María Isabel Hotel
Mexico City (modified)
José Adolfo Wiechers, José Villagrán and Ricardo Legorreta, Associate architects
pp. 22, 44, 58–63, 112, 217, 340, 381

1963
Villamagna Hotel
Madrid, Spain
pp. 22, 27, 44, 379

1963
Torremolinos Hotel Complex
Torremolinos, Spain
José Adolfo Wiechers and Imanol Ordorika, Associate architects
pp. 27, 44, 379

1968
Meliá Castilla Hotel
Madrid, Spain
pp. 22, 27, 44, 379

1969
Presidente Cozumel Hotel
Cozumel, Quintana Roo
José Adolfo Wiechers and José Ignacio de Abiega, Associate architects
pp. 22, 44, 217, 226–229, 341, 379

1974
Presidente Cancún Hotel
Cancún, Quintana Roo
José Adolfo Wiechers, Associate architect
pp. 22, 379

1977
Presidente Chapultepec Hotel
Mexico City
José Adolfo Wiechers, Associate architect
pp. 10, 22, 27, 44, 46, 78–83, 381

1993
Westin Regina Puerto Vallarta Hotel
Puerto Vallarta, Jalisco
José de Yturbe, Associate architect
pp. 218, 218, 378

1994
Westin Regina Los Cabos Hotel
Los Cabos, Baja California Sur
José de Yturbe, Associate architect
pp. 230–233, 339, 378

2015
Grand Hyatt Playa del Carmen Hotel
Playa del Carmen, Quintana Roo
Andrés Cajiga (architecture) and Nadia Borrás (interior design), Project leaders, Rockwell Group, Associate interior design firm
pp. 218, 234–241, 379

2018
Solaz Los Cabos
Los Cabos, Baja California Sur
Alejandro Coeto and Boris Pena (architecture), Nadia Borrás and Enrique Ralph (interior design), Project leaderso
pp. 11, 14, 15, 35, 218, 242–247, 343, 378

Saudi Arabia Hotel
Saudi Arabia (project)
Adrián Aguilar, Boris Pena, Diego Díaz, Fabiano Continanza and Jorge Gerini, Project leaders
pp. 35, 379

Chablé Sea of Cortez
La Paz, Baja California Sur (under construction)
Adrián Aguilar, Project leader
p. 37

HOUSES

1946
725 Sierra Fría
Mexico City (demolished)
pp. 17, 249, 252–255, 381

1952
2388 Reforma
Mexico City (demolished)
pp. 17, 43, 249, 250, 251, 381

1953
100 Conscripto
Mexico City
pp. 20, 249, 250, 256–259, 381

1956
940 Corregidores
Mexico City
Álvaro Ysita, Associate architect
pp. 20, 249, 250, 260–263, 381

1981
2076 Reforma
Mexico City
Javier Sordo Madaleno Bringas, Associate architect
pp. 12, 29, 251, 381

2007
Bosques de las Lomas
Mexico City
Álvaro Lebrija, Project leader
pp. 251, 264–265, 378

2009
Vistahermosa
Mexico City
Humberto Mendoza Mendoza and Andrés Cajiga, Project leaders
pp. 251, 266–269, 378

2017
Cozumel House
Cozumel, Quintana Roo
Andrés Cajiga, Project leader
pp. 270–273, 378

2021
Valle San Nicolás
Valle de Bravo, State of Mexico
Boris Pena, Project leader
pp. 251, 274–277, 378

APARTMENT BUILDINGS

1940
Monterrey and Álvaro Obregón
Mexico City (demolished)
Augusto H. Álvarez, Associate architect
pp. 42, 280, 282–283, 381

1943
Melchor Ocampo
Mexico City
Augusto H. Álvarez, Associate architect
pp. 19, 279, 280, 381

1945
333–335 Río Lerma
Mexico City
Augusto H. Álvarez, Associate architect
pp. 284–285, 381

1947
Río Ródano and Atoyac
Mexico City (demolished)
Augusto H. Álvarez, Associate architect
pp. 112, 381

1947
Edificio Larín
Mexico City (demolished)
Augusto H. Álvarez, Associate architect
pp. 280, 286–289, 381

1950
533 Insurgentes Sur
Mexico City (demolished)
Augusto H. Álvarez and Jesús García Collantes, Associate architects, demolished
pp. 43, 381

2006
Arbolada Lomas
Mexico City
Humberto Mendoza, José María Zarazúa and Javier Zarazúa, Project leaders
pp. 280, 281, 381

2006
Cumbres Residential
Mexico City
José María Zarazúa and Javier Zarazúa, Project leaders
pp. 280, 290–291, 381

2014
Artesia
Mexico City
Jorge Isaías, Project leader
pp. 281, 292–295, 381

2018
Alcázar de Toledo
Mexico City
pp. 281, 296–299

2020
225 Rubén Darío
Mexico City
Alejandro Quiros, Project leader
pp. 281, 304–307, 381

RELIGIOUS

1955
Sanatorio de la Sociedad de la Beneficiencia Española Chapel
Mexico City (modified)
pp. 43, 310, 314–317, 381

1956
Chapel Mausoleum in La Herradura Ranch
Huixquilucan, State of Mexico
Raúl Henríquez and Agustín Caso Bercht, Associate architects
pp. 310, 312, 318–321, 381

1961
San Ignacio de Loyola Church
Mexico City (restaured)
José Adolfo Wiechers and Ignacio Escalante, Associate architects
pp. 14, 311, 322–327, 339, 343, 381

1974
Santa Elena Chapel
Kingsville, Texas, USA
pp. 312, 328–331, 378

2009
San Josemaría Escrivá de Balaguer Parish
Mexico City
Jorge Isaías, Project leader
pp. 14, 313, 332–337, 378

OFFICE BUILDINGS

1945
15 Tonalá
Mexico City (partly demolished)
Augusto H. Álvarez, Associate architect
pp. 42, 381

1946
Reforma and Morelos
Mexico City (demolished)
Augusto H. Álvarez, Associate architect
pp. 9, 18, 27, 86–93, 137, 340, 381

1947
543 Mariano Escobedo
Mexico City (modified)
pp. 340, 344–345, 381

1953
Londres and Niza
Mexico City (demolished)
Jaime Ortiz Monasterio, Associate architect
pp. 12, 381

1954
Reforma and Versalles
Mexico City (demolished)
pp. 86, 88, 98–99, 140, 340, 381

1956
Dirección de Policía y Tránsito
Mexico City (demolished)
pp. 9, 21, 44, 48–51, 112, 340, 381

1956
Reforma and Lieja
Mexico City (demolished)
pp. 112, 340, 341, 346–347, 381

1956
Génova and Hamburgo
Mexico City (modified)
Álvaro Ysita, Associate architect
p. 381

1958
Anáhuac Tower
Mexico City (modified)
pp. 19, 44, 88, 89, 100–105, 140, 340, 381

1963
Ford Corporate
Mexico City (modified)
José Adolfo Wiechers, José Villagrán and Ricardo Legorreta, Associate architects
pp. 340, 381

1964
Palacio de Justicia
Mexico City
Imanol Ordorika and José Adolfo Wiechers, Associate architects
pp. 9, 21, 22, 44, 64–71, 112, 340, 381

1974
Bosques de las Lomas Complex
Mexico City
José Adolfo Wiechers, Associate architect
pp. 44, 72–77, 280, 381

1975
555 Palmas
Mexico City
José Adolfo Wiechers and José Ignacio de Abiega, Associate architects
pp. 12, 44, 112, 339–341, 343, 348–351, 381

1976
Centro Operativo Bancomer
Mexico City
José Adolfo Wiechers and Augusto H. Álvarez, Associate architects
pp. 22, 26, 44, 112, 341, 352–355, 381

1986
Centro Internacional de Prensa
Mexico City (demolished)
pp. 26, 27, 46, 342, 356–359, 381

1995
Herdez Corporate
Mexico City
pp. 342, 343, 381

1996
Cuervo Corporate
Mexico City
Humberto Mendoza, Project leader
pp. 343, 379

2017
Andares Corporate
Zapopan, Jalisco
Andrés Cajiga, Project leader
pp. 11, 343, 360–363

HEALTH

1999
Tlalnepantla CRIT
Tlalnepantla, State of Mexico
José María Zarazúa, Humberto Mendoza, Matteo Castelli Bullard and Cándido Hernández, Project leaders
pp. 365, 366, 379

2000
Jalisco CRIT
Guadalajara, Jalisco
Alejandro Coeto, Alejandro Quiros and Cándido Hernández, Project leaders
pp. 366, 379

2001
Oaxaca CRIT
Oaxaca, Oaxaca
Alejandro Coeto, Alejandro Quiros and Cándido Hernández, Project leaders
pp. 366, 371, 379

2002
Aguascalientes CRIT
Aguascalientes, Aguascalientes
Alejandro Coeto, Alejandro Quiros and Cándido Hernández, Project leaders
pp. 367, 369, 372, 379

2004
Guanajuato CRIT
Irapuato, Guanajuato
Alejandro Coeto, Álvaro Lebrija and Cándido Hernández, Project leaders
pp. 367, 368, 372, 379

2004
Hidalgo CRIT
Pachuca, Hidalgo
Alejandro Coeto and Cándido Hernández, Project leaders
pp. 366, 379

2004
Coahuila CRIT
Saltillo, Coahuila
Alejandro Coeto, Alejandro Quiros and Cándido Hernández, Project leaders
pp. 367, 370, 379

2006
Chihuahua CRIT
Chihuahua, Chihuahua
Alejandro Coeto and Cándido Hernández, Project leaders
pp. 366, 379

2006
Ángeles de Puebla Hospital
Puebla, Puebla
Alejandro Coeto, Project leader
p. 10

2006
Chiapas CRIT
Tuxtla Gutiérrez, Chiapas
Alejandro Coeto and Cándido Hernández, Project leaders
pp. 366, 379

2007
Quintana Roo CRIT
Cancún, Quintana Roo
Alejandro Coeto and Cándido Hernández, Project leaders
pp. 367, 375, 379

2007
Teletón Autism Center (CAT)
Ecatepec, State of Mexico
Alejandro Coeto and Cándido Hernández, Project leaders
pp. 366, 379

2007
Nezahualcóyotl CRIT
Nezahualcóyotl, State of Mexico
Alejandro Coeto and Cándido Hernández, Project leaders
pp. 367, 379

2007
Puebla CRIT
San Andrés Cholula, Puebla
Alejandro Coeto and Cándido Hernández, Project leaders
pp. 367, 369, 373, 379

2008
Tamaulipas CRIT
Altamira, Tamaulipas
Alejandro Coeto and Cándido Hernández, Project leaders
pp. 366, 374, 379

2008
Yucatán CRIT
Mérida, Yucatán
Alejandro Coeto and Cándido Hernández, Project leaders
pp. 366, 379

2009
Durango CRIT
Gómez Palacio, Durango
Alejandro Coeto and Cándido Hernández, Project leaders
pp. 367, 379

2009
Veracruz CRIT
Poza Rica, Veracruz
Alejandro Coeto and Cándido Hernández, Project leaders
pp. 367, 379

2010
Mexico City CRIT
Mexico City
Alejandro Coeto and Cándido Hernández, Project leaders
pp. 374, 379

2010
Sonora CRIT
Hermosillo, Sonora
Alejandro Coeto and Cándido Hernández, Project leaders
pp. 367, 379

2010
Baja California Sur CRIT
La Paz, Baja California Sur
Alejandro Coeto and Cándido Hernández, Project leaders
pp. 366, 379

2012
Guerrero CRIT
Acapulco, Guerrero
Alejandro Coeto and Cándido Hernández, Project leaders
pp. 366, 369, 379

2013
Michoacán CRIT
Morelia, Michoacán
Cándido Hernández, Project leader
pp. 367, 369, 379

2013
Teletón Infant Oncology Clinic (HITO)
Querétaro, Querétaro
Alejandro Coeto and Cándido Hernández, Project leaders
pp. 366, 379

2014
Texas CRIT
San Antonio, Texas, USA
Cándido Hernández, Project leader
pp. 367, 369, 379

2015
Baja California CRIT
Tijuana, Baja California
Cándido Hernández, Project leader
pp. 367, 373, 379

INDEX OF NAMES

NOTES ON AUTHORS

Barry Bergdoll is the Meyer Schapiro Professor of Art History and Archaeology at Columbia University, New York, and was the Chief Curator of Architecture and Design at the Museum of Modern Art in New York from 2007 to 2014, where he curated the exhibition *Latin America in Construction: Architecture 1955–1980* in 2015. He has published extensively on 19th and 20th century architecture and has curated exhibitions at MoMA, the Musée d'Orsay, and the Canadian Centre for Architecture in Montreal, Canada. He is a member of the American Academy of Arts and Sciences, the Royal Institute of British Architects, and the Society of Architectural Historians in the USA, as well as an honorary member of the American Institute of Architects in New York.

Louise Noelle Gras is a researcher at UNAM's Institute of Aesthetic Research, where she works as a professor and historian of architecture, and is the author of several books and articles on Mexican and Latin American architecture, including *Arquitectos contemporáneos de México* (Contemporary Architects of Mexico) (Trillas, 1989). She has been involved in various aspects of architectural research and criticism. She was a co-founder of the International Committee of Architectural Critics and an honorary member of the National Academy of Architecture in Mexico, and has done outstanding work in the Academy of Arts. Committed to the protection of 20th century architectural heritage, she is a member of Icomos and DOCOMOMO, as well as various other national committees.

Martha Thorne is Dean of the IE School of Architecture and Design in Madrid and Segovia, Spain. She studied Urban Planning at the University of Buffalo and the University of Pennsylvania, as well as at the London School of Economics. From 2005 to 2021 she served as executive director of the Pritzker Architecture Prize. She is the author of numerous articles and books, including *The Pritzker Architecture Prize: The First Twenty Years* (Next Door Publishers, 1999). She sits on international juries for prestigious awards, mostly related to urbanism, due to her keen interest in the role of architecture and design in contributing to making cities more sustainable and equitable.

Manuel Perló Cohen received a BA in Economy from UNAM and graduated with a PhD in Urban-Regional Planning from the University of California-Berkeley. He is a researcher at the UNAM Institute for Social Research and has been a professor at Berkeley and Stanford Universities. He is a member of the National System of Researchers of the National Council for Science and Technology, and his main areas of research is urban planning in Mexico, the contemporary history of Mexico City, the study of real estate markets, and the development of sustainable water projects. Author of numerous books, chapters and articles, he directed UNAM's University Program for Urban Studies, was director of the Institute of Social Research and has been a consultant for the UN, the World Bank and the Inter-American Development Bank.

Eduardo Alarcón Azuela graduated with a BA in Architecture from UNAM and has a MA in Heritage Conservation from UAM-Azcapotzalco. For more than ten years he collaborated with Dr. Juan Ignacio del Cueto on various projects related to Spanish-exile architects in Mexico, as well as in the edition of the *Candela Guide*, by the same author (Arquine, 2013). In 2018 he was invited by Sordo Madaleno Arquitectos to carry out historical research on the urban environment of the *Glorieta de Colón* in the 1950s and the following year carried out the classification of more than thirty thousand drawings belonging to the firm's collection, for which in 2021 he was appointed manager of the Historical Archive of this architectural office.

Juan José Kochen is an architect and editor. He studied architecture at UNAM's School of Architecture, journalism at the Carlos Septién García School of Journalism and received a MA in Analysis, Theory and History of Architecture at UNAM. He wrote for the newspaper *Reforma*, was editor of *Arquine* and consultant to Infonavit's General Subdirector of Sustainability and Technique. He is the author of *La utopía como modelo* (Utopia as a Model) (Arquine, 2015) and his research has been supported by the National Council for Science and Technology, the Graham Foundation for Advanced Studies in the Fine Arts and the Young Creators Program of the National Fund for Culture and the Arts. He is currently the general director of Fundación ICA and a professor at the Universidad Iberoamericana.

Rosalba Rojas Chávez has a BA in Architecture from Universidad Iberoamericana and a MA in Marketing and Brand Management from Universidad Anáhuac. From 2011 to 2014 she worked in Rojkind Architects, and since 2014 she has been Director of Marketing and Communication at Sordo Madaleno Arquitectos, where she also directs communication at SOMA (formerly Grupo Sordo Madaleno). In 2015 she began the project for the recovery and preservation of the historical archive of Juan Sordo Madaleno, which includes on-going research of his life and work. She has directed the project of this book since its conceptualization, as well as the exhibition of the same name at the Palacio de Cultura Citibanamex, Palacio de Iturbide in 2023.

Felipe Correa studied architecture at Tulane University and received an MA from Harvard's GSD. He is a founding partner of the New York City-based design studio Somatic Collaborative, through which he has led a wide range of applied research and design projects in several spatial contexts in the Americas, Asia, and Europe. He is the Vincent and Eleanor Shea Professor and Chairman of the Department of Architecture at the University of Virginia. He is the author of several books, including *A Line in the Andes*, with Ramiro Almeida (Harvard University Graduate School of Design, 2012), *Ciudad de México: entre geometría y geografía* (Mexico City: Between Geometry and Geography) (Applied Research and Editorial Design, 2015), and *Sao Paulo: una biografía gráfica* (Sao Paulo: A Graphic Biography) (University of Texas Press, 2018).

Kenneth Frampton studied architecture at the Architectural Association in London. From 1959 to 1965 he worked at the architectural firm Douglas Stephen & Partners in the UK, and from 1962 to 1965 he was the managing editor of Architectural Design Magazine. Among other titles he is the author of *Modern Architecture* (Oxford University Press, 1980), *Le Corbusier* (Thames and Hudson, 2001), *A Genealogy of Modern Architecture* (Lars Müller, 2015), and *The Other Modern Movement* (2021). He is Professor Emeritus of Architecture at the GSAPP of Columbia University, where he taught until 2020. He has also been Professor of Architecture at institutions such as the ETH in Zurich, the EPFL in Lausanne, the Accademia di Architettura in Mendrisio and the Royal College of Art in London.

Vera Simone Bader, an art historian, has been a curator at the Architekturmuseum of the Technical University of Munich, a research associate in the department of History of Architecture and Curatorial Practice since 2013, and has offered seminars on various topics, such as decolonial strategies in art and architecture. She has curated the exhibitions *Lina Bo Bardi 100: Brazil's Alternative Path to Modernity* (2014), *World of Malls: Architectures of Consumption* (2016), *Experience in Action: DesignBuild in Architecture* (2020), as well as the exhibition *Marina Tabassum Architects: In Bangladesh* (2023). Her dissertation "Modernity in Africa: Asmara - The Construction of an Italian Colonial City," presented in 2012 at the Humboldt University of Berlin, received the Hans Janssen Prize from the Göttingen Academy of Sciences.

Catherine R. Ettinger graduated with a BA from the Universidad Michoacana de San Nicolás de Hidalgo (UMSNH), a MA in Architecture, Research and Restoration of Sites and Monuments from the same university, and a PhD in Architecture with honors from UNAM. Originally from California, USA, she has lived in Morelia, Mexico since 1980, where she works as a teacher and researcher at UMSNH. She is the author of numerous articles and chapters, as well as several books, including *Richard Neutra en América Latina* (Richard Neutra in Latin America) (Arquitónica, 2018), *La Quinta Eréndira de Lázaro Cárdenas* (Lazaro Cardenas' Eréndira Ranch) (CREFAL/UMSNH, 2021) and *La arquitectura mexicana desde afuera* (Mexican Architecture Seen from the Outside) (Miguel Ángel Porrúa, 2016). She is a member of DOCOMOMO, Icomos Mexico, and the National System of Researchers of the National Council of Science and Technology.

Lourdes Cruz González Franco received a BA in Architecture, a MA in Art History and a PhD in Architecture at UNAM. She is a researcher and coordinator of the Archive of Mexican Architects of the Faculty of Architecture at the UNAM since 2002. She has written numerous publications on the history of 20th century Mexican architecture, including *Francisco J. Serrano, ingeniero civil y arquitecto* (Francisco J. Serrano, Civil Engineer and Architect) (UNAM, 1998) and *La casa de la Ciudad de México en el siglo XX* (Mexico City in the 20th Century) (UNAM, 2020). She is a member of the National System of Researchers, DOCOMOMO Mexico, Icomos Mexico and is an emeritus of the National Academy of Architecture. She has received several awards, including the National University Award in the area of Architecture and Design in 2020.

Sara Topelson has a BA in architecture from UNAM. From 1996 to 1999 she was president of the International Union of Architects and from 2001 to 2003 director of INBA's Architecture and Conservation of Artistic Buildings Heritage. She was named Woman of the Year in Mexico in 1996, is an emeritus academic of the National Academy of Architecture, and Knight of the Order of Arts and Letters in France. From 2007 to 2012 she was Undersecretary of Urban Development and Territorial Planning of Sedesol and from 2002 to 2007 President of DOCOMOMO Mexico. She is currently project coordinator at Grinberg and Topelson Architects and director of the House Research and Documentation Center, which since 2004 publishes the annual study "The Current State of Housing in Mexico."

Ivan San Martín Córdova has a BA in Architecture from UNAM and a BA in Philosophy from the Universidad del Claustro de Sor Juana, a MA in Urbanism from UNAM, and a PhD in Architecture from the Polytechnic University of Catalonia. Since 2001 he has been a tenured researcher at UNAM's Faculty of Architecture, where he teaches undergraduate and graduate courses, and since 2005 he is a member of the National System of Researchers of the National Council for Science and Technology. He is an author and contributor to several publications, and is the founder of the Mexican chapter of DOCOMOMO, of which he is secretary since 2010. He is a member of Icomos Mexico, the National Academy of Architecture and the International Committee of Architecture Critics. In 2010 he received the Juan O'Gorman Award from the College of Architects for his research.

Jose Castillo Oléa has a BA in Architecture from the Universidad Iberoamericana, with a MA and PhD in Urban Planning from the Graduate School of Design at Harvard University, where he has been a visiting professor for the last 10 years. In 2002 he founded (along with Saidee Springall) a911, an office dedicated to architecture, urban planning and mobility projects. His projects include the expansion of the Cultural Center of Spain, the Elena Garro Cultural Center and the Jaime García Terrés Library. His work has been widely published in national and international media and he has contributed articles to *The Endless City* (Phaidon, 2007), *Reinventing Construction* (Holcim/RubyPress, 2010) and *La casa latinoamericana moderna* (The Modern Latin American House) (Gustavo Gili, 2003).

Jimena Orvañanos is an architect from Universidad Anáhuac, graduated in 2015. She worked in marketing and communication at Sordo Madaleno Arquitectos from 2015 to 2021. In 2022 she collaborated as coordinator at Fundación ICA. She is currently in charge of the communication area at Cuaik CDS.

IMAGE CREDITS

When multiple images appear on the same page and are not designated by a letter, they are numbered from left to right and top to bottom.

Every reasonable effort has been made to trace copyright holders for the images and the authors of the photographs. If there are any inadvertent errors or omissions, please, notify us so that corrections can be addressed in any subsequent edition.

Eduardo Alarcón, private collection: pp. 86-B, 86-C, 86-D, 87-E, 87-F, 88-G, 230
Archivo Histórico Fundación Sordo Madaleno (AHFSM): pp. 19-C, 19-E, 21-F, 26-B, 27-D, 42-B, 54–55, 57-1, 60-1, 60-2, 62–63, 67, 68–69, 74, 75, 76-1, 77-1, 80, 81-1, 81-2, 82-1, 83, 92, 93-2, 96, 97, 98, 100, 102, 104-1, 104-2, 108-1, 108-2, 109-2, 111-A, 112-B, 112-C, 113-D, 187-E, 187-F, 190-2, 192-1, 194-1, 194-2, 194-3, 200-1, 200-2, 217-D, 222–223, 223-1, 223-2, 225-2, 227-2, 232-1, 232-2, 232-3, 232-4, 232–233, 233, 249-A, 249-B, 282-2, 285-1, 285-2, 286–287, 289-1, 289-2, 309-A, 312-F, 317, 321-2, 324, 325-1, 325-2, 325-3, 327-2, 328, 328–329, 330-1, 330-2, 331, 346, 355, 356, 356–357, 358-1, 358-2, 359-1, 359-2
© Barragan Foundation, 2014: pp. 114-F, 310-B
E. E. Barrios, photography, MexicoEnFotos: p. 215-A
Bozar, Centre for Fine Arts, Brussels, Producer, courtesy: p. 339-A
Joan Busquets and Felipe Correa (eds.), *Cities X Lines: A New Lens for the Urbanistic Project*, Harvard University Graduate School of Design, 2016: p. 163-B
Óscar Caballero, photography, SMA: pp. 116–117, 118-2, 120-1, 120-2, 122, 123-1, 124, 125-2, 126-2, 127, 137-A, 148-M, 153-R, 167-F, 168-H, 171-K, 181-N-1, 193-2, 204-2, 296–297
CGveron, SMA: pp. 35-I, 37-L, 129-1, 129-2, 138–139, 144-G, 145-I, 146-J, 146-K, 147-L, 148-N, 149-O, 154-T, 157-V, 158–159-W
Fernando Cordero, photography, SMA: pp. 368-B, 370, 372-2
Cordon Press: pp. 174-A, 174-B
Felipe Correa, *Mexico City: Between Geometry and Geography*, Applied Research and Design Publishing, 2014: p. 169
Paul Czitrom, photography, SMA: pp. 374-1, 375-1, 375-2
© F.L.C. / VEGAP, 2022: p. 280-C
Fundación ICA, Acervo Histórico, Fondo Aerofotográfico Oblicuas y Verticales: pp. 9-A, 41-A, 43-E, 45-F, 45-G, 48, 61-1, 72, 114-E, 118-1, 165-C, 166-E, 168-G, 170-J, 190-1, 191, 204-1, 216-C, 279-B, 353. Fondo Colección ICA: pp. 78, 193-1
Fundación Televisa: pp. 369-C, 372-1, 373-1, 373-2, 374-2.
Rafael Gamo, photography, SMA: pp. 11-C, 15-F, 31-H-1, 31-H-2, 31-H-3, 36-K, 121, 130, 130–131, 132, 133-1, 134-2, 135-1, 135-2, 175-C, 176-D, 176-E, 176-F, 176-G, 177-H, 178-I, 178-J, 179-K, 179-L, 202–203, 205-1, 205-2, 205-3, 206-2, 207, 208, 209, 210, 210–211, 212, 213-1, 213-2, 213-3, 242–243, 243-1, 243-2, 244-1, 244-2, 245-1, 245-2, 245-3, 246-1, 246-2, 247-1, 247-2, 270-1, 270-2, 270–271, 272-1, 273-1, 273-2, 274–275, 275, 276-1, 276-2, 277-1, 277-2, 300, 301, 302-1, 302-2, 303-1, 303-2, 304–305, 306, 307-1, 307-2, 307-3, 343-D, 360, 361, 362, 363-1, 363-2
© Gruen Associates, Victor Gruen: p. 186-C
© Gruen Associates, Victor Gruen, © Privatarchiv: Richard Longstreth, © Architectural Forum, Dezember 1956, S. 114–121: p. 186-D
Grupo de Diseño Urbano, Mario Schjetnan, courtesy: p. 165-D
Philippe Guignard, Air Images-Contreforts Production: p. 161-A
© Hotel Caribe Hilton: p. 219-H
Timothy Hursley, photography, SMA: pp. 264–265, 265-1, 265-2, 266, 266–267, 268-1, 268-2, 268-3, 269, 281-D, 290–291, 291, 332, 333, 334, 335-1, 335-2, 336, 337-1, 337-2
Jerde Architects, courtesy: p. 188-H
M. M. López, photography, MexicoEnFotos: p. 215-B
© Los Angeles Public Library: p. 185-A
Samuel Morales, illustration from *Chain Store Review*, september 1928, p. 29: p. 185-B
Samuel Morales, illustration from https://icaronycteris.tumblr.com/post/24224041128/edificios-en-la-plaza-melchor-ocampo-cuauhtemoc: p. 279-A
Alberto Moreno Guzmán, photography: p. 219-F
Lorena Moreno, design, SMA: pp. 366–367
Jaime Navarro, photography, SMA: pp. 195, 196-1, 196-2, 197-1, 197-2, 297, 298-1, 298-2, 299
Gabriela Quiroz Cázares, cartography, SMA: p. 47
Paúl Rivera, photography, SMA: pp. 126-1, 198–199, 201-1, 234–235, 236-1, 236-2, 237-1, 237-2, 240-1, 240-2, 241, 292, 292–293, 294-1, 294-2, 295-1, 295-2
© Ludwig Mies van der Rohe, VEGAP, Madrid, 2022: p. 311-D
© Royal Commission on the Ancient and Historical Monuments of Scotland: p. 188-G
Armando Salas Portugal, photography, © Fundación Armando Salas Portugal, AHFSM: pp. 73, 76-2, 77-2, 99, 101, 105-2, 249-C, 250-D, 251-E, 326, 347
Sebastián Saldívar, photography, SMA: p. 371
Servicio de Información Agroalimentaria y Pesquera, Mapoteca "Manuel Orozco y Berra": p. 85-A
Mariola Soberón, SMA: p. 123-2
Sordo Madaleno Arquitectos (SMA): pp. 88–89, 96–97, 119, 125-1, 128, 133-2, 134-1, 141-C, 142-D, 143-E, 143-F, 144-H, 150–151-P, 152-Q, 153-S, 155-U, 180-M, 192-2, 201-2, 206-1, 238–239, 272-2, 310-C (illustration from http://moleskinearquitectonico.blogspot.com/2008/08/capilla-de-las-capuchinas-barragn.html), 311-E (illustration from https://es.wikiarquitectura.com/edificic/capilla-memorial-robert-f-carr-de-st-salvador/), 351, 365-A, 369-D, 378, 379, 380–381, 382–383
José Abraham "Tex" Tejeda Meza, photography, AHFSM: p. 19-D
Universidad Nacional Autónoma de México, *Revista Arquitectos de México*, n. 27, may 1967: p. 45-H. *Revista Arquitectura México*: p. 106
Ignacio Urquiza, photography, AHFSM: pp. 28-E, 219-G, 231, 342
Ximena del Valle, photography, SMA: pp. 25-A, 28-F, 29-G, 36-J
Mariana Yáñez, photography, Arte Abierto: p. 181-N-2
Guillermo Zamora, photography, AHFSM: pp. 10-B, 12-D, 14-E, 17-A, 18-B, 22-G, 22-H, 23-I, 23-J, 26-C, 48–49, 50-1, 50-2, 51-1, 51-2, 52–53, 56, 57-2, 58–59, 61-2, 62, 64–65, 66-1, 66-2, 70, 71-1, 71-2, 79, 82-2, 90, 91, 93-1, 95-1, 95-2, 103, 105-1, 106–107, 109-1, 220, 220–221, 224, 225-1, 226–227, 227-1, 228, 229-1, 229-2, 252, 252–253, 254-1, 254-2, 255-1, 255-2, 256, 256–257, 258-1, 258-2, 259-1, 259-2, 260–261, 261, 262-1, 262-2, 263-1, 263-2, 282-1, 283, 284–285, 288, 314–315, 316, 318–319, 320, 321-1, 322, 323, 327-1, 341-B, 344-1, 344-2, 345, 348–349, 350, 352–353, 354-1, 354-2. Archivo Ragasol, courtesy: p. 94. Fototeca Tecnológico de Monterrey, Fondo Archivo Personal del Arquitecto Mario Pani Darqui: pp. 42-C, 43-D

Juan Sordo Madaleno (Mexico City, 1916–1985) was an architect from the School of Architecture at the National Autonomous University of Mexico (UNAM). In 1937 he started his own office, and two years later he entered into a collaboration with Augusto H. Álvarez. Together they developed a type of architecture with a clear functionalist style, such as the Reforma and Morelos' building (1946). He also partnered with José Adolfo Wiechers during the 1960's. The Palacio de Justicia (1946) is the most iconic building of this alliance. He taught composition at UNAM from 1954 to 1957 and served as vice president of the National College of Architects and the National Academy of Architecture. He was also enlisted as an honorary member of the American Institute of Architects in 1976. In addition to his body of work, and his important contributions to the international style that were mainly influenced by Le Corbusier and Walter Gropius, he focused on the creation of a unique type of architecture that went far beyond any established architectural style at the time, always bearing in mind human beings as fundamental to his design.

Javier Sordo Madaleno Bringas (Mexico City, 1956) trained as an architect at the Universidad Iberoamericana and graduated in 1979. In addition to winning numerous international awards, he is also a member of the main architecture and real estate sector associations. Of note is his appointment as an honorary member of the American Institute of Architects (AIA) and honorary professor of the International Academy of Architecture (IAA). His work includes the design of approximately 250 projects, the construction of more than nine million square meters, and the development of nearly three million square meters. He is president of SOMA (formerly Grupo Sordo Madaleno) and leads Sordo Madaleno Arquitectos (SMA) with a global perspective and visionary mindset. Along with his three sons, he created the Sordo Madaleno Foundation, primarily dedicated to promoting social and educational development using the transformative power of architecture.

Javier Sordo Madaleno de Haro (Mexico City, 1985) holds a degree in architecture from the Universidad Iberoamericana and since 2010 has been Director of Architecture at SMA. He is known for having a creative approach to architecture and real estate and his contribution to the development of SMA architectural projects has redefined commercial, residential, and land use for hotels in Mexico. He is vice president of SOMA and founder of Arte Abierto which is a non-profit art foundation dedicated to making art accesible to the public.

José Juan Sordo Madaleno de Haro (Mexico City, 1986) has a degree in Financial Administration from the Monterrey Institute of Technology and Higher Education. He is vice president of SOMA, and since 2010 he has led SOMA to be a leader in the real estate sector in Mexico. Since 2013 he has introduced different international brands to the national market in Mexico. In 2021 he managed the launch and consolidation of FibraSOMA, a real estate trust focused on the acquisition, leasing, and management of real estate in Mexico on the Institutional Stock Market (BIVA).

Fernando Sordo Madaleno de Haro (Mexico City, 1991) is an architect who graduated with honors from the Universidad Iberoamericana in 2014. He is the vice president of SOMA. Since 2016 he has been the Director of Architecture at SMA, where his innovative methodology based on research and sensitivity to context has been implemented into the design process. He has won major international architecture competitions in the Dominican Republic, Thailand, Saudi Arabia, and the United Arab Emirates.

Shaping Transformation
Sordo Madaleno Arquitectos

Edited by
Barry Bergdoll

Texts by
Eduardo Alarcón Azuela
Vera Simone Bader
Jose Castillo
Felipe Correa
Lourdes Cruz González Franco
Catherine R. Ettinger
Kenneth Frampton
Louise Noelle Gras
Juan José Kochen
Jimena Orvañanos
Manuel Perló Cohen
Rosalba Rojas Chávez
Ivan San Martín
Martha Thorne
Sara Topelson

Sordo Madaleno Arquitectos

Javier Sordo Madaleno Bringas
Javier Sordo Madaleno de Haro
Fernando Sordo Madaleno de Haro

Project Leader
Rosalba Rojas Chávez

Production Team
Angélica Chávez Escudero
Daniela Cruz Murillo
Daniela Rosas Zariñana
Eduardo Alarcón Azuela
Jimena Orvañanos Márquez
Lorena Moreno y Suárez
Óscar Caballero Herrejón
Vanessa Gutiérrez Tapia

Cover Image
Luis Miguel Ortíz Suárez

Consulting
Sara Topelson

Turner

Editorial Coordination
Armando López Carrillo

Graphic Concept and Design
David Kimura y Gabriela Varela

Translation
Philip Sutton
Kurt Hollander

Copyediting
Martin Fox
Rees Storm
Laura Badsey

Edition and Production
Laura Estévez
María José Fresneda

ISBN 978-84-18428-84-5
LD M-23139-2022

Distributed by
Turner
www.turnerlibros.com

United States and Canada
DAP
orders@dapinc.com
www.artbook.com

Europe
ACC
sales@antique-acc.com
www.accdistribution.com/uk

Spanish edition available
Spain
Machado Grupo de Distribución
machadolibros@machadolibros.com

Latin America
Océano
info@oceano.com
www.oceano.com

Cover Image

The graphic composition of this image, called *Trascendencia de un legado* (Transcendence of a legacy), shows the outline of three lines that constantly flow and stamp silhouettes corresponding to architectural projects of three generations, as links of a legacy that has thus cemented an urban transformation and has opened the way to a powerful present, preceded by 85 years of experience.

The publication of this book coincides with the exhibition *Transformación urbana. Sordo Madaleno Arquitectos* at Palacio de Cultura Citibanamex. Palacio de Iturbide, a co-production of Sordo Madaleno Arquitectos and Fomento Cultural Citibanamex, A.C., to be held in 2023.

Fomento Cultural Citibanamex, A.C.

citibanamex
El Banco Nacional de México

This book was printed in February 2023
in Madrid, Spain, under the supervision
of Turner. It was printed on 150 gr Novatech
Ultimatt 1.1 paper.